girlish

girl*ish*

❖ growing up in a lesbian home ❖

lara lillibridge

Skyhorse Publishing

Skyhorse Publishing books may be purchased in bulk at special discounts for sales promotion, corporate gifts, fund-raising, or educational purposes. Special editions can also be created to specifications. For details, contact the Special Sales Department, Skyhorse Publishing, 307.West 36th Street, 11th Floor, New York, NY 10018 or info@skyhorsepublishing.com.

Skyhorse® and Skyhorse Publishing® are registered trademarks of Skyhorse Publishing, Inc.®, a Delaware corporation.

Visit our website at www.skyhorsepublishing.com.

10 9 8 7 6 5 4 3 2 1

Library of Congress Cataloging-in-Publication Data

Names: Lillibridge, Lara, author.
Title: Girlish: growing up in a lesbian home / Lara Lillibridge.
Description: New York: Skyhorse Publishing, [2018] | Includes
    bibliographical references.
Identifiers: LCCN 2017050453 (print) | LCCN 2017053705 (ebook) | ISBN
    9781510723924 (e-book) | ISBN 9781510723917 (hardcover: alk. paper)
Subjects: LCSH: Lillibridge, Lara. | Children of gay parents—United
    States—Biography. | Lesbian mothers—United States—Biography. |
    Families—United States—Biography.
Classification: LCC HQ777.8 (ebook) | LCC HQ777.8 .L55 2018 (print) | DDC
    306.874086/6—dc23
LC record available at https://lccn.loc.gov/2017050453

Cover photograph: Lara Lillibridge
Front cover design: Jenny Zemanek
Jacket design: Mona Lin

Print ISBN: 978-1-5107-2391-7
eBook ISBN: 978-1-5107-2392-4

Printed in the United States of America

Author's Note

"I Used to Believe, Now I Know" was previously published on TheFeministWire.com on September 17, 2013.

A version of "Being Raised by Lesbians" was previously published on *Brain, Child* magazine's *Brain, Mother* blog on November 14, 2013, and reprinted on Australia's iVillage website under the title "How Having Two Mums Scarred Me."

"Cicadas" was previously published online on TheDrunkenLlama.com on December 30, 2016.

For Paul,
without whom this book would have taken a lot longer to write and
would have been a lot more difficult for the reader to follow.

contents

acknowledgments ix

introduction: a childhood crossword puzzle xi

notes from the fourth wall: this is how it feels to write
about lesbian parents xvi

the early years 1

elementary school 31

middle school 61

junior high 123

high school 159

college and beyond 259

acknowledgments

I am incredibly lucky to have the support of my family behind me. My mother, stepmother, brother, and half-sister have all given me their blessings, even without knowing what was on the page. There is no greater gift they could have given me.

I am beyond fortunate to have the support of my significant other and my two grade-school-aged children, who understand that Mama's writing is just as important as a job outside of the home. I'm also grateful that my children accept that this is a grown-up book and not appropriate for them just yet. I promise I'll write a book they can read someday.

Thanks, too, to my writing friends, who were willing to read early drafts, give encouraging words, and discuss at length the same sentences over and over again: Sandy Roffey, Sherry Dove, Andrea Fekete, Arlie Matera, and all my friends and advisors at West Virginia Wesleyan College's MFA program. I'm grateful, too, for my online writing community of Binders on Facebook, and the generosity of the many already published writers who took the time to answer questions from all of us newbies.

I will always be grateful to my editor, Chamois Holschuh, for her patience with my thousands of emails, and to Skyhorse Publishing for believing in me and helping bring my memoir to life.

Many names have been changed, and I attempted to leave people out as much as possible in an effort to protect their privacy. My focus was on my immediate familial relationships, and I included other people only when their story overlapped ours. The absence of friends or family members is not meant to deny their importance in my life, but an attempt to tell a complicated story as simply as possible.

introduction
a childhood crossword puzzle

LOLY

FOUNDAHALF

PEDIATRICGASTROENTEROLOGIST

MENTALILLNESS

LIBRARIAN

SEVEN

MATTHEW

ANCHOR

BADEYE

FIFTEEN

TW

RUSHLIMBAUGH

1. A description of my mother, starting with the letter "L." Not lesbian, that's too easy. Liberal is also good, but I'm looking for a physical description. Give up? Librarian. Yes, I know, she has never been employed at a library, but if you ask anyone at all to describe my mother, they all choose "librarian" as their first word. She is well-read and loves philosophic and political discussions. However, she is deceptively sweet—few people would guess how fiendish she is at Cards Against Humanity. A game that relies on shock value and twisted humor to win, my mother always wins.

2. My best friend, confidant, fellow rabble-rouser, and occasional arch-nemesis. Also, my only full-blooded sibling. Matthew, with two Ts. Want to know something funny? I didn't know about that second T in Matthew until I was in fifth grade. I'm not entirely sure he did either. No one paid much attention to Matt back then, unless he was in trouble. I always sort of

figured that's why he ended up six foot nine inches tall. He grew and grew until the world couldn't ignore him anymore.

3. What is wrong with my mother's partner, Pat, herewith referred to as my stepmother. But what about my father's wives, you ask? Aren't they also my stepmothers? Well, yes, but he was always switching them out for new ones. I think of them more as . . . numbers. Wife #4, Wife #5, Wife #5½, etc. The word "stepmother" in this book refers to my mother's one true love. She's been around the longest, anyway—from when I was three until the present. Now that we have that straightened out, let's get back to the crossword. What exactly is wrong with my stepmother? I guess it depends on who you ask. At first it was clinical depression, but that changed to manic depression. Yes, I know it's called "bipolar disorder" now, but that's not the word our family uses. We've always had our own preferred words for things, just like we said "gay" instead of "lesbian" when I was growing up. Yes, I do see how other diagnoses might fit her better, but I'm not a doctor, so I am not allowed an opinion, no matter how many online "diagnose yourself" quizzes I have taken on her behalf. Just write down "mental illness"; we'll sort it out later.

4. The city where I grew up. You don't need the specific suburb, no one can spell Irondequoit, not even spell-check. You give up? You don't like my game? Rochester. It's in New York, on Lake Ontario. No, I've never been to New York City. It's a six-hour drive and everyone I knew in college who went there got their luggage stolen. Toronto was only a three-hour drive, and everyone there knew how to use their turn signal. Rochester was the home of Kodak, Xerox, and Bausch + Lomb back then. My grandparents were given the chance to buy shares in Xerox before it was incorporated, but they felt it was too risky. Yeah, I know, pity.

5. My nickname growing up. No, not Lezzie. Four letters. Not slut, either, though I heard that a lot, too. I mean the one my parents still call me. The one that makes me cringe. Lolly. Isn't that sweet? It's downright gackworthy. Lolly is five letters? Okay, drop one of the Ls. That works, now, doesn't it? It's more important to be creative than accurate sometimes. At least that is what my father tells me.

6. One of my biggest childhood secrets. No, not the fact that my mother was a lesbian—that's too obvious, and it has too many letters. Not my stepmother's mental illness—they kept that secret even from me until I was older. I am looking for the answer to why my mother was in and out of the hospital and doctor's offices for most of my childhood—why she wore tape over the left side of her glasses and had four corneal transplants. I wasn't allowed to tell people my mother had herpes. They would think it was the sexual kind. It wasn't; it was the oral kind that settled in her eye and eventually took her vision. There are drugs for that, you say? She was ten months too early. You don't like the word herpes as an answer? Feels too gooey? Just write bad eye. That's good enough. If you leave out the space in the middle it will fit.

7. How I rebelled against my parents in high school. What, you didn't know me then so it isn't a fair question? Well, take a guess. Nope, not the time I shaved my head. That was accidental. Besides, how do you really piss off a lesbian? No, I mean piss them off more than just dating unemployed loser musicians. Teenaged sex, well, yes, but think bigger. Worse than smoking pot and skipping school. (Yes, of course I did that.) Give up yet? Rush Limbaugh. That's right. I became a "ditto-head" praising Jesus and hating "feminazis." Even voted for George Bush in my first presidential election. Take that, Mom! I'll rebel and screw up the country at the same time! I know, I know, you're thinking, *but she looks so sweet.* You have no idea how diabolical I can be.

8. My father's profession, in Latin. Okay, I can't spell it either, so I'll just copy and paste it for you. Pediatric Gastroenterologist—the digestive tracts of children. My father devoted his life to the study of burps, farts, shit, and vomit. He's very good at removing quarters from children's stomachs with a little tube called an endoscope. I've seen it done. I've also watched him stretch a child's esophagus, which involved a lot of vomiting and crying. He swore the boy was given an amnesia-inducing agent so he wouldn't remember any of it. I wish I had been given the drug as well, as I cannot forget it. Attachment disorder, he tells me, makes for a very good doctor. Dad could never be a vet; he could never hurt an animal, "even to save its life," he told me. Children, on the other hand, were something different entirely.

9. The city where my father moved when I was four years old. Hint: it's the biggest city in the only state in America that doesn't have counties. What, you don't remember high school geography? Anchorage, Alaska. Four thousand, one hundred and seventy-one miles away from my mother. Of course he wanted to be involved with his children—he just wanted them to experience the joy of commercial travel a few times a year. What kid doesn't like a twelve-hour trip without parents? Our mother gave us snacks for the plane. There were flight attendants to help us make connecting flights. Anchorage had mountains. It was beautiful. Don't tell me New York has the Adirondacks. My father doesn't believe in them. No, he told me so when I was a kid—New York has big hills, not mountains. He's a doctor—remember? An educated man. He wouldn't get that wrong.

10. The number of times my father has been married. Here, I'll help: Jackie, Sharon, Judy, Margaret, Jan, Theresa, Tricia. Seven. But it's not entirely his fault, he tells me. Jackie didn't really count. They had a marriage of convenience—he needed to move out of his mother's house, and she wanted to get into medical school. Two through five were legitimate, but his second ex-wife, Sharon, died and sent him Theresa, wife number six, to be his "one true love and his second chance at being a father." When that didn't work according to plan, she sent him Tricia, wife number seven, to once again be his "soul mate and second-second chance at being a father." It's not Dad's fault that Sharon's ghost was a lousy matchmaker; he could have reduced the total by one if she had been more skilled. What, you'll never be able to remember all those names in order? Fine. We'll just call them #One, #Two, #Three, #Four, etc.

11. The number of stepmothers I have had with my father. Hint: it's one less than my half-sister Juli had. Here, I'll help: four. No, Rose didn't count. They were engaged for five years but never married. Okay, four and a half then. Don't ask me how you'll make it fit. You were the one who insisted on accuracy.

12. The number of stepbrothers and -sisters I have had, combined. Don't count my half-sister Juli; we have the same biological father. *Step* is Latin for "not my family." You didn't know I took Latin? Well, maybe I didn't. Take four from Margaret, five from Jan, two from Theresa, and the current four

from Tricia. Fifteen. What about Stan and Tony? No, they don't count, I don't care what my father says. They are my half-sister's half-brothers on her mother's side. Juli and I have the same father, different mothers, so her half-brothers are not my blood. Their mother divorced my father before I was born, so they aren't step-anything. No, there won't be a quiz at the end. You can relax.

13. How many times I've been divorced. Just twice: Samson and Mike. When your father's been married seven times, you know that two trips around the carousel are all the rides you are allotted. I prefer to make my own embarrassing mistakes, not repeat his. No, three times is not a charm. Wedding rings have a habit of making husbands lose interest in me. I would never subject a good relationship to the court system—there is no part of me that wants to walk down that aisle again. Nope, no way. Except those wedding dresses are really pretty . . .

Did you like my little puzzle? What do you mean, I was supposed to sort them by "across" and "down?" Someone should have told me sooner. My family has never been good at fitting into boxes or following the rules. I'm glad I was able to have it make sense at all.

notes from the fourth wall
this is how it feels to write
about lesbian parents

It feels like strong female hands pushing you forward, while their hope presses down on your face and shoulders. It is your face they want to put on a poster, your voice they expect to proclaim to the world how normal and beautiful it is to be raised by lesbians. You can't breathe—the air is thickened with the expectation and hope of a generation of lesbian parents. You look back into their shining, happy eyes, these women who have been your extended family, who came to New Year's Eve parties every year and tied your shoelaces for you when you were small. You know you can't write the story they expect, these nice normal lesbians, because you don't actually know what it feels like to be raised by nice normal lesbians. You only know what it was like to be raised with a mentally ill lesbian stepmother and a mother trying her hardest to keep the family together. Their sexuality was far less significant.

You also know that if you write the truth, the anti-gay movement will put your face on their posters instead. It seems like there is no way to just write your story without becoming someone's poster child. You are not just your own voice, your own history—rather, you carry the expectations of both extremes.

The truth is that you don't know many lesbian parents. Your parents didn't have many friends with children. There was Marty, whose son Jim was a year older than your brother. There was Marilyn, who had a baby when you were eleven, but her child wasn't even close to being your peer. That was the circle you had growing up.

Once, in college, you met a girl your exact age who said, "It took me a long time to realize my mother wasn't a bad parent because she was gay, she was a bad parent because she was an alcoholic." Back when you were eighteen, this casual conversation in a parking lot gave voice to everything you had always felt but had not known how to say, except, of course, that neither of your lesbian parents were alcoholics. It was always murkier for you.

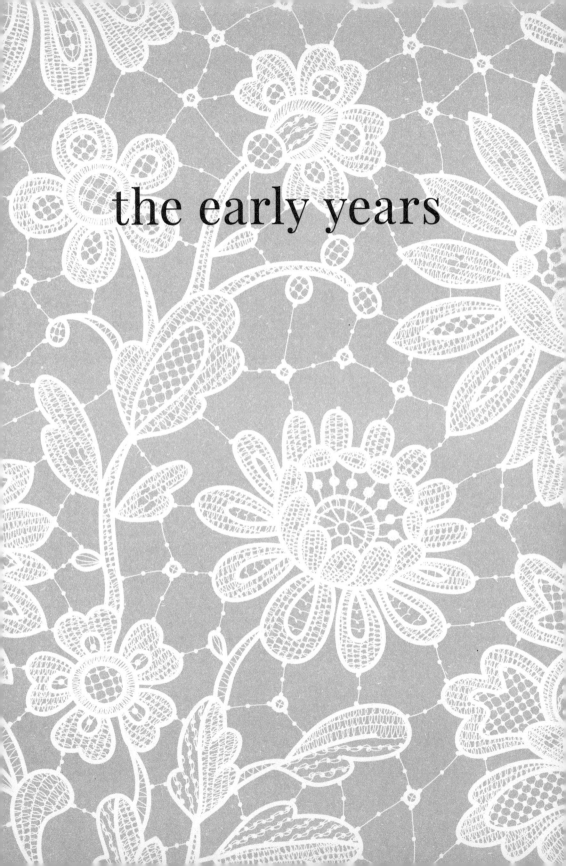

the early years

girl

Picture a scrawny little girl, with shoulder blades that stick out like chicken wings, an outie belly button, and detached earlobes. She has big brown eyes and messy brown hair. When Stepmother combs Girl's hair with a fine-toothed men's comb, it bites into her scalp and makes her cry, so she avoids combing her hair as much as possible. Her knees are stained brownish-green from playing outside, and her bathtub is filled with water-logged Barbies—her favorite toys.

Every night her family eats at the kitchen table—Girl in the seat up against the north wall, because she is the only one little enough to fit there; Brother to her right, pushed up against the western wall for the same reason; Mother across from Girl and closest to the fridge; and Stepmother, Mother's "wus-band" (woman-husband), at the head of the table next to the stove. The table is wood-grained Formica, the floor is green asbestos tile that wouldn't take a shine, and the overhead light is a circular fluorescent tube light that makes a *tttttts* like an electronic insect when the switch is flipped on. Girl's father lives far off in Alaska, the divorce so long ago that Girl can't remember when he and Mother were married.

Girl learned early on that she could tune out the world if she had a good book, but her room is always a mess and she always loses the ones from the library, or forgets how many she had to return, and the librarian sometimes makes her leave the library until she pays off her late fees, so she reads the books she already owns over and over. She tries to read at dinner to avoid talking to her family, but Stepmother says, "Put the book away. I'm afraid you will never develop social skills if you read all the time." Sometimes Stepmother gets a little teary-eyed when she tells Girl, "I just want you to have friends and not have your nose stuck in a book." This makes Girl want to fight and scream because she needs some way to stop her brain from thinking so hard: from replaying all the voices of the kids at school, or the sound of her Stepmother always criticizing, and mostly to drown out that small, sad conviction that she is not, and never will be, worth loving by anyone.

She wanted to run away from home. By third grade she had learned to read and write cursive, and could multiply three-digit numbers and do long division. She figured that she had all the skills she needed to make her way in the world. She tried to save her allowance in a plastic sandwich bag hidden in the backyard shed, but she always gave in and unburied the bag of nickels and quarters hidden under the straw. She walked two blocks to the corner store to buy candy, which she ate quickly, as was the house rule: all candy must be consumed on the walk home and the wrapper thrown away outside. She looked at the empty wrapper in her hand and wished she could remember tasting the second Twix bar.

When she opened the side door to the house, she didn't notice the smell of dog and dirty litter boxes. When the family got the second cat Girl promised to clean the cat box every week, but her resolve lasted only a few days. Stepmother always complained that the smell came up through the heat register and kept her from sleeping. This gave Girl a secret schadenfreude, though of course she didn't know that word yet, only the feel of evil pleasure. She "pretended" to forget to change the litter as long as possible, just as she rubbed her dirty-socked feet on Stepmother's pillow whenever she watched TV in her parents' bedroom.

Girl vacillated between fear, longing, and rage, but she learned to suppress the rage as long as possible, so the fear and longing flowed into the space that rage used to occupy. She wanted to be good. She did not want to be anything like Stepmother. When Girl was small, she had a waffle-knit blue blanket with a satin edge. She brought it everywhere she went, dragging it behind her until it turned gray and the original baby blue was only visible deep in the weft. The waffle-knit devolved into mostly strings in a vague blanket shape, and the satin edge was frayed. "When are you going to get rid of that rag?" the teen-aged girls who lived down the hill asked her. It was the same thing Stepmother was always asking. When Girl was four she summoned all her resolve and gave the blanket to Mother and told her to throw it away. Girl ran to her bedroom and threw herself on the bottom of the bunk bed she shared with Brother and cried facedown into her pillow so Mother wouldn't know that she had changed her mind. Mother had been so proud of her for giving up *bankie*. Girl missed *bankie* for weeks, months, years. She thought it was gone forever, so there was no point in saying anything to Mother. Besides, then Mother would no longer be proud of what a big girl she was. That was the start of the longing.

Years later, Girl learned that Mother kept the blanket in a paper bag in the closet until Girl graduated high school. She was surprised that Mother was so sentimental—it wasn't a side she had ever seen. And Girl was also secretly enraged to learn that her *bankie* was right there all along and she could have had that hole filled up inside her, if only she had asked.

The fear was as large as the longing. If Girl's closet door was open, she had nightmares. If she knocked on her parents' door, Stepmother would scream at her to go back to bed. She spent a lot of time awake in the dark.

At Father's house, she had the same nightmare every year. It was a parade of people wearing white dust masks and floating by on a river of smoke. She didn't know why it scared her so much, or why she dreamed it every summer. At Mother's house her dreams were all different. She didn't remember the plot lines when she woke up, but the feel of them would stay wrapped around her for days. Lingering terror lived in the tension of her small muscles, seeped into the marrow of her bones, and combined with all the real-world issues she worried about: bullies at school, nuclear war, getting lost in the grocery store, disappointing her mother, and of course Stepmother's erratic rage.

mother

Mother met Father when he was still married to Sharon, his second wife, although Mother thought Sharon was his first. She didn't know about Jackie until she and Father applied for their own marriage license. Father said his first was a marriage of convenience and barely counted. "She couldn't get into medical school unless she was married, I couldn't move out of my mother's house until I was married. That's all it was," Father told her. At that point, it was too late for second thoughts. Mother was eight years younger than Father, with long black hair down to her waist, an hourglass figure that she wished was a little less padded, and clear hazel eyes. "Your father told me he had an open marriage with Sharon, but I refused to date him until he was separated," Mother told Girl years later.

Juli, Sharon's daughter and Girl's half-sister, had a different story. "I remember when your mother first came around. 'Dad's got a new girlfriend,' my mom said. And that woman was your mother," Juli told Girl. Juli was eight years older than Girl, practically a grown-up.

There was a handmade kitchen table in Girl's basement, stained a pale blue, and on the bottom was carved, MADE BY CLINT LILLIBRIDGE AND HIS TWO WIVES, SHARON AND CARRIE, so at least the open marriage part of the story could be verified.

"Your father's marriage did not survive the death of Sebrina, Juli's older sister," Mother explained to Girl. "Most marriages fall apart when a child dies. It's sad, but it happens."

Mother and Father had a whirlwind romance, marrying at the courthouse. Mother wore a leopard-print minidress, and Father wore jeans. They brought Millie, Mother's mother, flowers on the way to the ceremony. No one could imagine a wedding with Mother's father so recently deceased. Mother thought she and Father had a good marriage, even though she thought it was a little unnatural that they never fought. Father was studying for his boards in pediatrics, and she got pregnant with Brother, and then Girl. Millie died before Brother was born, but Mother was close to her brother and cousins. She was not yet without family. Then one day she opened the glove box in her VW Bug and found a pair of women's panties that were not her own. There was a one-year anniversary card as well. Mother was six months pregnant with Girl at the time.

"I thought we had an open marriage," Father had said, although clearly this was wishful thinking on his part. Mother dragged him to counseling, where he wrote down only her name under "name of patient" on the intake form. By the time Girl was crawling, Mother asked Father to move out. As soon as Mother sorted out a place to live and had packed their things, she and the children left. It had been his house, after all, and it didn't seem right to keep it.

Mother stood at the top of the mountain, skis pointed downhill. She had buried her father, then spent two years watching her mother slowly die. She thought her happiness had ended with her marriage, but here she was. She looked down the slope at the white-frosted pines, the diamond snow, not just watching life out the window anymore, but being a part of it. She pushed off with her poles, the wind flowing across her cheeks, listening to the *shhh-shhh* of her skis as she pushed with one leg, then the other. She bent over in a crouch and let gravity do the rest. The universe was pulling her along, buoying her up, giving her what she needed.

Although Mother could provide adequately for the children, she wanted to do better than always living paycheck to paycheck. She wanted to raise them up to a higher standard of living, so she enrolled at the University of Rochester to finish her bachelor's. It meant signing up for food stamps and taking the last of her savings and buying a single-wide trailer. The day she walked into the government office and admitted that she needed help—there weren't words to describe the humiliation she felt. Afterward she took the last fifty bucks out of her checking account and bought a red sweater. It was dumb and frivolous and irresponsible, but somehow, it had felt necessary to do something that was for just her, not the children—something impractical that said she was still important, still visible, still deserving of nice things. She was flying on hope, flying down the ski slope and out of poverty and into a rich life filled with books and politics and new ideas. And she was carrying the children along with her.

It was hard being poor. She wanted to give the kids everything, but she had so little. Sometimes, at the end of the month, she pulled out the beige flannel bag that held her father's coin collection and cashed in a few to make ends meet. She made a sandbox out of uncooked oatmeal for her toddlers to play in at one end of the living room. She stapled blankets over the thin trailer walls in the winter to keep out the wind. But she could feel her mind expanding with every class: psychology, literature, the composition classes she was so good at, and the math her brother, Lewis, had to help her understand. Plenty of guys asked her out, and she dated a few of them, but she was protective of her time, her new life. And let's be honest, men didn't want to settle down with a woman who already had children.

Their first Christmas alone, Girl asked Mother, "What are you going to ask Santa for?"

"Oh, I don't know. A ski rack for the car," Mother said. She thought that would be the end of it, but Girl and Brother kept bringing it up, kept saying how they were sure Santa would bring her a ski rack. Eventually, Mother found one on clearance and wrapped it for herself, so they wouldn't lose their faith in Mr. Claus. Mother had a band saw and a jigsaw inherited from her father, and after the kids were asleep, or when they were at Father's, she made them wooden elephants on wheels, with a handle on top to roll them back and forth.

The night before Christmas, Girl woke up and had to go to the bathroom. Girl's bedroom in the trailer had a tiny half-bath, but for some reason, she refused to use it.

"I wanna use your bathroom, Mommy," Girl said.

"But you have a nice little bathroom all of your own right here!" Oh Lord, if Girl walked through the living room and saw the presents under the tree, it would be all over. Mother did not want to do Christmas at 2 a.m.

"Please, Mommy," Girl asked, her lower lip sticking out.

"Okay, okay," she said. Mother picked up Girl and carried her through the living room. Girl's big brown eyes looked at all the presents, but she didn't say a word. She used the bathroom, then Mother carried her back through the living room, and Girl looked and looked, but still didn't speak. Thankfully, she went back to sleep as soon as Mother tucked her in.

feminism

Mother discovered feminism in college. It was like discovering the atom bomb. Long conversations about inequality and overcoming society's mores kept her up late at night. She wasn't afraid to work for justice, carrying picket signs for the Equal Rights Amendment, taking the children along on protest marches and shushing them during the speeches at consciousness-raising rallies. She never burned a bra, because that would be completely impractical and uncomfortable, but she cheered while other women did. She threw out her makeup, high heels, and razor blade and became a *natural woman*. She had already cut her hair short as soon as the babies were old enough to pull it, but the style showed off her strong cheekbones. Her hair went gray early, but she liked how the white streaks at her temples contrasted with her nearly-black hair.

Mother went with a friend to a lesbian party and stood at the edge of the dance floor, not at all sure how she felt about this. All she knew was that every time she got into a relationship with men, she lost her voice and fell back into the same sex-stereotyped role she hated. And besides, none of the men she met wanted anything beyond sex from a woman with children. Her friend Marty convinced her to dance with a woman named Bonnie, and before the season changed Mother and Bonnie moved in together—just like the joke said: "What do lesbians do on the third date? Rent a U-Haul."

Girl wanted a baby doll, but Mother refused. She was not raising her daughter to be a housewife who wasted her life taking care of children. No dolls. None. No babies, no sex-symbol Barbies with their unrealistic proportions. That worked until Mother came home from class one day when Girl was three. Girl had taken a five-pound bag of kitty litter and wrapped it in her blankie. She was rocking her "baby" and singing it songs. After that, Mother gave up and bought Girl a baby doll. She even bought Barbies for her every Christmas. But she did not let the children watch *Hee Haw* or Archie Bunker. There was only so far she was willing to go.

Mother wanted the children to be sex-positive—no shame, no negative labels, no sexist expectations. She wanted Girl to phone boys she liked, not wait for them to call her. Nothing was more pathetic than a girl wasting her weekend waiting for the phone to ring. She told both kids the basic facts of reproduction when they were in preschool, before they asked too many embarrassing questions. She taught them the medical terms for their bodies—no dingle-dangle or boobs or titties. She gave Girl a book when she was in fourth grade. It said, "sex is for love, sex is for baby-making, and sex is for fun, and any of those reasons are okay, as long as both people are on the same page." She made sure Girl knew where her copy of *Our Bodies, Ourselves* was on the bookshelf, and encouraged her to look between her legs with a mirror so she would know what was down there.

Girl squeezed the back of her calf. Was that what her breasts would feel like? She wondered how the woman breathed when the man lay on top of her. She called boys, but they did not call her back. This whole free love thing, it was like Girl was doing the Macarena and everyone else was dancing the Electric Slide. She didn't know the choreography, and everyone knew she was *that kind of girl* long before she did. But she wasn't intentionally flouting the rules; she never knew they existed.

yearning

Mother divorced Father when Girl was eighteen months old, Brother three years, Mother thirty-one. Mother cried a lot that year—face-down on her bed, pillow muffling her sobs, the same way Girl cried. One day Girl toddled into her mother's bedroom and found Mother crying. Girl left wordlessly, then returned with her beloved blue *bankie* and handed it to Mother. It was the best thing she had to offer. Right then, Girl decided that it was her job to take care of her mother above all else, even above herself.

When Girl forgot and was pouty because she didn't get her way, or was lazy with her chores, or didn't work hard enough at school, later it would stab inside her chest, like a stick that was sharpened at both ends. Mother's disappointment spun an invisible line of remorse, connecting Girl's forehead to her navel, contracting her skinny, flat-chested torso into the letter C, Girl's insides filled with something that burned like acid. Shame. She wanted to die.

Mother stood in front of the white stove with electric burners, only some of which worked. There was always a shiny silver percolator on the counter. Under her feet was a cracked green asbestos tile floor. Masculine—and ugly—brown paneling went halfway up the walls. Limp, fly-specked, yellow-and-white-checked curtains with daisies on them framed the window. The white countertop was veined in gold like marble, but made out of a thin sheet of some smooth plastic-y stuff with a gray metal ribbed edge holding it down. Girl wrapped her six-year-old body around Mother's leg, and Mother dragged Girl around the kitchen as she cooked dinner. Girl was too needy, but somehow Mother tolerated it. Girl knew that she had to let Mother breathe, to step back, to stop hugging her mother as hard as she could, to just get enough Mommy to get by for a little while, even if it was not enough to feel full. She forced herself to let go when Mother said, "Girl, you're smothering me." Girl knew she needed to love Mother less, so she didn't devour both of them. And her inability to let go of Mother's leg filled her with the shame of over-wanting.

father

When Girl was three, Father lived a few miles away with his new wife, #Four. The children visited him every other weekend. At Father's house, Girl shared a room with Brother, which Father kept locked at night.

One morning the sky through the curtainless window was starting to grow lighter, but it wasn't bright enough to signal that the day had arrived. Girl knew that it wasn't time to get up yet, but she had to go to the bathroom. She rattled the white metal doorknob, but it was locked.

"Daddy? I have to tinkle!" she called through the closed door as she knocked. No answer came. Girl pounded the door with her fist. Pounding hurt less than knocking on the old wooden door. She shifted her weight back and forth in what Mother called "the pee-pee dance."

"Daddy! I have to tinkle! Bad!" Brother rolled over and faced the wall, ignoring her, but there was nothing he could do to help, anyway.

Girl held her hand between her legs, her fingers holding back the stream of urine. Father wasn't coming. She would have to use the mayonnaise jar he left between the children's beds when he locked them in last night. Her four-year-old brother could pee in the jar just fine, but it was harder for a girl. She pulled her nightie up around her waist and squatted over the jar, but she couldn't see down there and missed the small glass opening. Warm urine ran down Girl's leg and splashed over her feet, puddling on the wood floor as hot tears flooded her cheeks. Girl cried and called again for Father. *It isn't fair,* she thought. *I am a big girl, I know how to use the bathroom on my own, and little girls can't pee in jars.* She pulled her cotton nightgown over her head and tried to dry her legs off with it, then left it in the puddle of pee for Father to find when he finally woke up and unlocked the door.

That Christmas Father gave Brother an anatomically correct boy-doll with blond curly hair. It peed if you gave it a bottle. Father was very excited for Brother to open this gift in particular—it was the first gift Father pulled out from the pile. Girl was very interested in the naked doll's plastic molded penis, which was different from Brother's. It looked like a pink elephant trunk. Not understanding the difference between circumcised and uncircumcised penises, Girl wanted to look closer to see what was wrong with it.

"No, Girl! It's not *your* doll! Get back and let Brother see it!" Father held the naked doll in the crook of his arm. "Look, Brother, this is how you feed your baby." Father tilted the little white bottle up to the doll's open mouth. The instant the baby started to "drink," a stream of water arced out of the doll's plastic penis.

"Get a bucket!" Father yelled to #Four, jumping out of the old brown armchair. He held the doll at arm's length while it continued emptying its body cavity of water. #Four ran to the kitchen to get a bucket, but it was too late—Father and the rug were soaked. Girl was glad the doll peed on her father, even if it was really just water.

Girl and Brother watched as Father and #Four put the last few boxes into their yellow-and-white Dodge van they called Big Mama. They closed the doors with a final bang. Father had a scraggly hippy beard and his hair curled over his collar. #Four had long white-blond hair past her shoulder blades, straight and fine as corn silk. They were all smiles as they gave the children one last hug and climbed up to the white leather front seats. They were moving to Alaska. Father, #Four, and her teenaged children were driving from Rochester, New York, up the Al-Can Highway to Anchorage, over four thousand miles away. The van trailed dust clouds and exhaust as the children waved until Big Mama turned the corner at the end of the city block. Girl didn't know why Father didn't want them to go, too, and she wondered if she would ever see Father again.

After the van drove away, the children went back to Mother and Stepmother's house on Lake Road. Mother was in graduate school and worked as a nanny for a family with nine children. The two-bedroom house was part of her salary and sat at the top of her employer's property. They all shared the same yard, though the children knew the manicured lawn, like their house, wasn't really their own.

When the children got home, Brother went into the bathroom and turned on the faucet. The sink was old and it had two faucets, one for hot and one for cold, each with a white porcelain x-shaped handle. Brother took a photograph of Father that he was holding in his hand and held it under the running water. He rubbed his thumb over and over his father's picture until the color came off and Father's face ran down the drain. Girl wondered how he knew that would happen.

When Brother was five and Girl was four, they went to visit their father in Alaska. #Four's children were there: Jane, the oldest, was sixteen; Sara was fourteen; and Anne was twelve. Three girls with long, straight, white-blond hair. So pretty and cool in their hip-hugger bell-bottoms. Girl's half-sister Juli was twelve, the same age as Anne, and Juli was blood, not step, so Girl always loved her best. Father and #Four only had two bedrooms downstairs, so they split up Brother and Girl. In one room slept Juli and Sara, in the other was Jane. There was a brown couch in Jane's room, and a camper in the driveway. Brother and Girl alternated nights—one in the camper, one on the couch—then they switched, except neither of the youngest children wanted to sleep outside in the driveway alone. The camper smelled like mildew, it was scary, and there was no one nearby.

One night it was Brother's turn to sleep outside, but he cried to Father. "I'm scared, I don't want to sleep in the camper, I wanna sleep inside," he said. As usual, Father could not resist his only boy.

"Fine," he said, "Girl can sleep outside again."

"But it's not my turn! I slept there last night!" Girl protested. Her lower lip stuck out and her face melted into tears. It was so scary outside alone. It wasn't fair.

"Stop your blubbering!" Father yelled, scooping up Girl and throwing her across the room. Her small body thudded against the couch, then was still. Juli ran to her sister's ragdoll body, not sure if she should touch her, shake her, pick her up—willing her to cry, to speak, to breathe. Finally, Girl opened her eyes and put her arms around Juli's neck.

"She's sleeping with me tonight," Juli said, and that was the end of it. She wasn't going to let anything happen to Girl, not if she could help it.

juli and sebrina

Juli loved Girl more than anything. When Girl's mother got pregnant, Juli knew she would have a sister because she had prayed for a sister every night since God took Sebrina away. The first time Girl's mother was pregnant she had a boy, which was fine and all, but Juli already had two half-brothers from her own mother's first marriage. This time, she knew God would give her a sister, and He did.

Juli was eight when Girl was born, and she flew from Seattle to Rochester to see the baby. Juli was short—she hadn't outgrown her clothes in three years, but her parents didn't seem to notice—and she had coarse red hair and baby blue eyes behind thick glasses. She couldn't wait until she was old enough for contact lenses.

Juli didn't remember much about Sebrina. She had only one memory, really, of them sitting together in a red wagon. Juli reached back to hold her big sister's hand. Small hands sticky-warm, heads together, giggling. Knowing she was safe, because her big sister was behind her.

June 1967—Frankie Valli's "Can't Take My Eyes Off You" was top of the charts. The Six-Day War came and went in the Middle East. And Juli's sister Sebrina died of brain cancer. Blond hair falling out in long strands on the floor, leaving her naked head always cold—she never wore her little blond wig.

Sebrina was on morphine but it made her face itch and she scratched her nose raw and bloody, so Father and Sharon tried not to give her the drug unless they had to. Sebrina couldn't swallow very well and could only drink from a straw. Sebrina was not allowed to play with friends because the neighborhood kids would stand around gawking and hoping she'd die in front of them so they could watch. "Do you think she's gonna die today?" they whispered, but not quietly enough to keep Father from hearing—children poking each other, giggling, talking too loudly. Sebrina, scab-faced, shorn head, blue eyes looking hopeful.

Father was given a blank death certificate to fill in when the time came, which was not exactly legal, but a professional courtesy between doctors. Everyone knew it was just a matter of time.

Sebrina slept in bed between her parents. One night she awoke and asked for a glass of milk. This time, Father chose not to give her a straw. He gave Sebrina the cup of milk and watched her drown as she tried to swallow. There was no law that allowed mercy killing, and it seemed pointless to make her continue to suffer. Father did not wake up his wife when their daughter struggled and sputtered and died.

After Sebrina died, Juli escaped her bedroom every night to look for her missing sister. Sometimes they found Juli outside in the street, trying to find Sebrina.

Sebrina's body was donated to the local medical school. "Few kids have cancer, it seemed selfish not to," Father told Girl. "They would call us when they were done with this bit or that, and ask if we wanted it piecemeal. So we didn't bother to claim her body," he explained. Had Sebrina's mother wanted to donate her little girl, or had Father insisted on being pragmatic and she was too despondent to fight him?

Why didn't they at least claim her bones? What did the university do with her four-year-old skeleton when they were done dissecting Girl and Juli's sister? "We didn't bother to claim her body." No body, no grave, no headstone. The little four-year-old blond girl came and went with nothing to remember her by. She was the first child given chemo at the University of Washington. She's probably in a textbook somewhere.

But God gave Juli another sister, and this time, she would not let anything happen to her. When Father and Girl's mother got divorced, Juli refused to visit Father until he agreed that Juli could stay for a week in the trailer with Girl. She didn't mind getting up at 6:00 a.m. when Girl woke up. When Girl came riding up on her Big Wheel and gave Juli her found treasure—a dehydrated frog that had been run over by a car and was as flat and hard as a potato chip—she thanked Girl and told her what a wonderful present it was. She held the carcass between two fingers and only threw it out when Girl wasn't looking.

joyride

The carpet in the trailer was 1960s vintage, already a decade old and filled with musty smells and the stains of someone else's history. Mother and Bonnie, her first girlfriend, were still asleep, their bedroom door locked. When Girl and Brother woke up, Mother had carried them to the living room and sat them in front of the TV, then went back to bed, the same as always. Today, Bonnie's son, John, was there as well—it was a family sleepover.

"The rainbow bars. Turn it back to the colored bars one," Girl said to Brother. His longer arms meant that he always won their battles over the TV channel.

"No, the dots. The fighting dots," Brother said, holding the knob so Girl couldn't turn it back. The children watched the test pattern every morning as they waited for the broadcast to come on while they sat on the carpet eating Cheerios.

"This is stupid," John said. He was Bonnie's son, a soon-to-be-quasi-stepbrother. John was a year older than Brother and surly. He already went to kindergarten, not just nursery school.

"No, just watch," Brother told him. "Once we saw a rocket take off."

John rolled his eyes, but it was true—one morning the familiar black-and-white dots were suddenly replaced by a tall rocket erupting off its launch pad, the needle-tip rising into the clouds. Girl was there. She saw it. It could happen again.

John ignored the younger children and walked to the door, standing on tiptoe to slide the deadbolt to the right, the white metal door to the trailer swinging free. John walked outside, and the siblings followed into the chill of the early morning air.

They had a piece of straggled lawn outside their trailer with a good tree big enough to hold a swing, but the driveway and road were gravel. The siblings were lucky that John was tall enough to unlock the door. Outside was always better than inside, especially before cartoons came on.

That crisp, early morning, the three children found that Mother had forgotten to lock the door of her school-bus-yellow VW Bug. John graciously allowed the siblings to climb in first, sliding over to the passenger's side. The children were small and skinny and fit side by side easily on the dark gray seat. Girl could not see over the dashboard with its round dials and overflowing ashtray. John took the driver's seat, but he earned that right by providing those extra inches of height that bought their freedom. His five-year-old hand released the parking brake, and the tires crept down the incline, gaining speed, and now they were flying, soaring, as they rolled down the hill. A Herculean man loomed out of nowhere, his hands pushing on the hood of the car, shoulders bulging in his tank top as he caught the vehicle and stopped their joy ride. It was okay, though. Girl had felt that rollercoaster feeling in her belly and she had seen a man stop a car with his bare hands. It was enough. After that morning, Mother installed a slide lock close to the top of the trailer's door, where John couldn't reach.

two montessori schools

Brother went to preschool and Girl didn't, which she thought was completely unfair. There was no way Girl was being left behind while he got to do something as neat and fun as he made preschool sound. At drop-off one day Girl went up to his teacher and apprised her of the unfairness of the situation. The teacher said any child that could speak that well should be in school, regardless of her age, so Girl got to go, even though she was only two. Mother was cleaning houses and going to college, so having the siblings together made her life easier.

Although they were eighteen months apart, Mother always treated the children as if they were the same age. The children had the same bedtime, the same rules, even the same friends. Girl always got to do whatever Brother did, and Girl thought of them more like twins than older and younger siblings. She resented anything that implied otherwise.

Girl and Brother attended Trinity Montessori school. They poured water into little dishes of clay to learn the difference between islands and peninsulas. They shook buttermilk in jars with marbles inside to make butter. They traced letters made out of sandpaper and read *The Jet*, which had an orange cover and was clearly better than any other early reader in existence—it involved a man's hat falling into the mud—what could top that? But there was something weird going on at Trinity Montessori. There were a lot of parents with closed-up faces, mouths turned downward. Some of Girl's friends stopped going.

"Now, Girl, you may hear some people say bad things about the school director. Some people think she is a bad person and don't like her, but I think she's a nice person. She just had some problems and went a little crazy, but she's okay now. You are totally safe there."

Mother always talked to the children on an adult level. She explained to them how the director of their school had been a nun and had given birth to a baby in the cathedral of a Catholic church and then killed it, but Mother was really sure this was an isolated event and that the nun had probably been abused by a man so it wasn't her fault, and Mother was quite certain the director wasn't going to kill random kids, and the church was sure, too, or they wouldn't let her continue to teach at the school.

Girl wasn't bothered by it. If Mother said it was okay, it was okay, just grown-up stuff. What she hated was when she wore a leotard under her skirt and had to pee really badly and wound up hopping around on one foot trying to get everything off in time, and sometimes she didn't quite make it. The small spot of urine in her underpants humiliated her, because it wasn't her fault that not all her leotards came with snaps at the crotch and that she could never remember which ones did and which ones didn't. The other thing she hated were tights that were too short, and how her legs felt as if something was tied around her thighs, making it harder to run or climb things. Girl loved to climb things. But she was a little wary of Sister Maureen, in spite of what Mother had said, and kept a suspicious eye on all of her teachers.

Next door to Mother's white trailer was a pretty yellow one. Girl wished their trailer was a real color, not just white. She wished the trailer park had a paved road instead of a gravel one, because she had to push the blue pedals of her Big Wheel extra hard to make it go, and sometimes the front wheel would spin but the rest of the three-wheeler wouldn't move at all. In the yellow trailer next door lived two women with a couple of dogs—one nice black-and-white one and one mean-sounding German Shepherd that barked all the time. The neighbors also had a rabbit that hopped around the living room without a cage and chewed up their telephone wires.

When Girl's family first moved in one of the neighbor ladies had come over to introduce herself.

"Hi," she said, with a southern accent. It sounded like "haah" to Girl. "I just fried up some milkweed buds and thought I'd share," the neighbor said.

"Uh, thank you," Mother said, waiting for the woman with the sporty-short brown hair to leave before she threw out the cooked weeds. Honestly, some people were just too strange.

Girl liked when the woman in the yellow trailer let her pet the rabbit, but if Girl woke that lady up on a Saturday when she and Brother were swinging on their tire swing—man, could she yell. A year later Mother ran into this neighbor lady (who had since moved away) at a lesbian social. She asked

Mother to dance and they wound up kissing, even though they both were living with different partners.

Mother went home and told Bonnie that very night that they were through, and she and the children moved into a little yellow two-bedroom house with bunk beds. Stepmother came over to the little yellow house shortly after Mother and the children moved in. Mother made lasagna, and everything was going fine until Girl threw up all over the table. Do you know what thrown-up lasagna looks like? Pretty much the same as a dish of lasagna after a few slices have been cut, when it's goopy and unfurled, the noodles and ricotta swimming in an oily red sauce. Stepmother asked for seconds anyway, while Brother jumped up and down singing, "Stinky noodle! Stinky noodle!" over and over again. That second piece of lasagna won Mother over, and Stepmother moved her boxes of art supplies and clothing and musical instruments in, taking over the side of the bed closest to the door.

Girl and Brother were sent to a new school, Webster Montessori, where they had to sit still in little chairs, and Girl was told not to make her eights by stacking two circles on top of each other but instead to make the twist that was always so hard. They had to learn French and when the children talked too much or got out of their seats, the teacher would grab their earlobes and pull down hard, making them burn long after they were released from her grip.

"Teacher threw Billy's shoes out the window today," Girl told Mother on the ride home.

"Why would she do that?" Mother asked.

"Because he untied them during class. And there's a dog outside that eats shoes." One of the schoolchildren's favorite ways to interrupt class was to untie their shoes, requiring the teacher to stop and retie them.

"Did she ever throw your shoes out the window?"

"Yeah, but the dog wasn't there that day so she just pulled my ear." Mother had no idea what Girl was talking about, but it sounded crazy.

Girl could tell Mother didn't believe her, but it was true, exactly like she said. The teacher was mean and Girl missed Trinity Montessori, even if the director killed her baby. Girl thought that it didn't make sense that nice people sometimes did worse things than mean people.

stepmother

Stepmother had become Mother's same-sex life partner, or "wusband," as she liked to call herself after they had their own private commitment ceremony in the woods. When Girl said "her parents," she meant this woman and her mother. She never considered her father one of her real parents. He was just Father, who lived far away and had a new family. Although she visited him, he was mostly important for his absence. Day-to-day life was Girl, Brother, Mother, and Stepmother. She didn't remember much of life before they became a family, just little snippets of things, but Girl did remember how happy she had been in the single-wide trailer before Stepmother came to live with them.

Girl remembered one nice woman Mother dated, who played the guitar and sang songs. She liked her a lot better than Stepmother, but that woman went into the hospital and died. It would be many years before Girl learned that this woman and Stepmother were the same person—the woman who went into the hospital to have a hysterectomy came out someone with a hormone imbalance that turned her into someone unrecognizable.

Girl didn't care that her mother was gay—it was the way her mother had been for as long as she could remember. But everyone else made it a big deal. Girl cared that Stepmother was always yelling, and that Mother loved Stepmother best—more than she loved Girl and Brother, it seemed. Girl cared that Stepmother appeared to hate Brother and hit him all the time. Stepmother told Girl over and over that she loved her, but her words felt like nothing.

Stepmother was what they called "Baby Butch" back in the 1970s. This was the best kind of butch to be; tough and strong but with a cute face. In the lesbian world, she was a catch. Throughout her life, a lot of men asked Girl why lesbians were so ugly, by which they meant masculine, and if ugly women became lesbians because they couldn't attract men. Men asked, "Have you ever noticed that most lesbians are women that men wouldn't want to fuck?" The truth was that while the lesbians Girl knew were a few decades behind in their fashion role models (think mullets, lots of mullets) they had a different scale of attractiveness. Many didn't want to look feminine, not because they were bad at it, but because they did not subscribe to the fashion industry's sexualization of women. The butch look was popular because women still wanted to feel like their partner could protect them and kick some ass if need be, but there was also an appreciation for the androgynous, the gender-bending.

Stepmother wanted to be a 1950s-style husband. She wore burgundy sweater-vests over pale yellow button-down oxfords, and jeans or polyester slacks that hugged her fat stomach. Her small feet were always in loafers or sneakers, never heels. When Stepmother went to work she wore skirted business suits under duress, and she always wore the same small, gold hoop earrings. Her hair was short and dark brown, parted on the side. Everyone in the family had the same haircut: Mother, Girl, Brother, Stepmother. Only Girl hated it. Girl wanted long hair and ponytails, but she wasn't allowed to grow it until third grade, or until she stopped crying when Stepmother combed it, whichever came first.

Stepmother often went to the library to find home repair manuals. She liked to fix things. She got a book on how to patch concrete and repaired the basement wall, saving them five thousand dollars. But she must have missed something, because by the time Girl was twenty, the house had slowly collapsed inward, so that the light switch plate in Girl's old bedroom was half-buried behind the door frame.

Once, Stepmother was repairing a rusted-out hole in her Datsun station wagon. Girl stood nearby, watching and chewing gum.

"Girl, give me your gum," Stepmother said. Girl pulled her gum out of her mouth with her thumb and forefinger and handed the wad to Stepmother. Stepmother balled it up and used it as filler for the hole in the car, painting over it with touch-up paint.

"Hey! That's my gum!" Girl protested, poking the repair with her finger.

"Look what you did! You dented it! Now I have to do the whole thing over again. Do you have any more gum?" Stepmother asked.

notes from the fourth wall
10 steps to raising children
who behave properly

1. It is good if you can procure children who are already slightly damaged by other people, say, a father who abandoned them or a parent who has untreated mental illness or alcoholism. In our experience, this will cut their learning time by half.

2. Yell often and randomly. This is so obvious that it almost doesn't merit writing down. Keep in mind that all yelling is not created equal. For example, constant yelling can be confused with hearing loss, and is therefore ignored. To be truly scary, the yell needs a narrowing of eyes to provide an edge of meanness. Fun words to yell: loser, wimp, pussy, or WhatTheFuckIsWrongWithYou. Yelling without possibility of following up with physical harm is all foam and no latte, which leads us to #3 . . .

3. Corporal punishment. This is a no-brainer, but for those of you who are faint of heart, please keep in mind that one need not draw blood or leave a mark to provide psychological damage. Spanking hard enough to sting will suffice, particularly if it is carried out in a basement or other scary place. Best practices include changing up the requirements for spanking/hitting/ et cetera so that the children never know what will result in physical punishment. Further information on this technique can be found in several popular dog-training manuals under *intermittent negative reinforcement*. Think of yourself as a slot machine that randomly punches the player.

4. Never underestimate the power of negativity. If you don't have the physical stamina required for #3, it can be just as effective to ensure that the child knows they are a failure, preferably in everything. All-pro parents know that there is

always one good child and one bad child, so it's not hard to find reasons to draw everyone's attention to the loser child's errors. If done properly, one only needs to throw a handful of criticism in the direction of the good child to scare them into submission. The good child knows that if they cross over into bad-child territory there is no redemption. Helpful phrases: it is all your fault, you can't do anything right, I should have known you'd screw this up, etc.

5. Privacy is for the weak. While some advanced parents actually remove doors from bedrooms, we have found that walking in on naked teenagers works just as well, especially if you pause and linger for conversation. Long conversation. With roving eyes. Also effective is the Stand Silently and Stare While Scratching Your Own Butt technique.

6. Blow your nose at the dinner table, open the Kleenex, and look at it. Manners, like all rules, are just for children. "Do as I say, not as I do" sounds better than "we don't hit people in this family unless I am the one doing the hitting."

7. Do not, under any circumstances, defend your children from bullies at school. They might get the idea that bullying is not an effective behavior management technique. Better yet, make sure they know that if they stand up for themselves, they will be punished even more once they get home.

8. Don't forget to take everything personally. We all know that everything children do is just to spite their parents: hair styles, clothing, music. They need to consider your feelings in every decision they make, because you really do know better than they do. If they can anticipate your judgment, they will self-correct before disaster strikes.

9. If you have not yet made fun of your children, please put this book down now and do so immediately. Scorn, ridicule, tease. It teaches them to have a thicker skin and also provides endless hours of pure enjoyment.

10. In all of your behavior modification/training of the children, don't forget their mother. The more you berate her in front of the children, the more complete your power is over the entire household. They will quickly learn that they have no advocate, that there is no one who can influence or sway your opinion.

no one minded the children

There were two black grand pianos placed back-to-back, the keyboards opposite from one another. The floor was shiny hardwood, and Girl's and Brother's three- and four-year-old feet echoed as they ran underneath them. Girl could run beneath the pianos without ducking. She and Brother ran up and down the room and laughed, even though they weren't supposed to laugh, because this was a funeral. Mother's only brother had died suddenly of pneumonia, a complication of chicken pox. He was thirty-seven. No one minded the children running beneath the pianos. Girl's shoes were shiny black patent leather and she wore white tights that were too short in the crotch and constantly needed to be tugged up when no one was looking.

The moment the children missed when they ran under the pianos was the harsh record player screech of the words, "I am Mother's lover/girlfriend/we are lesbians," spoken by a woman to the mourning relatives milling around in the Jewish funeral home. Like a bell, the words couldn't be un-rung. After the funeral, all the cousins leaked out of Girl's life like water in a sieve, some fighting to leave faster, some dribbling slowly, until they all were gone eventually—all except Girl's uncle's widow. She and her children alone remained family. Maybe if Girl was sitting like a good girl on the sofa she would remember the sound of her relatives turning their backs on them.

Parsky Funeral Home was the only Jewish funeral home in town. There were deep blue curtains for the immediate family to sit behind if they chose, so no one could witness their grief. Mother did not pull the curtains when her father died when she was twenty-five, and she did not pull the curtains when her mother died two years later, but when her only brother died Mother pulled the curtains and stayed alone in her grief. Girl and Brother sat outside the curtains with a friend Mother would never name in the years to come—it was this nameless friend who outed her and chased all of her relatives away. Girl never pressed for details—she was too afraid of making Mother cry.

Stepmother liked to tell a story of two cousins who came over for dinner, holding hands and giggling uncomfortably on the couch. Stepmother said the word *giggle* with derision. Was it Mother and Stepmother who walked away from the extended family, disgusted by their discomfort? The cousin-couple did come to dinner. They were trying—was their effort just not good enough to make them worth keeping? Or did they refuse to return after that one awkward dinner?

When Girl was ten her family was invited back to the annual family reunions where everyone was nice to her but too old to be of interest. She was suddenly supposed to care about these cousins she didn't know, people who still did not invite them over for holidays but always showed up at funerals. Girl always had trouble letting go of resentments.

Mother had a lot of cousins. Back in high school, Mother was forced to take a first cousin to her school dance, and had to wear knee socks instead of pantyhose. When she was first divorced, a female cousin moved in with her to help Mother with the children in exchange for rent. With the death of her brother, Mother became the only surviving member of her immediate family, and then was cut off by all the more distant relations with the utterance of that single word, "lesbian." Only her brother's widow and their children remained.

Girl had no people. They were lost to her when whomever they sat with on the day of the funeral outed Mother.

Years later Girl finally asked Mother, "Who did we sit with at Uncle Bear's funeral?"

"You sat with me," Stepmother said.

"It was Bonnie Mason," Mother answered.

elementary school

the deconstruction of a male child

Brother was older than Girl, but somehow more fragile. He was afraid of dogs, and wouldn't even hold their kitten unless she was wrapped in a towel. Because he was older, he had to do things like go to school first and alone. Because he was always in trouble, Girl's transgressions were often overlooked as inconsequential by comparison. Girl got to trail behind in the wake he broke for both of them, but she made up for it when they were together. She made friends at the day camps they were sent to over the summer, in both New York and Alaska, and introduced them to Brother. She defended him and covered up for him at home. Girl even occasionally did his chores to keep life somewhat on an even keel. It was her job to take care of Brother—no one else was going to.

Stepmother hated everything about Brother. He was a weak little weenie, just as disgusting as that silly bouncing appendage he had between his legs. He wasn't good at sports or making friends, and he wasn't motivated to do his chores or his homework.

Brother was a scrawny boy-child, and he grew so tall and so skinny that Girl called him "the evolution of a pencil—proof that people came from writing implements." He didn't have many friends before high school, and someone was always chasing him or stealing his shoes or sitting behind him in class talking about all the ways they would disembowel him. When he got home, Stepmother constantly told him what a waste he was. "If I were a boy, I could have been a doctor, or a lawyer. You were born with all the privilege I never had, and you just squander it! You are an asshole, just like your father!"

But unlike Girl, Brother sometimes yelled back or got on his bike and rode away. Girl wished she were as brave.

In sixth grade, Brother stopped doing his homework. He just stopped bringing it home or worrying about turning it in. Girl wished she could be so blasé about it, but she hated to be in trouble, hated the teacher's disapproval when she missed an assignment. Brother just stopped caring. Stepmother was enraged, and he was more or less permanently grounded. Stepmother threaded a tiny luggage lock through the hole of the TV plug to keep them from watching it after school.

"I know it's not fair to you, Girl, but Brother is grounded, so neither one of you can watch television," Mother said. Brother didn't mind that, either—when their parents were gone, he just straightened out a paperclip and picked the lock.

Stepmother and Brother fought often and loudly, screaming throughout the house. When Stepmother yelled, Mother grabbed her keys and left.

Girl didn't know what Brother had done this time—or hadn't done, most likely. Chores, homework, or both maybe. This time, Stepmother took him to the basement.

"I refuse to listen to this!" Mother yelled, slamming the green side door behind her. Girl ran outside, but by the time Girl got there, Mother's car was pulling away from the curb. She was never entirely sure if Mother was coming back.

Girl could hear Brother scream from the basement, but she was too afraid to go downstairs. She stood frozen in the kitchen, listening, loathing churning her stomach for her own inaction. Someone needed to save Brother, but she wasn't brave enough.

Years later Mother told Girl, "Stepmother always knew where I was. I went to the movies, always at the Webster Theatre. I'd get a large popcorn and watch a movie by myself—whatever was playing at the time. If I was really mad, sometimes I'd watch two. But I always came home."

When Girl went into the basement the next day, there was a blue wooden paddle broken in half on the ground, the end splintered and frayed. She didn't throw it away—it was the only proof they had. She wanted to outline it in chalk like a crime scene, so Mother couldn't ignore it.

"The paddle wasn't that thick. You are always so dramatic," the children were told.

camping

Every summer, the family went camping. Stepmother's bronze Datsun station wagon left the paved road and turned down the dirt path into the trees. The turnoff was marked by a small green sign that only said, Welcome Friends of Sabra. The sign was round and only a foot wide, hidden among the wildflowers at the edge of the woods. No one would notice it if they weren't looking. Grass and small flowers grew in the hump in the middle of the dirt road, and the trees were so thick they formed a dark tunnel speckled with sunlight. Bushes and branches sometimes brushed the sides of the car, and the children reached their hands out the windows to grab them. The dog sat in the middle of the back seat between Girl and Brother, and once they turned off the main road, the dog whined and wagged, the wispy fur of her tail slapping the children in the face.

When there was no longer any danger of being seen from the main street, Girl and Brother were finally allowed to shed their clothing. Girl frantically pulled off her too-short pants and marginally fashionable shirt in a race to return to her natural state before the car stopped. Her chest was as flat as Brother's, but she was only eight. Their limbs were long and thin and their round bellies stuck out. They both had outie bellybuttons and dark brown hair, but hers was long and his was short.

The children hurled themselves out of the car, untangling their long legs from the balled-up clothing at their feet, and ran down the hard-packed path toward the pond. Their bare feet slapped the powdery dirt as they ran through clouds of gnats congregating in sunbeams that filtered through the forest canopy. There were evergreens and maples, oaks, and trees Girl didn't know the names of. Blackberries and raspberries grew wild at the sides of the path, and they'd stop to pick them, staining their fingers and chins before they ran off again, racing to get to the beach first. The gnats chased them, but the children were too fast.

They couldn't swim in the avocado-colored pond until their parents came down to the beach, so instead they looked for their summer friends, Stephanie and Steven. They said *hi* to the adults they knew, too. Vicki was pregnant, and she didn't mind Girl looking at her popped-out bellybutton on her naked belly. It looked just like a brown barnacle. Vicki's nipples were brown, too, and her breasts high and firm, her bottom round and full with pregnancy. Vicki was beautiful with long brown hair, and she was thinner and younger than Girl's parents. There was no Sabra of Sabra's Pond. Vicki and George owned the campground and they were gentle and kind people with no tan lines, their skin evenly golden brown all over. Girl's arms were darker than her chest and belly from having to wear clothes all the time at home.

There were a few men at the beach lying on their backs in the sun, their soft penises flopping to one side and resting on their legs. Girl looked at them out of the corner of her eyes. She knew not to stare, but penises were fascinating, even if they were attached to ugly old grown-ups. They were all circumcised. Did men have to put sunscreen on their testicles so they didn't get sunburned? No one looked twice at her here. She was just a naked kid in the woods.

You couldn't tell it was the seventies—without clothes or TVs or radios, the family belonged to no decade. No one could tell Girl was a nerd without her out-of-style clothing. She could be anyone or anything she wanted, and what she wanted to be right then was an Indian princess, or maybe a forest nymph.

Mother and Stepmother finally came down to the beach with a blanket to sit on. Mother was big, round, and naked, her breasts resting on her stomach and her privates hidden by thick, curly hair. Stepmother was still wearing her white cotton underwear, white bra, baseball hat, and sneakers. Stepmother was always slow to undress. Maybe it was because she was from West Virginia, or because her father was a minister, or maybe just because she didn't realize or care about how badly Girl needed to get in the pond.

"Hurry up and take your bra off so we can go swimming!" Girl yelled across the beach. Stepmother's cheeks got a little red as everyone turned to look at her, the only clothed person at the nude beach. Sometimes she even swam in her underwear, though it clung uselessly and sagged at the bottom when wet. It embarrassed Girl. Both of the children were good swimmers but they weren't allowed in without a grown-up watching because you couldn't see through the greenish-brown water. Someone had to count their heads and make sure they surfaced.

"It's okay, you can go ahead," Stepmother said, and the children ran into the pond. Girl dove down to find the cool water close to the silty bottom and swam underwater as long as she could hold her breath, pretending to be a frog princess. Water streamed from her hair when she surfaced, and the sun was hot on the top of her head. The pond was sun-warmed and opaque, filled with tadpoles and fishes the size of her hand. If you could swim in the clouds and the birds were fish it would be just like this, she was sure of it; only the smell would be brighter.

Girl got a big inner tube to float around in, careful to make sure the valve stem was pointing toward the water so it wouldn't scratch her back. She stuck her butt through the hole in the middle and leaned her head back against the hot black rubber, her feet hanging over the other side. She paddled her hands to make the inner tube float in lazy circles. The best part about swimming naked was that she didn't have a bathing suit going up her crack. She closed her eyes and breathed the warm tire smell blended with the scent of diluted mud and sunshine.

Brother swam up to Girl. He had the littler inner tube around his stomach, the top half sticking up in the sky like a skinny black donut. "Let me have a turn in the big one," he whined.

"No. I got it first," she said, kicking her feet to get away. *Thwunk!* A wad of wet mud hit Girl in the back of the head.

Girl scrambled out of her tube so she could chase him properly. As soon as she was free, Brother doubled back and snatched the big inner tube, leaving the little one floating nearby. Girl grumbled at him, but knew that it wasn't worth chasing him. His legs were longer and he could swim faster than Girl could. She pulled the smaller tube over her head, forgetting to check for the valve stem and scratching a red line down her stomach. She dog-paddled around the lily pads and daydreamed about Indians and wolves, wondering when she'd be old enough to get her own Swiss Army knife. There would be marshmallows later, and singing around the campfire, and swinging with Stephanie in the white rope hammock that left cross-hatched lines in the backs of their legs as they tried not to breathe in too much scratchy wood smoke.

Stepmother was still sitting on a blanket at the nude beach, trying to get up the nerve to get fully *nekkid*. Stepmother had thought she had left behind all the hang-ups from her southern Methodist upbringing, but she couldn't quite bring herself to unhook that bra. She watched Girl raise her knees high as her daughter entered the pond, mud dripping from her feet and falling with a glop into the greenish-brown water. The little girl's bottom was still white—it was the beginning of summer—but her forearms and legs were browning up in the sun. Stepmother wasn't sure that a nude campground was such a good place to take a little girl. She didn't like the idea of adult men seeing her daughter's vulva even if she didn't yet have breasts to speak of, but Mother had been going here for years and it was important to her, so Stepmother had caved and said okay. Besides, she loved camping and singing songs around the fire and collecting pinecones and little bits of things she could glue together into animals or whatnot. Once she found a burr and told the children it was a "porky-pine egg," and they watched and waited so long for it to hatch that she worried they'd never give up.

Stepmother had brought her canoe, strapped to the top of the station wagon. It had been hard to get up there—she was only five foot two—but she had managed it like she managed everything else. She was strong—even though she was well-padded, thick muscles lined her shoulders and arms under her pale white skin that always freckled and burned in the June sun. She didn't need a man for anything—she was the man, only with these breasts that hung down nearly to her waist and got in the way of everything. Stepmother had been a professional Girl Scout, going through all the ranks until she was employed full-time as a camp director. She had always been happiest walking down dirt paths inside the cave of the forest branches. Stepmother looked for white fungus growing along the sides of fallen logs, and when she found one, she took her pocket knife from her front pocket and pried it from the rotten log. That was another problem with being naked—she had nowhere to store her stuff. She always kept her sneakers on and stuffed her penknife in her sock.

When Stepmother got back to the campsite where they had an army-green, four-person tent for the kids and a pop-up camper for Mother and herself, she sat in the folding chair outside and carved pictures of mountains and rhododendron into the face of the fungus, then set it on the folding tray table to harden. The woods always reminded her of the good parts of back home: the mountains and flowers and camping with the Girl Scouts, and the smell of the mildewed tents.

That night, at the campfire, she brought her guitar, but Michael was the king of the group and always led the songs. She could sing much better than he could, but what could she do? She hadn't been there as long, and he stayed all summer, as opposed to the week or two she managed. Still, one day she'd get her chance to sing John Denver or Judy Collins and strum the chords, and then they would see all that she had to offer—see that she was better than Michael by a long shot.

Earlier that day when she snuck away to the two-person outhouse—she was always constipated out here, because the outhouse had only three sides and no door—Michael had walked in and plopped down on the second seat next to her, chatting as he made a BM. Stepmother finished up as quickly as she could and decided to try again later, hoping he didn't notice how red her face was.

Mother had found this place back when she was in college. She told her brother about it, and he had gone, too, but they always coordinated their schedules so they'd never run into each other. Or they had tried to, until her brother's wife decided that was silly and had made them go on the same day. Mother still laughed when she thought of it—her brother sitting on his blanket next to her, both of them staring straight ahead, so careful not to look at each other. She missed him.

Mother worried that her children suffered from the lack of a strong male role model, and wished yet again that her father or brother were still alive. Her father had been the best man she knew, and she had always been "Daddy's girl," calling him Pop, or Popsicle when she was feeling silly. Her brother had been four years older, and he had always looked out for her. Once, back in high school, he hit his best friend in the mouth and knocked out a couple of his teeth when his friend wouldn't stop kissing his girlfriend in front of her. Mother's brother had been an Eagle Scout, and he had helped her with math in college, and she, in turn, had helped write his essays. If only he had lived . . . but he got chicken pox, and that led to pneumonia. Her brother had gone into the hospital one day and died the next. When a nurse pulled Mother aside and told her that she could sue, that mistakes had been made, Mother had walked off, refusing to listen. There was no point in thinking about things like that— no point in blame or what-ifs.

Mother liked going camping—Stepmother was happy, the kids played by themselves, and she could read a paperback novel all day long with no chores or guilt about what she should be doing instead. Mother wore thick prescription glasses, and the sunglass tint was on the purple side of black, tinting the pages of her book slightly lavender. She swatted absentmindedly at a mosquito buzzing around her thigh and glanced up at the children. The sun picked red tones out of her daughter's brown hair. Her son's glasses were slightly askew, and Mother smiled her closed-lipped smile as she watched them standing on the raft. Brother used the long pole to push them around the pond, and Girl lay on her belly, her head hanging over the edge, watching the opaque water flow by.

That night in the tent, after Brother went to sleep, Girl's hand went between her legs as she thought about penises and wondered what they felt like. They looked so vulnerable, flopped over on the legs of the men at the beach. She wondered if testicles felt like hardboiled eggs (they seemed to be the right shape and size). That night, she fell asleep and dreamed that she was a doctor. She carefully slit Batman and Robin's scrotums open and removed their testes, replacing them with assorted objects: golf balls, cherry tomatoes. Then she carefully sewed them up and put the superheroes in little cradles hanging from a tree, where the wind could rock them softly until they healed up enough to put their tights and shiny crime-fighting briefs back on and return to the TV show she watched every afternoon with Brother.

alaskan unease

There was something creepy about Father that Girl couldn't quite put her finger on. He told too many dirty jokes and he talked too often about sex. He never wore clothes around the house or hid the fact that he and #Four smoked pot and had sex with other people. The children knew that Wanda with the long, gold fingernails slept in Father's bed with and without #Four. Father always stayed at Sarah and Ira's house on the occasions he came to Rochester, and Father and Sarah weren't embarrassed when the children caught them taking a nap together in the afternoon while Ira was at work. No one asked the children not to tell Sarah's husband. Girl assumed they slept all together in one big bed.

Once when Girl and her brother were young, maybe seven and eight, they were spending the summer in Alaska at Father's house. They snuck into the living room where Father and #Four slept on a king-sized futon. In the corner was a heap of multi-colored floor pillows #Four had made that they used instead of a sofa. Brother and Girl burrowed into the mound. The children hadn't gotten dressed yet, and wore the big T-shirts with no bottoms they had slept in.

"Shhh!" Girl hissed at her brother, "We'll get caught." Brother hit her with a cushion and they both buried their faces in the fluffy pile, which only kind of worked to stifle their giggles. The children were about as quiet as a pack of chattering squirrels, but they were bored and wanted Father to get up; they just didn't want to get in trouble for rousing him. The children could hear Father and #Four stirring and knew they had succeeded.

Instead of getting out of bed, though, Father and #Four started kissing. #Four lay on top of him, their uncovered naked bodies squishing into each other and moving back and forth. Girl and Brother watched silently. She had never seen anyone have sex before, but based on the description in the books Mother gave her, she knew that was what they were doing. Girl was fascinated—it had never occurred to her that women could be on top during sex.

When they were done Father called "Good morning" to the children. "Come snuggle," he said, and Brother and Girl climbed into the futon bed with them, even though it didn't seem quite like something they should be doing. After a few minutes, Father went to pee and everyone got off the futon. Girl had heard about condoms but didn't see one. She didn't know there were invisible ways to prevent pregnancy, so she wondered if Margaret was going to have a baby now.

"I went inside #Four," Brother told her later, but she didn't believe him.

"Father rubbed between my legs," she lied, trying to keep up with Brother. She knew any flopping contact was accidental . . . probably. She told herself that she should have been wearing pajamas bottoms or underpants, like a normal girl. She knew that if they told anyone, they would be told that they should have known better, and if they told Stepmother they wouldn't ever be allowed to go to Alaska again.

listwood

During the school year, Girl walked one of two ways to Listwood Elementary. Normally Girl went down Belmeade to the path—a cut through between two houses with a dirt track worn in the grass by dozens of children's feet. From there it was three more blocks to the main entrance. Sometimes, though, Girl turned left on Gardham and walked four blocks straight over, then cut behind the high school to arrive at the back of the elementary building. It was the same distance either way, but the walk got boring, so she mixed it up. If Girl went behind the high school, she passed the smokers on the corner, just off school grounds. She was afraid of the loud teenagers with their tight jeans and denim or leather jackets, because sometimes they'd jump out at the little kids and yell, sticking their tongues out like Gene Simmons. Sometimes Girl saw her cousin Peter, with his black curly hair and athlete's build—he was so cool. If she saw him she knew she was safe. He'd always say *hi*, even though Girl was just a dorky kid and he was a teenager. Once past the smokers, Girl cut across the high school running track, walking on the top crust of the deep snow. Mostly she was light enough to walk on the ice layer on top of the snow, but sometimes the ice crust broke and she fell into the snow up to her crotch. Girl was proud to be so little, and never wanted to be tall. Her sister Juli was a dwarf, and she wanted to be just like her. The snow on the field was blinding white, like being inside a diamond. She had to squint as she walked in her ugly, cheap, brown duck boots. She wore bread bags over her dirty socks because her boots never stayed dry.

Girl never had enough socks, so the ones she had turned permanently gray from too few washings. She hated when the colored bands at the top didn't match. More than that, she hated when she wore the tube socks the wrong way and the heel was on the top and it rubbed a red spot on her skin and wore a hole in the sock. Girl couldn't figure out how to put her socks on the right way, even though she was in third grade. She'd hold them up and look for the dented-out heel part, but because she got it wrong so often, Girl could rarely find it just by looking. Once on her feet, she didn't have time to take them off and try again. When Girl walked across the snow in her brown duck boots the heel of her sock rubbed the top of her foot raw, and she wished she had turned the sock around before she left.

Girl liked to lie on her back and make snow angels before dinner, looking up at the stars. She wanted to make a snow fort, and had a plastic brick-making form, but her endurance never matched her ambition. It was better to find a drift left by the snow plow on the six-foot-wide strip of lawn between the side-walk and the street. If Girl and Brother found a big enough pile, they would hollow it out together, making a fast though inconveniently located fort. She was a girl who liked taking shortcuts.

The best thing in winter, almost as good as Christmas, was when Mother half-woke Girl, whispering, "You don't have to get up, it's a snow day." Girl's bed was pushed up against the wall, and the window gently seeped cold air onto her cheeks and the tip of her nose, her body warm in footie-pajamas and wrapped in her puffy comforter. Everything good about childhood was wrapped up in her mother: her kisses, her lap, her pillowy body covered in a yellow bathrobe that went all the way to her toes. Mother smelled of Jean Naté and Nivea hand cream, and when Mother wasn't home, Girl would go into the bathroom, open the After Bath Splash, and smell the bottle. Girl rubbed the thick, white Nivea cream into her own hands and put them to her face, some-times getting cream on her nose in an effort to get closer to her Mother's scent. An extra day of Mother was all that Girl ever wanted in the world.

sleep

G irl woke up in the dark with a sharp inhale, the fear clawing at her
ribs, burning in her chest. Terror was acid and Girl felt it in her lungs.
The fear was all around her and inside her and she had to make it go
away, she had to make it stop before its heaviness smothered her.

"Mommy?" Girl said her name softly and it made her blink fast—when she
said the name aloud it made the fear more real, made her voice box get heavy
and sore.

Girl tiptoed down the hall to Mother and Stepmother's room in her Strawberry Shortcake nightgown. She stopped in front of the heavy white door, held
her breath, and turned the doorknob as quietly as she could. Stepmother slept
closest to the door, and she was a light sleeper. If Girl woke her up, Stepmother
would stand at the doorway in her underpants yelling for Girl to go to sleep
and leave her mother alone. Then there would be no Mommy, no making the
fear go away. If Girl eased the door open really quietly, tiptoed past Stepmother's side of the bed, and got to her mother first, Mother would hug Girl and
tuck her in again and make the scared feeling disappear until morning. "It's
all right, Stepmother," Mother would say as she padded on bare feet around
their bed in the dark bedroom—she never wore slippers. If it was a really bad
night, Mother would put on her yellow bathrobe and take Girl downstairs and
make them both hot spiced milk in a pan on the stove. Girl didn't know why
Mommy slept on the side of the bed farthest from the door.

Girl held her breath, leaned back, pulled the door toward herself, and
turned the knob up and to the left so it wouldn't creak, but the door was locked.
The eye-hook rattle woke up Stepmother, who unlatched the door and pulled
it open before Girl could run back to bed. Girl couldn't believe how quickly
Stepmother went from dead asleep to standing straight up in the middle of the
night—like a jack-in-the-box.

"What? What do you want?" Stepmother demanded, her hair sticking
up in all directions. "Mother needs her sleep. She has to work tomorrow.

Go back to bed!" Stepmother loomed above Girl, angry in her men's cotton undershirt and white underpants that sagged in the back and had a rip along the waistband, so a strip of her stomach was visible. (She never wore a nightgown like Mommy, and never wore the satiny underpants Mommy liked. Stepmother despised all things pretty. She often told Girl that she was pretty.)

Girl raced back to bed before Stepmother turned meaner. She pulled the covers up and promised herself, *when I have kids I will never forget what it is like to be scared in the dark.* Stepmother slammed their bedroom door shut and dropped the lock back into place.

Alone in her bedroom, the open closet door made a dark mouth against the wall. All of Girl's bad dreams lived in the closet, and if she couldn't get it closed, she knew they would come out as soon as she fell asleep—they always did, just like if she fell asleep with the light on she knew that she'd wake with a headache. Girl threw her weight against the closet door, but it was stuck on a stuffed animal or a Barbie dress, or maybe a paperback book. It wouldn't close, and she couldn't bear to be uncovered and vulnerable so close to the closet for very long. She dived back into bed and hugged Scooby-Doo, who was two feet tall and filled with tiny Styrofoam balls so he was hard, not soft, but he was still her favorite and Girl slept every night with her head on his muzzle, which was forever smooshed into a very un-dog-like shape. Girl had her parents' old bed and their old, light-blue-and-white comforter, not that Girl could see it in the dark. But Mother used to sleep under it, so it kept some comfort trapped deep in the cotton batting. Girl grabbed her stuffed weasel that had been loved from white to gray, its hard plastic nose tucked up by her face so Girl could find that extra-soft fur behind the ear and rub it on her cheek. She clenched the tail between her knees. Mother bought her plenty of stuffed animals but it was always the ones from Father that became Girl's favorites. She closed her eyes tight-tight-tight until she saw stars behind her scrunched-up lids. In the dark of her bedroom Girl created an even darker dark inside her tightly closed eyes, lit with retina bursts that looked like jellyfish. Girl filled the void with scrolling lyrics, like the prologue in *Star Wars*. Words from "America the Beautiful," or "My Country Tis of Thee"—her fear-crazed brain could only think of the stupid songs they learned in school. Girl never sang in her head any of the songs her mother sang, only empty repetitive ones that held no meaning. An empty structure to hold the fear at bay. "Oh beautiful, for spacious skies . . ." The tune was easy to remember. The lyrics dismissed Mother as easily as she had abandoned Girl to the night. Girl's hands finger-spelled the first letter of each word with both hands at the same time, concentrating as hard as she could. Gradually her fingers relaxed, then her shoulders, and finally she slept.

notes from the fourth wall
this is a story about mothers and children who are very bad at sleeping

2008

"The closest I ever came to losing it was at bedtime," my mother said. "This was after I divorced your father, before I met Pat. Matt would not go to sleep and I spanked him, and I felt like I could have spanked him forever. So I stopped myself and took you both over to Aunt Kiki's house and went off on my own for a few hours. The next day I signed up for counseling. I didn't want to be a person who could even imagine abusing her kids."

I left my husband when my youngest was four months old, a few months before my eldest's third birthday. I worked two jobs. I nursed my baby and tried to get my toddler to eat and we slept all three of us in my double bed. My big boy could only sleep wrapped around my body, one arm underneath my shoulders, the other across my torso, his little hand buried underneath my side. "Don't burrow!" I'd admonish, but when I was the one holding him, I always tucked my fingers under his back in exactly the same way. We were burrowers, we couldn't help it. My baby wasn't a burrower. He would crawl to the end of the bed (which was pushed up against the wall both for safety and because the room was only ten feet square) and sleep far away from us. If he was feeling needy, he'd come sleep on my pillow, his stomach draped across the top of my head.

2015

Every night that I don't take melatonin I have nightmares. Maybe it works, or maybe it's just a placebo. If I skip my pill, I wake up gasping, my heart thrashing against my ribs like a trapped bird. I should be too old for this shit. I generally can't remember the dream, just the feel of it. Fear is heavy, like breathing in steam or smoke. I look at my left breast—I can see it pulse above my pounding heart. Little rabbit jerks. *Breathe, Lara.*

"You always say you never slept when you were a child," my mother told me in what she considered affectionate teasing. "You would insist that you didn't close your eyes all night." Her look is slightly vengeful, like she's been waiting for years to show me what a silly child I was. "I'd go into your room at night and you were always asleep, but you'd never believe me when I told you so."

"I've done research, Mom. I was a frequent night waker, and in children, they often don't realize they slept, because they are awake so much."

"I didn't know that," she said, with a look that told me she was appeasing, not conceding. "All I know is that it was so funny, how you said you never slept, but I always saw you asleep, your bed covered in stuffed animals."

"I always thought you'd sleep better if you got rid of half of those stuffed animals," my stepmother said. I changed the subject.

Do most people wake as frequently as I do? I woke so often as a child; I really did believe that I didn't sleep. All I knew was that I was always staring at the ceiling. My light fixture was a fluted square with flowers etched into the glass. The plaster ceiling had brush-stroke swirls I knew like my own fingerprints. I always left my door open and the hall light on, so I could still see, but when my parents came to bed, they shut the light off, and the room was only dimly lit by the streetlights outside. I fell asleep staring at the ceiling and woke staring at the ceiling, so it didn't feel like time had passed.

Now I know when I wake. I fall asleep on my right side, my body wrapped like a backpack against my lover, my hand tucked under his chest. My stomach fits perfectly in the small of his back. I tuck my left arm up under the pillow, and I wake when it goes numb. Then I flip over to my left side and reach my arm back to rest on his hip. He wakes up and turns over and encircles me with his arm. Later, we move to our backs, and our arms drift across the bed to hold each other's hands. All night we wake and flop and grasp and touch and sink back into down pillows. When he is out of town, I still wake, my eyes hunting the clock instead of his body. Knowing the time grounds me, returns me to my present self, pulls me back from the dream world that feels more real than this one.

Whether he is home or away, every night I tune the television to a documentary or podcast before I close my eyes. I cannot sleep in silence. I need sounds to drown out my thoughts: the lists of things I need to do, the essays I don't know how to finish. Quiet makes my brain louder. If I forget my melatonin, I wake in the early morning darkness with a sharp inhale, the fear clawing at my ribs, the burn in my chest, terror in my lungs. It feels like a craving, but for what, I don't know.

2009

When my youngest was eleven months old, I got him to sleep regularly in a crib, and instead of nursing from my body, he drank soy formula from a bottle. My breasts could not keep up with shared parenting. I put an extra "baba" in his crib, so when he woke up, he could find it on his own and go back to sleep. The baby was the best sleeper of the three of us. Once he was down, I carried my three-year-old down to the living room and put on my *Pure Eighties Dance Mix* CD. I swayed to the opening stanzas of "Video Killed the Radio Star," holding my big boy to my chest. This was how I got him to sleep every night since he was an infant. I did aerobics—lunges, knee lifts, and side-steps as the song changed to "Hungry Like the Wolf." My son and I both had a need for mother-love, we had touch-hunger, empty holes inside our chests. As I danced, I held his head gently against my breast. The CD player spun into track three, and my son's arms went limp, his head lolling as I swayed. I carried him back upstairs and laid him in his bed. Only then was the night my own.

2015

Most of the time I remember only fragments of my dreams, just one or two images, maybe the thread of plot, but I awake swollen with the emotion of it. I wake with the taste of sadness, or love. Sometimes I dream the same dream over and over all night, always waking at the same place. I often wake myself with the word I spent my whole dream trying to enunciate, but instead of *help* it sounds like *hnnnnuh*. I will carry a bad dream for a day, sometimes two, unable to leave that murky world that exists on the other side of awake. My boyfriend thinks it is unfair that I tend to blame him for actions he performed only in my dreams. I tell him my dream is a microcosm of my thoughts and unresolved feelings, therefore I can blame him. I think I must be a very hard person to live with.

2009

My big boy didn't even have a bed at his father's, so he thought this idea of sleeping in his own room at my house was exasperating and ridiculous, not that he used those words. I was trying to stop dancing him to sleep every night, so I laid down in bed next to him, curling my five feet seven frame to fit in the four-foot-long toddler bed. It was a good thing I didn't weigh much. He rested his head on my shoulder, his arm across my body, fingers tucked in underneath my side. His light-brown hair smelled like boy-child, like his very own person, like mine. I hated when he came home smelling like Daddy's house, or when his hair kept the musty smell of church, or the powdery smell of Grandma Kathy. To help him fall asleep, I told him a story I crafted off the top of my head about a pet guinea pig—our agreed-upon reward for when he finally slept in his own room all night long. I made up grand adventures for the pig and the boy until my son fell asleep. The pig went to playgrounds, got pulled around in a little red wagon. The pig went to nursery school. Half the time I fell asleep beside my son in that tiny bed, exhausted from his constant night waking. But it was not always this ideal. Some nights consisted of stories and songs and creeping downstairs only to hear him cry, "Mama!" as soon as my foot hit the bottom step. Many nights were filled with his tears and my begging him to please, just this once, couldn't he go to sleep?

How do you tell an unbearable story? If I don't write it down, maybe he will forget the time he wouldn't go to sleep and I was screaming and he was crying and it was eleven at night and I swatted his bottom through his pajamas once, twice, before I left him sobbing alone in bed, retreating to the porch and dragging the sharp biting smoke of a cigarette deep into my lungs. I needed the smoke to burn me, I needed the ten-minute break to return to who I meant to be. I went back upstairs and held my little boy and told him I was sorry and that he was good and it wasn't his fault and I held him and rocked him until he fell asleep. He was four years old and this was wrong and I knew better. I knew better because I remembered what it was like to be small and scared in the dark. I never hit him again, and when I ask him about it now, he doesn't remember it happening. That isn't enough to absolve me.

2015

"Mama, I can't sleep," my oldest child, now ten years old, says. "Honey, I can't make you sleep. This is something you have to figure out on your own," I answer. "I'm not a good sleeper, either. I used to sing songs in my head. You are going to have to find something that works for you."

"Well, if I can't sleep, can I read?"

"As long as you don't wake up your brother and stay in bed, you can read as long as you want."

Should I have sleep-trained him as a baby, like some of my friends did with their infants, forcing him to cry alone in a crib until he learned to soothe himself? I didn't have the heart for it. Had all of my bedtime ministrations left him permanently sleep-scarred? Slowly, I have backed away at bedtime. This is the first year I no longer sing lullabies, though I still read a chapter of *Diary of a Wimpy Kid* to my seven-year-old every night. I've outsourced bedtime to the iPod, and let them play talking books on repeat. Now, unless they are sick, once the boys fall asleep, they stay asleep until morning. It's been years since a nightmare has sent them racing for my bedroom door. If one does have a bad dream, he walks across the bedroom to his brother's bed and lies down beside him and falls back asleep. Maybe I should encourage them to wake me up instead, I don't know. I don't know the first thing about sleep.

with his free fist, but she hung on until he called for Mother. Girl couldn't outhit him, but she could outlast him.

Brother was cross-eyed and started wearing glasses when he was three, whereas Girl didn't wear glasses until she was ten. He wouldn't play *Star Wars* with her, even though Girl had a Jawa and Princess Leia and promised not to touch his precious AT-AT or Tauntaun. He made her watch *G.I. Joe* on Saturdays instead of *Strawberry Shortcake*. There was no taking turns; there was only who got to the TV dial first, and his arms were longer. The rule was, if the children woke Mother up the television went off, so Girl had to give in even though she didn't want to. Still, though, they walked to and from school together every day, traded books back and forth, and occasionally had to wear each other's socks.

The children thought they were poorer than everyone else at school. They weren't, really, but their parents scrimped and saved for summer vacations and future college expenses. Their parents didn't lavish the children with Jordache jeans, like their classmates wore. The children's Toughskins jeans and shirtsleeves were never long enough for their gangly limbs, and their clothes weren't cool by a long shot—which their classmates were quick to point out with colorful word choices and scornful glances. Brother and Girl despised each other as much as everyone else at school despised them, hating the mirror of uncool they reflected back at each other.

"Why couldn't I have been an only child?" Girl asked Mother on an almost-daily basis.

"Because if I only had one child, I would have only had Brother. He's oldest. That's how it works."

"That's not fair!" she protested, even though she was old enough to understand basic biology and timing. Girl occasionally prayed that Brother would get hit by a car, though she knew this was evil and wrong.

The turning point came when Girl was in fourth grade. It was her birthday, and she wore her favorite pink dress to school. She loved pink, and her sailor dress was dotted pink-on-pink cotton, and even though it didn't have lace or ruffles, Girl felt pretty in it. That day she wore her pink dress with her pink sneakers and the corsage her father had sent. She didn't understand the purpose of the pin-on flowers. It wasn't nearly as good as the new Barbie dolls she had been coveting, but at least he remembered her birthday this year.

brother and girl against the world

Brother was always a head taller and a grade ahead, but otherwise he and Girl were as identical as opposite-sex siblings could be: straight brown hair, brown eyes, gawky knees and skinny backs, long stork-like limbs and round stomachs that stuck out like children from Ethiopia on TV commercials. They both had double-jointed thumbs. Like the two-headed dog Orthos in Greek mythology, they were often treated as a conjoined set—*Brother-n-Girl*, one word, one identity. They played together, bathed together, sometimes even peed at the same time when they had been toddlers, sitting back-to-back on the toilet seat if Mother was in a hurry, Brother's hot stream splashing Girl's bottom.

Brother and Girl were made of the same genetic flotsam. Mother was a separate person from Girl. Father was even further removed. Brother was made of the same DNA and dirt as she was.

He was the only other person who had the same life as Girl. Mother and Stepmother had never been to Father's house in Alaska. They had never smelled the odor of jet fuel inside of Father's plane or felt his condo's rough carpet itch their bare legs as they sat on the floor watching TV, because Father had no couch. Mother and Stepmother didn't know how the sun glinted off the water in Alaska's Prince William Sound where Girl and Brother sailed every summer. Father didn't know the color of the dirt in the backyard of Mother and Stepmother's house that got lodged under the children's fingernails and no one made them clean. Father hadn't seen the view from Girl's bedroom window and had never run his fingers over the 1945 inscription in the base-ment wall behind the water heater.

Brother was companion and adversary, playmate and competitor. By the time the children entered grade school they fought viciously every day over TV channels, toys, who got the front seat of the car, who looked at the other the wrong way. Brother could hit harder, but Girl grabbed onto his upper arm and dug her fingernails in as deep as they could go. He hit her over and over

Normally he sent a box in the mail a week or so late, but the flowers had come on time, and she liked being the only one wearing a corsage to school, as if she were someone special.

Girl and Brother walked home from class together, the strange, old-lady flowers still pinned to Girl's dress. Rogers Middle School was a mile and a half from their house—they missed the cutoff for busing by three blocks. Girl and Brother always met up in the halls filled with slamming lockers, swinging backpacks, and yelling voices. Even when they were in the middle of a fight, they would never leave the other behind to walk home alone.

Brother seemed kind of nervous when Girl met him in the hall. He didn't confide in his sister about his problems, but she could tell he was eager to get out of there as quickly as possible. "Let's go," he said, banging closed his gray locker door that still smelled like back-to-school paint. They went out the side door into the sunshine. It was the first week of school, what they called autumn but was still technically summer. Their house was a mile or so from Lake Ontario and the warm wind had just a kiss of September coolness at the edge of it. They walked on cracked sidewalks in and out of shadows cast by maple and oak trees. Brother and Girl cut through the Catholic school parking lot and through the break in the fence behind the plaza. Lots of kids took the same path in sets of twos and threes and fives, leaving a few feet between each cluster.

When Girl and Brother reached the big, empty parking lot behind the shopping plaza, most of the other kids had turned off toward their own houses—there weren't that many kids who walked as far as Girl and Brother, and she envied those who had parents willing or able to pick their kids up after school. Girl hated this section of the long trek home. It was ugly and gray and the sun was hot with no trees to give them shade. There were a few scraggly weeds that managed to push their way up through the cracks in the broken concrete and old rusted lampposts to break up the view of the back of the stores. As they got near the shipping doors for Irondequoit Plaza, a kid on a white bike pulled ahead of the siblings and stopped suddenly, cutting them off and almost knocking Girl down.

It was Richie, one of the school bullies. He was in Brother's grade but was shorter than Girl, and he rode a girl's bike that had a tall pole topped with a triangular flag on the back of the white banana seat.

"Look who I found! Brother Lillibridge and his sister. Nice floods, Brother." Girl's hands balled up into round, hard apples at her sides. She had never been in a fight with anyone besides Brother. Her hands might have been ready to brawl, but Girl was too scared to raise her fists to beneficial height, and they hung uselessly at the end of her arms. Girl could no more break her paralysis than she could scream in dreams. Richie was short, dark-haired, and squinty-eyed with a chip on his shoulder the size of Texas. Everyone was afraid of him and his friends. He only hung with the coolest and toughest kids in school, and Girl and Brother were neither cool nor tough.

"Can't your mother afford to buy you new clothes? Four-eyes."

Girl's eyes narrowed—no one could pick on Brother besides her. She hated Richie, and hated that Brother couldn't stand up to him, even though he was more than a head taller than the bully. She knew it wasn't in Brother's nature to fight back. He was afraid of dogs and was too shy to make friends easily. Girl wasn't very tough either, but she was their only hope.

"You're riding a girl's bike," she sneered.

"It's my sister's. Got a problem with that?" Richie spat on the ground. Fear blanked Girl's mind of any more snappy comebacks. Turns out she wasn't any better at this than Brother was.

Brother's moist fingers closed around Girl's. *Run*, she could feel him think, his terror fusing with her own as the fear-sweat of their hands acted as a conductor for action. Fight or flight. They flew.

The siblings ran holding hands, Girl's red book bag bouncing and thumping into her shoulders. Her corsage turned sideways, dangling from the pin that secured it to her birthday dress. Girl's pink Keds slapped the concrete as she pumped her legs as hard and fast as she could. She wished for the wind to sweep them up into the sky. Brother's legs were longer, and he didn't let go— his hand pulled Girl along faster than she could have run on her own. He was the wind that bore them both to safety. Neither of them would ever leave one another behind, not even to save themselves. Never. At home and at school it was Brother and Girl against the world. From that day on, Brother was Girl's best friend. He stopped pummeling her when he was mad and she dug her fingernails into him no more.

the pool

"The pool is kidney shaped, like a bean," Mother said, but Girl didn't know what that meant. Mother had signed up for a family pool membership at the Sheraton Inn by the airport. "And it has skylights," she added. Girl had never seen a kidney, but she knew what beans in chili looked like, because she carefully ate around them, leaving them in a red pile at the bottom of her bowl. She had only seen round or rectangular pools—a kidney seemed like an inefficient design for swimming laps. When they walked into the pool area Girl fell in love with the graceful curves of the pool, mimicked in four bubble skylights above it. She understood instantly that kidney-shaped pools were the best kind of pools there were.

Mother and Stepmother swam laps, but mostly they sat on beach chairs and read books or sat in the hot tub and talked. Girl and Brother played Marco Polo and if there were other children around they had chicken fights, which they almost always won as long as Brother was the horse and Girl was on his back. Sometimes they would "polar bear," which meant they sat in the sauna as long as they could stand, then rolled in the snow outside and jumped in the pool. Girl didn't like breathing the hot sauna air and she was a little afraid she'd get locked in there, even though the door didn't have a lock. The wooden benches inside smelled good and cedar-y, but if she accidentally sat on a nail head, it burned her leg. Brother liked to sit on the top bench, but it was harder to breathe close to the ceiling. Girl liked best to sit on the floor under the bottom bench if there weren't any grown-ups in there with them. The snow part of the polar bear was terrible, and Girl never really rolled; instead she ran outside, the snow burning the bottoms of her feet, and rubbed some snow on her legs and arms. She could not willingly lower her body full-length in the snow like Brother. A grown-up was always willing to man the sliding glass door from the courtyard to the indoor pool—for some reason grown-ups always loved to watch the children do the polar bear, even though once a woman said they might have heart attacks from the temperature change. Girl ran as fast as she could, the cold crotch of her too-big bathing suit hanging down just a little and slapping her legs. She leapt into the pool, not bothering to dive or pull herself together into a cannonball. She crashed feet-first into the water, all the stress of the running and the cold leaving her body. Floating underwater, all the parts that the snow had touched were hot now—the children called it floating in marshmallows. Dreamlike, soothing, it felt something like love.

Mother had a swim bag filled with flippers and masks and goggles, but there never seemed to be enough to go around. Stepmother taught Girl to spit inside the goggles and rub it around with her fingers to keep the lenses from fogging. Stepmother swam laps with a mask, snorkel, and flippers. Mother used only a pair of goggles. When Girl didn't have goggles she opened her eyes underwater anyway, until her eyes turned red and one of her parents sent her to the drinking fountain to rinse them. Girl couldn't ever bring herself to open her eyes in the cold stream of the drinking fountain, but it felt good on her closed eyelids, and she thought her eyes could somehow absorb the benefits of clean water if she blinked with her eyelids almost touching the stream.

Sometimes there were other children at the pool. Girl looked closely at kids with tubes in their ears, the ones who had to wear red or blue ear plugs to stop them up. The plugs looked like Play-Doh, or chewed-up gum.

"Do they hurt?" she asked every kid she saw who had plugs.

"Not really," they always answered, but Girl didn't believe them, because how could sticking tubes into your ears not hurt? It was one of the things she was afraid of when she went to the doctor. Mother never made the children use Q-tips at home, so when they went to the pediatrician he always used a long metal tool that had a tiny spoon at the end to get the wax out, and it hurt a lot.

"Dang, I got a sunburn!" a black boy around Girl's age said to her once, pushing his fingers into his forearm. In the summer, they went out and played in the grass when they were bored with swimming. "You probably don't think black people can get sunburned," he said, and he was right. Girl thought he was joking—she had never gotten a sunburn in her life, and she was a lot lighter than he was. All she knew about black kids was that they wore swim caps at the pool more often than white kids, but they mostly didn't mind playing with her. Not like at day camp, where the kids segregated themselves by race and she was stuck with the few white kids in the urban program. At the pool there weren't enough kids to be choosy. "Look," he said as he held out his arm, and pressed his fingertips above his wrist. Girl did the same to her own arm. "See? You can tell by your fingerprints on your arm if you have a sunburn." Girl looked at his arm, and back at her own, but didn't see what he was talking about.

Mother always took a long time getting into the pool. She'd walk in slowly, making cold "Ah! Ah!" noises, and splash her body with water for a few minutes, then go "ooooo!" and slide up to her neck all at once. Girl loved to pick Mother up in her arms like a baby and carry her around the shallow end, but Mother only tolerated that for a little while. Sometimes Girl would hold the back of her mother's bathing suit straps and go for a dolphin ride when she swam laps.

"This is how your grandmother taught me to swim," Mother said. "I held onto her straps when she swam until I could do it on my own." Mother's back was broad and soft, with only one tiny flat mole on her lower right side, so small Girl could only see it when she hung on her back. Mother's skin was darker than her daughter's, prettier, Girl thought, and faster to tan. When Girl held onto her mother's straps they pulled back a little, and she could see the permanent red indentations on her mother's shoulders from wearing a bra. Girl hoped she never got shoulder indentations, but she did hope she got big boobs, like Mother.

Mother looked different in the pool. It was the only time she didn't wear glasses, and her mouth was softer, like her lips always wanted to smile. At home, her brows always pulled slightly toward each other, and her lips made a straight line. If you asked her to smile for a picture, she wouldn't show her teeth. In the water, she smiled with her mouth open and Girl could see all of her teeth.

"Is that your mom?" a new girl asked as Mother walked toward the pool. Girl sighed. She knew what was coming. Mother was fat, but proportional, like a big, soft peanut, and she didn't dye the gray in her hair, but that wasn't the major problem. It was her body hair. Under each arm was a round black bush the size of Girl's fist, and at the bottom of her swimsuit curly hair escaped down her thighs. Her shins were covered in dark hair.

"Why doesn't she shave?" the strange girl asked, her long, brown ponytail dripping water.

"She doesn't believe in it. She's a feminist," Girl answered, as she had been taught to. She was never, ever to say they were gay. Girl hated anyone to look at her mom like that, like she was weird, or ugly. Mother was the best person in Girl's whole world. Stepmother didn't shave either, but her hair was sparser and lighter in color, and because she was a lumpier kind of fat than Mother was, her hair got lost in the folds of her body. You couldn't see it across the pool as easily.

"Who's that with your mom?" the other child asked.

"My aunt," Girl said, telling the Official Family Lie. "My parents are divorced," she offered, to justify it. Almost nobody she knew had divorced parents, but Mother promised that by the time she graduated high school half of her friends would have divorced parents. Girl swam away from the questions. She'd rather play by herself anyway. Girl ran back to her mother, her swimsuit dripping down her legs, and asked her mother for a penny. Girl threw the coin into the deep end and dove after it, trying to catch the spinning copper before it hit the bottom. When she got close to the bottom, her ears felt overfull and made a tinny, throbbing sound. If she missed the penny and it floated all the way down to the square grate of the filter nine feet below, she'd try to pick it up with her toes, or convince Brother to get it for her. Girl exhaled on the way up, racing the silver bubbles to the surface. If she twisted quickly enough, sometimes they would get caught in her hair.

Before she took a bath the next night, Girl dug through the drawer in the bathroom cabinet and found an old, orange Bic razor. She pulled the single blade over her wet shins, leaving them red and stinging. She could see why Mother didn't want to shave, if it hurt so much, but Girl did it anyway. She shaved her thighs and her arms as well. Girl knew that she wasn't allowed to shave until seventh grade, three years away, but she could not stand the boy-like black hair on her limbs. The next day Girl pulled her socks up to her knees so Stepmother wouldn't see that she had defied her.

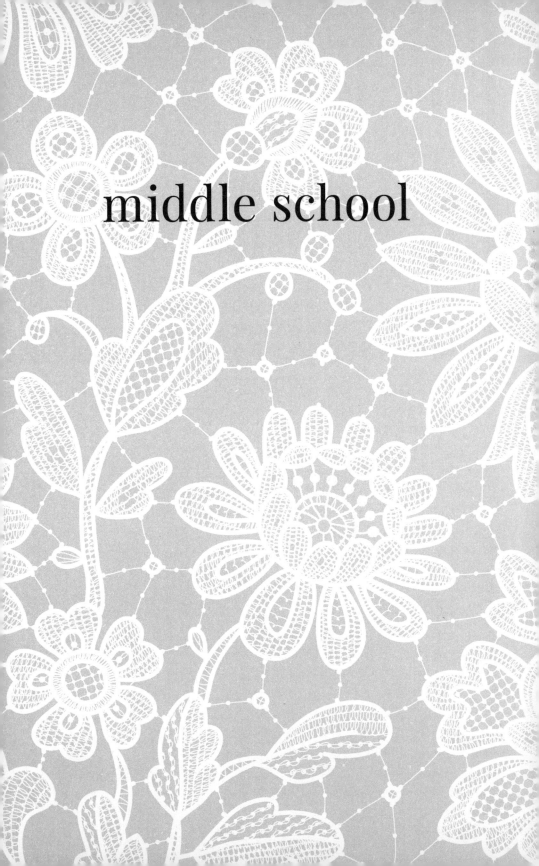

middle school

naked sculptures

Stepmother was a Great Artist. The house was filled with her landscape paintings and clay sculptures of naked women.

Some of the girls at school were no longer allowed to play at Girl's house once their parents heard about the statues. "The human body is a work of art! You go tell your friends to tell their parents that all great artists study the female nude. No, it is not weird!" Stepmother explained to Girl and Brother. But Girl's friends only looked at her funny when she said it, obviously unconvinced.

One of the sculptures was of Mother seated in a chair, large breasts splayed on her large stomach, legs slightly spread to reveal the pubic hair Stepmother had carved with a special metal sculpting tool. Stepmother had lengthened Mother's hair—Girl didn't know if this was meant to disguise Mother, or if it was wishful thinking. Stepmother often asked Mother to grow her hair long and dye it red. Girl didn't think it was nice to imply her mother wasn't good enough as she was.

"Don't tell your friends that is supposed to be me," Mother told the children.

"But isn't it supposed to be a beautiful work of art?" Girl asked, not entirely innocently.

"It is absolutely a beautiful work of art. But it makes me look fatter than I am in real life," Mother replied.

Girl had seen Mother naked plenty of times and she thought the statue was pretty spot-on, but she knew better than to contradict her. She didn't want her friends to know what Mother looked like naked anyway, so Girl wouldn't have told anyone even if she hadn't been forewarned.

Because Stepmother was a Great Artist and understood the importance of naked statues, she was very understanding when Girl made a sculpture of her own in fourth-grade art class.

Mr. Bailey taught art to all the grades, traveling from school to school. Back when Girl was in second grade, her class painted pictures of autumn trees. She had red and orange for the leaves, and purple for some violets she was planning to add around the bottom. Mr. Bailey dipped his paintbrush in the purple paint and added some purple leaves to Girl's tree. She was livid, but didn't say anything. She just iced him out. For the next few years, anytime Mr. Bailey spoke to Girl, she'd turn her head fast in an obvious, hair-flouncing fuck-you.

Once she knew that she had made her point, Girl graciously began speaking to him again, and he was pathetically grateful for it. He'd smile at her and allow her to ignore his assignments and make whatever she wanted during art class, as long as she was quiet. Girl spent her entire fourth grade year drawing life-sized pictures of girls with braids and roller skates and cool clothing. Art was a pass/fail class anyway. If she liked an assignment she'd try it, like when the class made piñatas. Girl made a brown rat head and was quite pleased with herself—it turned out exactly like the vision in her head. Mr. Bailey felt she should have made ears that stuck out using oaktag as he had instructed, and when he gave her a B on it, he earned another month of glowering stares.

Girl was excited when he announced the unit on clay. She had liked making pinch pots and little animals over the summer at the Art Gallery, and she had been hankering to make a very specific sculpture for quite some time. She had it all worked out in her head. She wanted to make a penis sculpture, and she could picture exactly what it should like: it would sit on the rounded V-shaped testicles, the shaft of the penis pointing up at a right angle. Girl and her best friend, Gretchen, talked a lot about penises and how to make a sculpture of one without getting caught. They needed a statue because they couldn't agree on what a penis looked like, and their drawing skills were not good enough to resolve the disagreement to either's satisfaction. Girl decided she could make one in art class and just tell everyone it was a Chinese man. She figured the acorn head of the penis resembled the large circular peasant hats in the pictures of farmers in China she found in her Social Studies book. Girl knew Mr. Bailey would never question her.

"What are you working on, Girl?" Mr. Bailey asked cautiously.

"A Chinese man. This is his peasant hat, and these are his legs," she explained as she attached the testicle "legs" of the penis sculpture to the shaft that she was pretending was the man's body, pressing the clay firmly so it wouldn't fall over.

"Aren't you going to give him arms?"

"He doesn't need arms," Girl scowled.

"What about shoes?" he tried.

"He's too poor to afford shoes," she answered, and he had no comeback for that. Girl knew enough about art to know it didn't have to be realistic. Her "man" had a head, a body, and the suggestion of legs. It was interpretive art, or modern art, or something. Picasso's people didn't always look real, either.

Mr. Bailey dared not question her. Unfortunately, she could find no justification for making a pee hole at the top of the "hat," so she had to omit it.

When the class's projects returned from the kiln, it was time to glaze their creations. Girl looked through the white plastic bottles for something flesh-colored.

"Do you have any peach?" she asked Mr. Bailey.

"Everything we have is out," he said, moving on to help someone else. Girl rummaged through the bottles, but there was no peach, or even tan. How could that be? What if Girl had made a deer statue, or a person, or a peach tulip? Had he hidden the flesh tones? She rummaged through the glazes, and finally settled on a greenish-brown with flecks of black. Not her vision, but it would have to do. It was somewhat skin-colored if you let your eyes blur to slightly out of focus.

Mr. Bailey was back again, looking over her shoulder.

"How about you use blue for the pants, red for the shirt, and yellow for the hat? You know you can use several colors of glaze. They won't bleed into each other. Then it will be more obvious that it is a Chinese man."

Girl just stared him down. She wanted peach. There was no peach. She suspected there might have been peach, but Mr. Bailey hid it when she was in the art room, so she ignored him entirely as if he had never spoken.

When Girl brought her sculpture home and explained once again that it was a Chinese man, her parents graciously put it on the mantel for a while, until it magically disappeared one day. Naked women were great art, but penises were just embarrassing.

fourth of july

Brother tiptoed into Girl's pink bedroom and tugged at her shoulder to wake her. Brother and Girl shared a box fan at the end of the hallway and slept with their bedroom doors open to catch the hot moving air. Mostly, they just got the buzz of the motor. Mother and Stepmother had a window AC unit that came with the house. All summer their door was closed tightly so as not to let any air out. Girl loved waking up in the hot summer air that did not feel different from the temperature of her skin.

In front of their house was a busy street—a double-yellow-line street, not just a white-dashed-line street. It was the Fourth of July, and the road in front of their house was closed, but the parade hadn't started yet. Brother and Girl padded down the hallway in bare feet, stepping around the squeaky places on the hardwood floor and placing their feet carefully on the stairs so that no one woke up and told them "no." They walked outside through the prickly gravel at the edge of the road. Girl looked left and right even though there were no cars because she didn't know how to *not* look both ways. The pavement held the warmth from a month of sun and radiated up through her calloused feet. The siblings crossed the oncoming lane as quickly as they could without scraping their toes. They had a destination: the double yellow line. It was ugly gold and grayed out on the edges, and it, too, had retained heat. When Girl prodded the line with a toe it squished just a little under her toenail—not as hard as the concrete, and not quite as soft as when she had stuck her thumbnail into a glob of old green paint on the bench at the playground. Girl had been waiting all year to see what it felt like. Brother and Girl stood with their feet on the dividing lines and there were no cars anywhere, just people starting to walk with lawn chairs down to the parade route on Titus Avenue, the main road with traffic lights and small stores. Hawkers were already selling red balloons to tie around children's wrists. Girl always untied hers and released it with a wish, and she always cried with regret when it went up so fast into the sky and got lost in the clouds. Mother knew she did this every year, and before buying a red balloon at the parade she made Girl promise that this time she would not let it go and she would not cry and they both knew this was going to happen regardless, but Mother bought one for Girl anyway, tying a shoestring bow around her summer-brown wrist.

Brother and Girl had to hurry now, because the sidewalk on Titus was filling up and the good spots were already taken. The siblings ran back into the kitchen to urge their parents, "faster, come on, hurry up, we are going to miss it, we don't want to miss it, hurry up." They never brought lawn chairs because by the time they got there the crowd was at least one or two rows deep, even though the family lived closer than most all of them. But it was okay, because when the people marching in the parade threw candy, their arms arced wide enough for at least a few pieces of candy to land where the children stood. They watched their friends march by with Girl Scouts, or dance troupes, or Pee-Wee cheerleader squads. Brother and Girl had marched in parades, too, but only in the Memorial Day parade, not the sacred Fourth of July one.

"You will not be a cheerleader," Stepmother told her daughter as little girls went by shaking their navy-blue-and-gold pom-poms. "Their outfits are a disgrace to women! No daughter of mine is going to wear a short skirt and cheer for boys." Girl wanted to be a cheerleader more than anything, but she didn't say a word. She practiced doing the splits with her best friend Gretchen, and someday when Girl was able to get her crotch all the way down to the ground, she planned on bringing it up with Stepmother again, but she couldn't do it, not quite yet. Cheerleaders were popular and cute and when they stood up in class they tossed their hair with the same right-to-left flip as the models in shampoo commercials.

Shriners rode by on tiny motorcycles with their silly red fezzes, and the children could clap for them, because Mother said that they had a great-uncle who was a Shriner, and Shriners raised money for sick children. Girl thought the old men on their knee-high scooters were embarrassing and she didn't want anyone to know that she was related to one, but Shriners always threw the most candy, so Girl yelled loudly so they'd make sure to send some her way. Girl felt the rat-tat-tat cadence of snare drums in her teeth, but the deep bass drum got trapped inside her chest where she felt everything. She didn't know why bass drums made her cry but it had something to do with expectation. When Girl felt the bass drum she did that ugly, nose-wrinkle don't-cry-face and turned away so Brother wouldn't mock her. She loved the feather caps of the majorettes even though Stepmother said that majorettes were as stupid as cheerleaders, with their fake white guns and knee-high boots and miniskirts. Girl also loved the dancers that waved double-sided flags until they almost touched the street and then back up with a swirl as the band played behind them. Girl swore that someday she would dance down the street in knee-high boots and a miniskirt twirling a flag because she was really terrible at spinning her baton in the backyard, and she knew baton-girl was beyond her abilities. When she threw that shiny metal rod up into the air and spun around, the white rubber ends hit her on the head as often as they bounced on the grass.

The veterans went by, and the crowd quieted slightly in respect.

"Don't clap, yet," Stepmother said. "Wait, I want to see . . . okay, they are World War Two vets. You can clap for them."

Korean vets were iffy, but Stepmother told the children to never, ever clap for Vietnam vets. Girl clapped anyway, saying, "It's a free country," under her breath, and everyone else was clapping too so Stepmother couldn't hear her. Even though Mother always said the children could clap for whomever they wanted, Girl wasn't sure what was right. She didn't want to clap for war, but a lot of these men were the fathers of her classmates. Girl couldn't always remember which vets were okay to clap for and which were not, so sometimes she refused to cheer for any of them—it was too hard to figure out. Why was it permissible to clap for very old soldiers and not young ones? Girl had seen the old vets at the drugstore and they always had blurry green tattoos and a lot of them had the red blotches Mother said was scurvy, and their skin was always dry with white flakes on their arms. Girl clapped quietly, her sticky palms barely touching, not making much sound, unless they had a tank or big military vehicle. Then she couldn't help cheering but was a little afraid at the same time.

The children could cheer for Campfire Girls and Girl Scouts and Boy Scouts, and Girl clapped for all the teenaged girls who wore prom dresses even though she didn't know what they were queens of. Girl promised herself that someday she was going to wear a crown in a parade and sit on a float and wave, just like them. When the politicians came by with their big signs on the sides of their convertibles, Girl wondered if they had to find a friend with a convertible every year or if they tried to be nice to people who had convertibles just to keep their parade options open. Girl was not supposed to clap for Republicans but if they threw candy her way, she clapped anyway and didn't care.

"Pinny Cook!" Stepmother yelled and walked up to her car to cheer up close while the politician was stopped behind a dance troupe for a minute.

Pinny Cook was a Republican but she was also a woman and Stepmother voted for her but Mother didn't because Mother said that being a woman wasn't as important as being a Democrat. Louise Slaughter drove by slowly and the whole family all clapped for her, even though Louise wore too much makeup and everyone could smell her perfume a mile away. "Hi, Judy!" she yelled to Mother, and Girl felt famous because her mother was on the Democratic Committee and made the children walk around the neighborhood and put fliers on houses every fall. But Democrats didn't throw as much candy.

At the end of the parade came all the kids on bicycles who were in the decorating contest, with red, white, and blue streamers woven through their spokes and dangling off their handlebars. Brother entered the contest once—a year before Girl was old enough to—and she had watched him weave blue and white crepe paper between the spokes of his red dirt bike. Now that they both could enter, neither of them wanted to. The other kids had sparkly garlands and Mylar streamers—much fancier than Brother's—and Girl didn't know where to buy things like that. She felt sad for Mother, because obviously she didn't know either, and Girl didn't want Mother to see that their crepe paper decorations weren't as good at the other children's.

The family had a cookout in the backyard after the parade, and Girl and Brother rode their bikes down to the town hall for the craft fair and street party and the fried dough. The siblings watched people throw balls at the dunking booth, but they never tried because they were both very bad at throwing baseballs and the firefighter in the booth always made fun of the people who missed. They very much liked to watch him suddenly drop down into the tank because he was so mean and obnoxious and the children knew that water was cold and grown-ups were always big babies about cold water. Girl and Brother rode back and forth between the front yard of the town hall and the backyard of their parents' house, where Mother and Stepmother had grown-up friends over. Their parents didn't have many friends who had children.

Everyone went down to the town hall together for fireworks: the children, their parents, and their friends, Shirley and Betty. They always got a good seat on the curb. They never brought a blanket because the grass was full by the time they get there, and more importantly, Stepmother said that the view was better from a little way back. Girl looked scornfully at those people on blankets who didn't know they were sitting too close. Girl and Brother always saw someone from school and said "Hi" and then stood there awkwardly for a minute before running back to their parents to wait for full dark.

"Don't cheer when he gets dunked," Stepmother said as they passed the man in the dunking booth. "They are poor migrant workers and they deserve respect. I just wish they found a way to raise money with more dignity." She didn't realize that the "Point Pleasant Pea Pickers" were the local firefighters' union, not people who picked vegetables.

The fireworks started and Mother's friend Shirley asked Girl, "Which ones are your favorites?"

"Bacons," Girl said, knowing it was a silly made-up word, but not knowing how else to describe the ones that sizzled on the way down like bacon grease in a black cast-iron skillet. "Like that!" she explained, pointing her popsicle-sticky index finger up at the white balls, the sizzle lighting up inside her in the same place that the bass drum hit, but fireworks made her soar inside like she was coming out of her body entirely.

"More bacons!" Shirley yelled, as they clapped wildly. Girl loved her so much for not laughing at the silly word. The white bursts snaked down the blackened-blue sky and the grand finale went up, one firework after another after another, colored ones that opened like paper umbrellas, each one larger than a house, ones that cracked and boomed. Smoke trails snaked down and hung in the air brownish-black, before they wafted away. When it was over Girl was surrounded by too many grown-up legs moving too quickly, and Mother took Girl's hand and pulled her close, like she knew that the crowds had turned her small, like Girl was too precious to lose.

flying to alaska

Girl and Brother had started spending every summer as well as a week or two every winter in Anchorage back when they were four and five years old. At first, they made the eleven-hour flight with various chaperones, then graduated to Unaccompanied Minor status when Girl was seven or eight. They flew every summer, leaving right after the Fourth of July and returning at the end of August.

Girl and Brother ran across the wet lawn in their socks. Girl was excited to get going and Mother and Stepmother were taking forever to load the car and Girl knew she'd be sitting for a long time. She decided then and there that socks were just right for running in the grass. They were warmer and softer than bare feet, but without the loss of the texture and sensation of the grass stems, anthills, and rocks. It was perfect, but she never did it again.

When the children returned to the house, Mother and Stepmother were in a tizzy. Every stitch of clothing the children owned was packed in two powder-blue Samsonite suitcases so full their sides curved out into a rhombus and they had to be duct-taped shut. The children had no other dry socks. Stepmother was so mad she had drops of spittle on her lips, but then it never took much to send her over the edge. It would be five more years before Girl was given the words *clinical depression* as rationale for Stepmother's constant anger. All Girl knew then was that Stepmother had a very short fuse, and just about everything the children did would turn Stepmother's face red and her words harsh and full of fury.

Today Girl wasn't concerned in the least. Stepmother could yell, but she could never strip away the feeling of the grass beneath Girl's socked feet, and she couldn't stop the children from going to Alaska. Her power over them was about to be lifted for the summer, traded in for that wielded by Father, and that knowledge trumped Girl's usual strong desire to behave properly. Girl didn't have to listen to Stepmother anymore, and there wasn't anything Stepmother could do about it. The wet sock problem had to be resolved without opening those cases, the closing of which was a family affair. Mother would pack them full, then the children sat on the top of the light blue plastic-y lids while Stepmother strapped duct tape around them and swore. Swearing made the duct tape stick better.

At the airport, Mother and Stepmother walked Girl and Brother through security and all the way onto the plane. The stewardess wore too much makeup, and Girl longed to wipe off her face and see how old she really was underneath. Girl suspected that the stewardess was a lot older than she was pretending to be. The dark blue polyester uniform was ugly, and her pantyhose sagged at the knee. It was the late 1970s and all the flight attendants wore ascots, regardless of gender. Girl hoped she would never have to wear such a manly uniform no matter what career she chose someday. The stewardess gave Girl and Brother Unaccompanied Minor pins, and Girl was enveloped in heavy perfume as the flight attendant fastened her seatbelt. Mother turned to leave with a closed-lip smile and her eyes were wet behind her thick glasses, but Girl's were dry. This was the children's adventure; there was no place for Mother or Stepmother in this and she was eager for them to leave. Girl and Brother were starting their day of limbo, which would end with them in the possession of their father. On the planes and in the airports in between, the children belonged to no one.

The plane started to taxi, going faster and faster, and Girl and Brother leaned forward as long as they could, fighting gravity until the speed pushed them back in their seats, unable to even tilt their heads forward. Joy rose in Girl as the front wheels left the earth. *Here we go, into the wild blue yonder! Climbing high, into the sky!* Girl sang freely now that the engines were too loud for Brother to hear and tell her to stop, like he always did. The children held their hands on the silver armrests in what Brother said was "pilot style" and pretended they were the ones flying the 747. Once the plane leveled off and their excitement with it, the children dragged their carry-ons from under the seats in front of them and looked at the surprises Mother had packed: a few small toys, some candy, and an *Archie and Jughead* comic book. The children only got comic books for trips—Mother said that they were for people who weren't smart enough to read real books, so it was a good treat to have one.

Girl's carry-on was dark blue and white and said TWA (Trans World Airlines) on it. The letters formed the shape of a swan. Brother had an ugly, white bag from Northwest Orient. Girl's bag was prettier and sleeker, but the children had never flown TWA and Northwest Orient was by far their favorite airline. Northwest Orient stewardesses wore white dresses and they all had long, shiny, black hair and almond-shaped eyes. They smiled a lot and were super nice to the children, and pinned gold pilot's wings to their shirts to identify them as passengers needing assistance. When the children flew Northwest Orient, they were always the only Unaccompanied Minors and got to hang out in the first-class club lounge on long layovers. The flight attendants let the children lie on the white shag carpeting and watch the big, wood-enclosed console TV that sat on the floor, and they even brought the children orange juice in real glasses with ice.

By far the worst plane to fly unaccompanied was United Airlines. Instead of gold pilot wings they gave out ugly, red-and-white, diagonally striped tin buttons with "Unaccompanied Minor" printed in bold type. On Northwest Orient the stewardess would take the children off the plane as soon as they landed, before the rest of the passengers, but on United, Girl and Brother had to wait for the plane to clear of people before they could leave.

When the children got to Chicago they had to walk quickly to keep up with the flight attendant who was overseeing their plane change. Flight crews all had small rolling bags they trailed behind them with one hand, so Girl and Brother dragged their carry-ons, too, even though theirs had no wheels.

"Stop dragging your bags!" the stewardess reprimanded them. "You are going to rip them!" Girl and Brother listened for a while, but the Chicago O'Hare terminal was big and their bags were heavy, and they knew the stewardess had no real authority over them. By the time the stewardess delivered the children to the United Airlines Unaccompanied Minor room, Girl was out of breath and the bottom of her bag was streaked in gray.

The room was small and smelled of old shoes. There was a red-and-blue rug printed with the stylized tulip-shaped UA insignia in the middle. It had stains from spilled drinks and black spots of ground-in chewing gum. Eight or ten other kids sat in armless chairs upholstered in red-and-blue, nubby fabric like polyester terry cloth. A few looked up when Girl and Brother entered, but no one said hello or even nodded an acknowledgment. A television hung from the ceiling blaring a baseball game. Girl didn't recognize either team, but then no one in her family watched sports.

"Where're you from?" an untidy boy around her age asked Girl. His hair was rumpled brown and his face was splattered with freckles.

"Rochester, New York," she said. Her brother ignored the new child and pulled out a book.

"I'm from Minneapolis but I'm going to Atlanta! That's in Georgia," he bragged.

"We're going to Anchorage," Girl answered, wishing he would go away.

"Yeah, well, I'm going almost a thousand miles!"

"Yeah? Well, we're going over three thousand." The Atlanta boy spit on the carpet and walked away. Girl didn't want to take her Barbies out to play with on the carpet now, so she dug through her carry-on for a book. The chairs were too close to the wall to allow her to lean back on two legs, so instead Girl curled forward, her book on her lap.

None of the other kids approached the children. Girl and Brother weren't the kind of kids that made friends easily anyway. Brother wore glasses and Girl's hair was never well-combed, and their pants were always a few inches too short for their long, skinny legs. Girl and Brother were kids who read books and played by themselves, not kids who cheered for sports teams and made friends with strangers. They didn't particularly like other children or want them around. It was better when it was just Girl and Brother.

They had two or three flights to get from Rochester, New York, to Anchorage, Alaska, depending on whether Father had gotten the children a direct flight from Chicago or if they had to first go to Seattle. One and a half hours to Chicago, then a layover for an hour or two; four hours to Seattle, then another layover; three more hours up to Anchorage. It was around eleven or twelve hours altogether, but inside the aluminum tube of the jet, time seemed to dissolve into the static of the engines. *Bing!* Girl pushed the flight attendant call button to ask how much longer the flight would be. The attendants often stopped answering, so Girl and Brother pushed the button over and over until they got a response. *Bing! Bing! Bing!* Once a flight attendant gave Girl her watch to hold for the entire flight so she'd stop binging the call button. The watch was slender gold with a tiny metal buckle—nicer than Mother's silver Timex with the expandable, accordion-like band. Soda pop was free and the children never got to drink it at home, so they'd ring the bell for pop, and more pop, and more peanuts, even though the nuts were honey-roasted and tasted gross. Back then a meal was served on the long flights, too, which was always some sort of inedible meat, but it came with a cookie or dessert of some sort.

Brother would race his Matchbox cars down the aisles, and they'd fight and call the stewardess to referee.

There was a train that ran beneath the Seattle-Tacoma airport, and Brother and Girl had to ride it between terminals when they changed planes. Another Unaccompanied Minor told Girl about the passenger that fell on the tracks and was run over by the train. They used sawdust to soak up the blood. Girl thought a lot about this every time they rode the train. It was nearly impossible for passengers to gain access to the tracks. The train was hermetically sealed in its tube, with automatic sliding doors and whatnot. A passenger would have to work very hard to wind up on the tracks and get run over by a train and require someone to soak up their blood with sawdust. It could not have been accidental.

Girl didn't know why they used sawdust to soak up blood but it seemed feasible. She often saw sawdust in the tunnels of the SEA-TAC subway. What else could it be for? The subway car smelled of oil and unwashed hands, and the carpet was always stained from too many feet.

Brother was nine or ten the year they started flying unaccompanied, and travel transformed him from the family's problem child to the leader. Brother was not put off by blood-soaked sawdust or changing terminals all alone in strange airports or reading diagrams of the subway stops. They took the train—Girl looking suspiciously out the window, keeping an eye out for sawdust and wondering how someone could get inside the tunnel to get hit by a train anyway—and Brother in his glasses, thinking about being capable or something.

Brother wasn't made anxious by airports or maps or directions to places they had never been. Girl followed him because she had to. She certainly couldn't navigate strange places and large airports on her own.

At Mother's house Brother was always in trouble for things he did or did not do: he did not do his homework, he went to the grocery store after school and someone stole his shoes, he did not do his chores, and he once asked a police officer to give him a ride home when a group of boys were chasing him. Stepmother's conclusion: Brother was not tough enough and he did not work hard enough and therefore he was a little weenie, and did not deserve respect. It was only Stepmother who thought so, but she was the one who hit the hardest.

Brother's competence—no, his superiority—started when they boarded that first plane in Rochester and it grew with each connecting flight. By Seattle, he was the one in charge. Girl could not change planes without him.

When they reached their gate, Girl and Brother sat alone on the floor, digging through their suitcases for toys and candy. An adult interrupted them with a grunt and handed Girl a card that read: *I am deaf. I am selling these sign language cards to support myself and live independently.* Girl didn't know how to say no, so she bought a card with line drawings for the alphabet. She and Brother studied it during the long layover until they could finger-spell pretty fluently, and they used it as their secret language well into high school.

The Anchorage airport was filled with large taxidermied animals: a mountain goat, a Kodiak bear, maybe an eagle. The carpet was modern and in shades of orange and brown.

Father kept dog biscuits in his pocket for his husky and always offered them to the children as a snack when he picked them up. Girl ate them. Brother did not. The dog bones tasted like grit and shame and nothing. At Father's house, Brother was the son, and Girl lived in his shadow.

Girl always figured that she'd grow up to be a stewardess. She didn't want to, but she flew so much that it seemed like she was already training for it. She thought it was a boring job, and Stepmother said it was for people who weren't smart enough to go to college, but stewardesses got to fly everywhere, and in spite of the boredom, Girl liked to fly. The smell of jet fuel at the airport would make her smile even if she wasn't happy. Girl loved the shiny airport halls filled with rushing people going places, and the feeling that Girl was one of the people going somewhere, too. She never thought about being a pilot. Girl had taken the controls in her dad's two-seater plane plenty of times, so she knew flying itself wasn't hard, but all those instruments looked complicated. Girl didn't want to have to think that much and she had no sense of direction and maps made her so frustrated she cried. There were no street signs in the sky to tell pilots where to go. Stewardess, then, was probably going to be her lot in life.

Once Girl sat next to an Asian man, almost old enough to be her father. It was on the way home from Alaska the winter that Girl was ten. Girl and Brother often went to Alaska separately in the winter to have "alone time" with their father. The stranger spent hours coloring with Girl in her coloring books. Girl knew Mother wouldn't think it was appropriate for a grown-up to want to play with her so much, but Girl didn't know what to do—they were assigned seats next to each other, and Girl was bored.

"What's your name?" Girl asked, but the man wouldn't answer. He just kept coloring.

"Here," he said, "take this to the bathroom." He had written something that looked like a foreign language in her coloring book, maybe Chinese. "Hold it up to the mirror, then you will see my name."

Girl took the book to the tiny plane bathroom. She never locked the door, because more than anything Girl was really afraid of getting locked in small places. If she didn't lock the door, though, the light wouldn't turn on, so in order to see the book Girl held the door open just a tiny bit with her foot. Girl saw his name in the reflection clear as a bell: NICHOLAS. Girl went back to her seat, impressed that he could write backward, but a little scared. Grown-ups shouldn't be so tricky about their names.

Girl slept the rest of the flight, and Nicholas woke her up only when they landed. Girl looked around for her blue knit hat that said Go Kiss a Moose, a present from her father that Girl used to carry her Smurf figurine collection. There was nothing Girl loved more than the Smurfs. She had gotten a few new ones on her trip, so now Girl had eight of the two-inch-tall, blue, plastic creatures. Girl had put her hat full of Smurfs under the seat in front of her next to her carry-on—she was sure she had—but it was gone. There was nowhere else for it to be, and the stranger helped her look for a minute but he wasn't happy or friendly anymore. "It's time to leave the plane," he said sternly. Girl knew he had taken them. She didn't think he wanted to play with them—Girl figured he wanted to use them to make friends with another child. Girl hated him and she wanted her Smurfs and her new hat but everyone was filing off the plane, and who would believe a grown-up would want a hat full of Smurfs anyway?

notes from the fourth wall:
fragments on flying
on the planes and in the airports in between, matt and i belonged to no one

I feel the shift in my thighs first, long before the pilot announces that we have begun our descent. Right above my knee the pressure changes as the angle tilts slightly forward. Now my weight is balanced between my thighs and the top of my back, and gravity pulls at the balls of my feet, but not the heels. I fly like other people take the bus. And this fall I have been flying every week. Sundays I leave Cleveland for Florida. Wednesdays I leave Key West to return to Ohio. October, November, half of December, and here it is January and I'm on a plane. The pressurized cabin is the same air I breathed in childhood.

When I smell jet fuel, there is a commotion inside my rib cage, soaring up, up, up. If happiness were visible, it would gush from the top of my head like those mega-sprinklers they advertised on TV in the 1980s. As a child, airports and airplanes were a liminal space between parents. As an adult, the encapsulated time in flight is a respite from emails, text messages, housework, and long lists of things I should be doing but don't want to do. It's a release from guilt and the privilege of being alone with my thoughts and books. The freeze-time is as prized as the destination.

Rochester, New York, to Anchorage, Alaska was 4,486 miles: 1,047 miles to Chicago, 1,976 miles to Seattle, 1,463 miles to Anchorage. Of course, we always had layovers at the airports in between.

When I was a child, we didn't have to take off our coats and boots to go through security—we just emptied our pockets, and made sure the straps of our carry-ons didn't snag as they went through the X-ray. We scorned grown-ups who made the machine beep and did that cartoonish "D'oh!" face as they slapped their back pockets and removed their wallets and coins. We never made the machine beep. Now security requires tiny containers of liquids kept in a Ziploc baggie, no shoes, no belt, no coat, take your laptop out of your bag, stand with your hands above your head like you're freeze-frame in a safety dance while the scanner moves around you. I still have no patience for people who make the machine beep.

As an adult, I mostly fly south. My nostalgic airports from childhood—Chicago, Seattle, Anchorage—have been replaced by Fort Meyers, Miami, and Atlanta. I know each one's quirks: where to eat, where to smoke, where to shop. I never take the train in Atlanta because I am always trying to lose weight. I can cross three terminals in under fifteen minutes if I wear the proper shoes, and if other travelers heed the loudspeaker that advises us to *stand right, walk left* on the escalators and conveyor belts. If I have to take the train, I test my balance by standing without holding on, leaning into the acceleration, embarrassed if I do that off-balanced wobble step that shows how out of practice I am.

Airplane orange juice bears little resemblance to real orange juice. When I pull back the hermetically sealed foil, it makes a light hiss that sounds vaguely carbonated. It's syrupy and sour, but I drink it anyway, hoping the vitamin C will ward off the germs of my fellow passengers. As a child, I ordered it over and over, hoping it would be the same sweet drink we were only allowed on special occasions, and the half-full cup of disappointment slid around on my tray until it ended in my lap.

I have learned to wear white headphones on the plane, from the moment I take my seat until the moment I exit the plane. Most of the time they aren't connected to anything, but they stop my seat mates from treating the airplane as a flying confessional. I've heard about how ballroom dancing saved one man's marriage. I've been told about a job interview that went poorly and the man's fear that this wife would leave him if he didn't find employment soon. It was after one man tried to recruit me for a blackmail scheme that I stopped talking to people on planes. This passenger wanted me to find an older, married man to buy me a drink in a hotel bar when we landed, and then invite him up to my room. My fellow passenger would snap photos, which would be "good for $5,000, usually." He wound up next to me on the shuttle bus to the car rental pavilion. "Lillibridge," he said, looking at my luggage tag. "I'm going to look you up later." After that, I flipped over my luggage ID so that only the words "see reverse for info" were visible, and I stopped talking to strangers on planes.

After my divorce, I flew with my sons from Ohio to Florida to visit my parents. I pushed one toddler in a stroller, carry-on bags hanging off the handles.

I wore the baby in a sling across my chest and a backpack diaper bag on my back. I told my three-year-old that TSA was looking for hamsters when we went through security—he was too young to have to worry about bombs and other implements of terror. My son stood there looking confused, trying to figure out why so many people were smuggling rodents, but he knew if he had been given the opportunity to bring his guinea pig he certainly would have. I packed toy surprises and snacks for my children, just like my mother did for me years ago. The children and I flew every year, and gradually they grew into two boys that could walk on their own holding my hands, then eventually into two boys who could carry their own luggage. They are quiet and polite and never complain about delays, and even as infants they did not scream in flight. They, too, love the transitional space of airports, the timeless feel of encapsulated air travel. But on the planes and in the airports in between, they always belong to someone—they belong to me.

loon landing

Father and #Four bought an old hunting camp on Lake Louise, a four-hour drive from Anchorage, and named it Loon Landing. There were four little log cabins, each with its own wood-burning stove, because there was no heat or electricity. Outside each cabin was a paint bucket with a toilet seat on top—there was no running water, either. One cabin was set apart on its own, and Father rented it out to fellow campers. The other three cabins sat all in a row, halfway down the hill, overlooking the lake. #Four and Father shared the Taylor cabin, which had the biggest stove and shelves of canned and dehydrated food. There was a counter that ran the length of one wall, and that was where everyone ate. Next to the Taylor cabin was the Lillibridge cabin—Father had carved signs for each cabin out of wood, named for all the family's last names: #Four's name was Taylor; Father, Juli, Girl, and Brother were all Lillibridges, and #Four's children shared the surname King. Girl and Brother shared the Lillibridge cabin, sleeping on metal cots. Father hung posters over their beds—golden retriever puppies on Girl's side, *Battlestar Galactica* on Brother's. #Four covered a small table with contact paper so the children had a place to draw. The contact paper had giraffes and zoo animals all colored orange and yellow and brown. Father locked Girl and Brother in at night, but he left a bag of granola mix for the morning, and a pee bucket in the corner, which was an improvement over the jar.

The third cabin was the King cabin, where Juli and their stepsister, Anne, stayed. Of their three stepsisters, only Anne came to Alaska regularly. Jane and Sara were older, and often stayed home with their father in Toronto, with whom they lived full-time. None of #Four's children lived with her. Juli and Anne were both the same age—fifteen. Anne listened to Pink Floyd and smoked pot. Juli listened to Barry Manilow and did not smoke anything. No one minded that Anne smoked pot, though, because Father and #Four did too. Girl spent a lot of time trying to figure out how they smoked a pot—did they leave it on the stove until it burned? All she knew was that when pot was being smoked, Juli came outside the cabin and played with her.

At dinnertime the family would turn on the radio to listen to "Caribou Clatters," which were messages read over the air to all the people who lived in the bush and didn't have telephones. Sometimes Mother and Stepmother would send a message to the children over the radio—just a sentence or two saying they missed them and hoped they were having fun. Hearing her name on the radio made Girl feel important. Father and #Four had set up tent sites on their ten-acre property, and someone had to stay at the campground all summer, in case anyone wanted to rent a campsite. Father and #Four still had to work, though, so they split up the season between them. One week was #Four and Brother, one week was Juli and Girl, the third week was Father and everyone all together. Once, when Juli and Girl were at the campsite alone, Brother sent them a Caribou Clatter. "I hope you are having fun with Lucifer," he said. Juli was livid, but that was the name of Juli's cat, so Girl didn't understand what she was so mad about. Girl hadn't ever read the Bible.

Juli was sixteen and Girl was eight when Big Mama, as they called the van, pulled away and left them behind at the campground. There was no car in case of emergency, but there was a canoe Juli could row to a nearby hunting lodge. Juli let Girl stay in her cabin, so neither of them had to sleep alone. Every morning Juli read the Bible to Girl, starting from the very beginning. Girl knew Juli was dyslexic and this was a big deal to her, so she listened closely even though it was boring. At night the sisters wrote letters back home on pale lavender stationery.

One night two drunken campers came to their campsite. The men ignored the barricade that separated the family's area from the campground itself, and walked down as if they were invited guests. "Is your father here?" they asked Girl in gruff, slurred voices. She said no, but the men didn't leave. They were tall with untrimmed beards, smelly and unwashed from living in the bush country. They found Father's Reiner beer in the cooler and sat down at the picnic table to hang out for the night. They told Juli that she was very pretty, and Girl agreed. Juli had long, red hair and baby blue eyes. Even though she was short—only four-foot-nine-inches—she had really big breasts, so big that even at eight years old Girl knew they were impressive. The sky doesn't darken during an Alaskan summer, so there was no easy way to end the evening. The stars don't come out, there's no feel of time passing—it is like one very long day. Eventually, Juli told the men that she had to get her little sister to bed. Still they did not stand up and go, but kept drinking beer around the campfire, trying to convince Juli to hang out with them longer.

Juli and Girl went into the King cabin, and Juli locked the door from the inside. There wasn't really a doorknob, but there was a metal latch and Juli hooked the Master lock through the hasp and shut it. The sisters stood quietly as the door, listening for the men. Girl kept her arms wrapped around her big sister, trying to slow her thumping heartbeat, afraid the men could hear it. Juli told Girl, "If I tell you to run, go out the window as quietly as you can and climb in the window of the cabin next door. I'll meet you there. Don't look back or wait for me in the woods, just run as quickly as you can."

Girl wasn't sure about this. What if Juli couldn't get in the window? What if the men caught her? Girl went and laid down on her metal camp bed as quietly as she could, hoping the men would think they were asleep. Juli stood by the door, one eye on the peephole. She did not lie down until the men gave up and walked away.

pearl the squirrel

There was a fat, dead squirrel in the trap Father had set in the storage area of the Taylor cabin. The oversized mousetrap had caught him behind the head, and he wasn't moving or bleeding.

"Dad!" Girl called. "You got a squirrel!" She went outside so she didn't have to watch him take it out of the trap and she tried not to cry.

"Why do you have to kill them?" Father didn't hunt. He hardly ever fished. He loved his dog more than he loved just about anyone or anything. How could he do this?

"Girl, you know I have to. They eat our food."

She didn't see how a squirrel could get into all those cans, and he kept the dehydrated meat and noodles and stuff in sealed plastic containers. What was even here for an animal to eat? Some candles? The squirrel had looked soft and cuddly, even though you couldn't hug a squirrel. Girl balled up her hands in her pockets, kicked the gravel at her feet, and didn't look up. She puffed out her lower lip and blew her tangled, dirty hair out of her eyes.

"Look, I know you love animals, honey. But it wasn't a pet. It was a wild animal, and if I let them in here they'd eat everything."

She still wouldn't look at him. It wasn't fair.

"Hey, I have an idea—we could stuff him and make him into a stuffed animal," Father said.

"Really? We could do that?" A jolt of longing banished Girl's melancholia. She loved stuffed animals. A real squirrel would be the best thing ever.

"Sure! We can go down to the lodge later and ask Linda for some button eyes." Father was cheerful, his big blue eyes looking into Girl's brown ones. She swore he never blinked, or at least not as much as normal people.

"But only if you dissect it with me first." Father longed for one of his children to follow him into medicine someday. As far as bribes went, it was an easy one. Girl wasn't afraid of entrails, especially if she would get a real stuffed squirrel afterward.

Father carefully took the squirrel out of the rattrap and carried it into the cabin.

"Brother? Do you want to help dissect a squirrel?" Father asked as he laid the carcass on the white Formica counter.

"No way!" Brother dropped the book he was reading and ran outside. Good. If he thought Girl was going to share the squirrel with him he could think again.

"Get my purse," Father said, as he always referred to his camera bag, much to Girl's embarrassment. The bag held everything he ever needed: wallet, camera, film, reading glasses, stethoscope, scalpels, bandages, and stitches— all sorts of medical tools and even packets of Betadine for cleaning wounds. He laid out a couple of sterile-packaged scalpels and his locking scissors with teeth that seemed to come in handy for a multitude of things.

"Come outside and wash your hands with me," he said, walking out the door to the picnic table outside. He turned the knob on the big plastic jug of water and handed Girl a surgical scrub brush. It had a soft yellow sponge on one side, and white plastic teeth on the other.

"But the squirrel's dead. It's not going to catch germs."

"It's good practice," he said in the voice that meant no arguing. They scrubbed their hands clean under the cold water and finally got to the good stuff.

"We can tan the skin with Betadine," Father said. Girl stood close to his elbow and looked over his shoulder. The skin on Father's neck was pebbly and red, and he smelled warm and comforting—that special Father smell that wasn't cologne or sweat, but just the body warmth of hugs and infrequently washed wool shirts. Without running water, no one bathed that much at Loon Landing. His hairless, knobby hands cut smoothly through the squirrel's belly in one neat motion.

"Hand me the hemostats."

"The what?"

"Those curved scissors with teeth."

"Okay." Girl leaned her elbow on the table so she could see closer as he peeled back the skin and pointed out the various organs.

"This is the esophagus, and stomach." Girl was surprised that there wasn't a lot of loose blood. "Look, it was female—here is her uterus, and back here are the kidneys." The organs were super tiny—smaller than she had antici-pated. Father carefully dissected the carcass and removed the innards, setting them aside. "Look at the spine." He named off each vertebra as he pointed with the tip of the blade: cervical, thoracic, lumbar. One of the eyeballs was on the counter. It was a cloudy blue-gray, like the lake outside. When he wasn't looking Girl poked it with a pen, expecting it to roll like a marble. Instead it squished like a tiny fragile grape. She hadn't meant to dishonor the squirrel by mutilating it and she didn't want Father to know, but at the same time she craved absolution.

"I thought eyeballs were hard," she said, "like marbles. But it squished when I poked it."

"That's right. They're really bags of fluid." He scraped the skin clean and reached for the Betadine. Girl watched him rub the orange disinfectant all over the inside of the squirrel pelt, then hang it up to dry by the wood stove. "We have to let it cure for a while." He took the guts and threw them in the woods for an animal to find.

In the days it took the skin to cure, it smelled like rotting food and antiseptic inside the Taylor cabin, and Girl found excuses to be outside as much as possible. Father had lost the majority of his sense of smell in a high school chemistry accident when an experiment he was working on blew up, so it didn't bother him as much as it bothered everyone else.

After a few weeks the skin was dry, and Father stuffed it with cotton balls and sutured it closed with his strong, deft fingers. Girl was surprised by how much it had shrunk. The pelt had half the girth of when it was alive—it was a good thing the squirrel had been so fat. They found blue buttons for eyes. Girl had hoped for buttons that actually looked like stuffed animal eyes, but it was the best they could do out in the woods and everything. She named the squirrel Pearl and slept with her every night, rubbing the soft body against her cheek. Pearl was Girl's most prized possession.

On the plane trip home to New York, Girl and Brother got into a fight, as they always did. Brother was bigger and stronger, but Girl could generally wear him down enough to win by just letting the blows fall on her and not giving in. She wasn't above cheating to win, either, and that day she took her home-taxidermied squirrel and used it like a scythe, slicing his arm with the crisp, dried claws of Pearl.

"You are *so* getting in trouble for this," Brother gloated. "I'm calling the stewardess." *Bing* went the call button, and Girl knew she was in for some serious shit.

"I probably need a rabies shot or something!" *Bing. Bing. Bing.*

"Yes?" The stewardess flashed a wide, fake smile but her eyes were squinched and she looked angry. The children always binged the call button too much.

"My sister scratched me with her squirrel," he said, pausing dramatically and shooting Girl an exaggerated glare, "and I need a Band-Aid." He held out his forearm, which was indeed bleeding.

"Squirrel?" She was confused, so Girl held it up to clarify. She might as well face the consequences. It wasn't like she did it by accident, but she figured that she had good reason. He started it, after all. Girl finished it.

"Oooh! It's so cute!" the stewardess exclaimed, taking the squirrel from Girl and holding it up. "Jane! Come see this!" She called another stewardess over to pet Pearl.

"It's adorable," Jane said. "We should show the Captain. Do you mind?" Jane asked Girl.

"It's okay," she said, shrugging. She was getting off scot-free.

"But—" Brother whined, but was cut off by the flight attendant.

"We'll be right back with this," the first stewardess said, walking down the aisle with Pearl.

"You suck," Brother said. "You always get your way. Everyone always loves you." Girl ignored him, smiling sweetly at the stewardess when she returned the squirrel. Brother never even got his Band-Aid.

car rider

Girl and Brother lived 1.3 miles from Rogers Middle School—two tenths of a mile short of the busing requirements. Girl was always jealous of the kids who got rides home, but there were plenty of other kids who walked, too. Poor Tim lived three blocks past Girl—he had missed the bus cutoff by half a block.

One day, though, Girl was going to be a car rider. It was her first day back to school following a week of the flu, and Stepmother said she would leave work early so Girl didn't have to walk in the cold. This was unheard of, and all day long Girl would stop working and remember, "I don't have to walk today!"

After school, she stood outside in her pink-and-purple-striped ski jacket. The sun was out, and it was so cold that the snow squeaked under her moon boots. She had wanted moon boots more than anything, but they got heavy when she walked, and she wished she had just bought normal ones.

She kicked the snowy sidewalk as she waited, watching the other kids get picked up one by one. She looked at the clouds as the teachers pushed through the school doors a half-hour later, their arms juggling papers and tote bags as they fought to unlock their car doors.

"Hey, are you okay?" one of the teachers asked. All the other kids were gone.

"I'm fine! My stepmother is coming to get me today!" she called back cheerfully. Stepmother was late, but she was always late. Girl coughed into her mitten. When the janitor locked the double doors, she started to worry. After he drove off, Girl only lasted a few more minutes before she gave up and started walking home. When she got halfway she started to cry, snot and tears covering her face in the icy wind.

Girl was halfway down the row of shops at Irondequoit Plaza. The strip mall had a large cement awning, so it was a little warmer. Stepmother pulled up in her bronze Datsun station wagon, but Girl ignored her and just kept walking. Stepmother trailed her for a few shops, then stopped and got out of the car.

"I'm so sorry!" she cried, tears running down her face. "I'm sorry, I'm so sorry, I got carried away at work, I didn't know what time it was. I am so sorry." Girl wanted to punish her more, refuse to get in the car, make her suffer, but Stepmother was crying harder than Girl was, so she got into the front seat and they drove home.

the ghost

When Father and #Four divorced, they sold Loon Landing and Father bought a boat. The *Ghost* had a single wooden mast mounted to the top of the enclosed cabin, a teak deck, and a pale gray, fiberglass hull the color of a seagull's wing. Navy blue letters spelled out *GHOST* in fancy script, painted above smaller lettering identifying the previous owner's home port of Kodiak, Alaska. Father never got around to correcting the letters to read Seward, Alaska, where he docked the boat. There were white plastic-covered wires called stays at various places to mount the smaller sails, and a fence-like wire in the same white plastic-covered metal that ran around the edge to keep the children from falling off. White rubber buoys were used as bumpers off the sides, and the dodger, a canvas windscreen at the back of the boat, was bright blue. They steered the boat by way of a wooden handle called a tiller that attached to the rudder at the very back of the vessel. The steering area was called the cockpit, and it had a recessed deck framed by storage benches made of teak. If Girl stood on the floor in the cockpit, she was too short to see over the dodger, so mostly she stood up on the benches. The cockpit was the only access into the cabin of the boat by way of a three-rung ladder followed by two conventional stairs. The ladder could be flipped up to access the hidden storage compartment inside the wooden steps where her father always kept lemon-flavored hard candies to combat seasickness, among other things. To the left was the tiny two-burner stove they cooked on. Girl liked the way the metal cooktop moved freely with the waves so as not to spill the soup, and the fence around the burners that kept pots and pans from flying about if they hit a swell. Girl loved using the foot pedal at the galley sink that brought up ice-cold Alaskan seawater to wash dishes, saving the fresh water for the final rinse only. To the right of the stairs was the built-in chart desk where Father kept maps and the radio. The children were forbidden to sit at the built-in seat of the chart desk, though, and Girl developed an aversion to it much like a dog with a shock collar. Girl avoided looking at the desk entirely if she could help it, and she had no interest in learning how to work the finicky radio that was always on the fritz.

The main cabin had a foldable table and two benches that converted into sleeping berths when they attached the canvas sides that connected with ropes to hooks in the ceiling. They had a tiny bathroom with a hand-pump toilet and minuscule sink, but Father had chosen the mirror for authenticity, not function. Girl could not see her face in the cloudy glass, but it didn't matter. Girl would start fifth grade in the fall, and she didn't care much about brushing her shoulder-length hair, though she did feel guilty if she didn't brush her teeth. Father didn't mind if the children avoided all forms of brushing on the *Ghost*, and they generally ended the summer with a new cavity or two from their neglect. Guilt was no match for laziness. After a week or two her hair had divided into clumps approaching dreadlocks, but Girl liked how the clumps gave a curl to her straight hair and made it seem thicker.

Behind the bathroom was Father's bed, which reached from wall to wall in a big triangular shape, fitting into the nose of the boat. The walls around it had built-in cubbyholes and a small wooden bookshelf where he kept his book of dirty limericks as well as other books by Ogden Nash and Jack London. Above the bed was a square hatch that could be opened for air or escape, if necessary. Underneath Father's bed were storage tanks for water. They carried all their freshwater with them, and the fluid was doled out like liquid gold, though Girl hated the plastic-y taste.

Father insisted that Brother and Girl learn the nautical vernacular for everything and had even sent the children a young sailor's dictionary to New York for them to memorize, but they didn't. Girl thought it was dumb to call ropes *lines* or, even worse, *halyards*. They were just white nylon and cotton ropes with a hint of blue thread running through them. They didn't need a special name, in her opinion, but if Girl used the word *rope* her father would suddenly act as if he was struck deaf—same thing if Girl said *bathroom* instead of *head,* or called the *galley* a *kitchen*. Front was *fore* and back was *aft, port* meant the left and *starboard* was the right. That made Girl mad. She was left-handed, and she wanted the left side to be called starboard. It was so much prettier sounding than port.

Girl straddled the empty space of the cockpit with her legs, each foot solidly on one of the teak benches that had roughened to gray in the salty air. Girl first came to know teak in this dried silver state, her hands and feet learning its texture as she traversed the boat monkey-like on all fours when they were underway. When they oiled the deck and benches at the end of each summer and returned the brown tackiness to the boards, Girl was always disappointed. The chore of rubbing linseed oil by hand into the wood in long, even strokes wasn't an unpleasant one, but it gummed up the feel of the wood and held the soul of the teak at bay, trapped beneath a layer of emollient. Besides, the boat was named the *Ghost*, and ghosts were white, gray, or silver. They were never golden brown. Girl steered the boat with the five-foot-long tiller, made of varnished wood as thick as her forearm, coming to a phallic knob at the end.

"Most people stand to one side to steer with a till," her father said, "but if you stand like this, with one foot on each side and the tiller between your legs, you can feel the rhythm of the waves in your body, and you'll make course corrections instinctively. Besides, you aren't tall enough to see over the dodger if you stand in the cockpit itself."

Girl was ten in 1983, and not yet five feet tall. With one foot on each built-in storage locker Girl added eighteen inches to her height, just enough to see over the blue canvas windbreak at the very back of the forty-four-foot sailboat. The tiller rose between her legs and Girl gripped it in front of her stomach, slightly uncomfortable about the sexuality of it. Her shadow rendered her a long-haired boy with a foot-long erect penis. Girl disliked looking down at her hand holding this rod in the same way her father and brother held their bodies when they peed off the deck, so Girl kept her eyes on the horizon and avoided looking at the tiller. It wasn't that Girl minded steering this way, actually, but she didn't want her father to make a joke about her having a penis, and Girl hoped he didn't notice her shadow. Girl and Brother had seen strippers rubbing poles between their legs on a dirty movie their father had left in the VCR for a week the year before. Brother was one year older than Girl, and he watched that tape over and over in the living room until Father returned it to the video store. Girl wanted to watch the cartoon movie they rented, *Shinbone Alley*, but Brother was bigger and always got his way. The dirty movie was called *The Van*, and it was kind of fascinating, but Girl could only sit through it once. The movie caused a tickling between her legs, and she didn't like to feel that while sitting next to Brother. Girl was never sure if her father left the dirty movie accidentally or as a gift to his son.

Actually, the *Ghost* wasn't really forty-four feet long. Years after the boat was sold, Brother looked it up in the Alaska registry of vessels, and they learned the sailboat only measured twenty-eight feet. Their father had inexplicably added sixteen feet to the length. As a child, though, forty-four was the number

Girl took as fact as solidly as she knew her address or age. As a child, forty-four feet was the length of her yard back home, almost, or as big as a floating Winnebago. Girl told everyone, "My dad has a forty-four-foot yacht," which they probably didn't believe. Some of the kids thought Girl had made up her father entirely. What kid in suburban New York has a father who lives in Alaska, let alone one who purportedly owned a plane and a boat? Even Girl recognized the incredulity of it.

After they cleared Seward's harbor Dad gave Girl the helm and went below decks to unpack. Girl was outside alone in the cockpit, her eyes focused on an island on the horizon. Steering was easy—Girl just kept her eyes on a landmark, and the boat seemed to follow her gaze. The *Ghost's* bow sliced silently through the waves when under sail or with a soft, steady chuffing if the diesel motor was engaged, as it was that day. Girl liked using the inboard motor, even though clouds of diesel exhaust sometimes blew forward. She didn't mind the smell. It was the scent of adventure.

Father and Brother were below decks playing cribbage in the cabin where the wooden walls glowed golden with old brass trimmings and there was an abundance of cubbyholes and hidden cabinets. The porthole windows were oval, not round, but their glass could swing open to let in the salty air that turned the brass fittings green.

"Brother, Dad, come quick! Porpoises!" Girl was first to see the dolphin pod surround their boat, and it was like they had come just to see her. Brother's head popped out the companionway door, quickly followed by the rest of him.

"Here, Girl, I'll take the helm. You can go look," Father said when he emerged, and Girl scurried around the boom to the foredeck, Brother racing up the other side to join her.

"Five of them, Dad!" Girl called, the wind carrying her voice back to the cockpit.

Girl climbed around the sail bags hanging from the stays on the bowsprit so she was at the foremost point on the ship. The bowsprit was narrow, maybe two feet wide, with a metal railing. Here Girl could lean over and watch the dolphins play in the wake of the bow. They crisscrossed under the boat, swimming alongside, their gray dorsal fins coming out of the water when they rose to take a breath. If Girl could get down to water level she would touch them, if only her arms were a little longer. Girl sat on the hammock-like sail bag that hung from the stays, rocking back and forth until the dolphins tired of the boat and swam away.

"Move over, Girl, give me a turn!" Brother wanted her spot, but Girl was there first. Even though Father always sided with Brother, he wouldn't tolerate any shoving on the boat, so there wasn't much Brother could do about it. Girl hated the way Brother always walked around with his two front teeth sticking out, and how he never let her play *Star Wars* with him, at least not very often, and how he never let her pick what they watched on TV back home. He smelled like farts and dirty socks but Father still loved him best—his only son. Well, this time Girl had beat him to the bow and she wasn't giving in.

"I was here first!" Girl said, and stuck her tongue out for good measure. He gave up and left Girl alone, just the way she liked it.

The bow cut through the waves and the sea splashed her face when they hit a swell. The waters of Prince William Sound were an opaque jade green, without any light or warmth. It wasn't pretty and didn't hint at mermaid songs or submerged forgotten cities like the turquoise beaches they had seen in Mexico with Mother and Stepmother. Girl didn't hold it against the water, though. Like her, it had the misfortune to be the kind of water that was strong but not beautiful. Girl bobbed and traveled the currents of childhood unable to steer her own course or choose her own ocean, and she understood that the surrounding sea didn't get to choose either. It was an ugly body of water bullied by winds and pulled by moon tides, reactive and unable to pretend any form of deliberation. Dad said it was the vegetation on the bottom of the ocean that gave water its hue, and this was another way the sea and Girl understood each other—both of them colored by what was below their surfaces.

They anchored overnight in Sunny Cove, her least favorite place. It always rained there, in spite of its name, and today was no exception, so they decided not to go ashore. That night after dinner, as they did every night, Girl and Brother folded up the solitary leg on the table and latched the wooden tabletop into its position on the wall. After they were snuggled into their sleeping bags, Father pressed the play button on the cassette deck mounted over Brother's bunk and went forward to his cabin. They were listening to *The Hobbit* on tape, and the narrator's voice filled her dreams with dwarves and magic and vast rooms of treasure.

Girl liked the way the boat rocked when they slept in their narrow bunks. After the first week they no longer bothered stringing up the hammock sides meant to keep the children in their beds at night. Their bodies had melded into the constant pendulum of the sea that rolled the boat cradle-like from side to side, and falling out of her bunk was no longer a danger. Besides, first thing in the morning the beds needed to revert to the benches they sat on for meals, and it was faster to reassemble the small cabin if they didn't string up the hammocks. As it was, bedding had to be stowed in the secret cabinets behind the cushions along with their pajamas, books, and teddy bears. They dressed quickly and went out into the cockpit, where Dad was already. Dad always woke up super early.

"Good morning, Girl!" Dad hugged her too hard, his wool shirt scratching her cheek as he crushed her to his chest. Girl pulled away and sat down to eat a granola bar in her favorite corner of the cockpit, leaning against the cabin. There was something different about the air over Prince William Sound. It was clearer but colder, and the light itself was lacking in the familiar warmth of New York's summer skies. The Alaskan sun never set from June until early August, only dimming slightly from 2:00 a.m. until the sun rose again at 4:00 a.m. But the sunlight wasn't yellow, it was a whiter sun that didn't heat the air or hurt your eyes. July and August on the boat were mainly in the high sixties where you were neither warm nor cold, and the air was indistinguishable from your skin.

"Well, the weather report is good today. We'll have a good stiff wind at our backs, so I thought we'd raise the sails and go like a striped ape." Father always said stripe-ed like it was two syllables instead of one. Girl sighed. She really didn't like to sail. It was too much work. Girl preferred motoring along lazily, but Dad had to get to Cordova to do a clinic, and they had only a few days to get there.

Cordova was a small fishing village that could only be reached by boat or small plane. No roads connected it to anything else. The town was so small that they didn't have a pediatrician, only emergency medical technicians and nurses in their small clinic. Once a month Dad would sail down and see all the kids in town. If Juli wasn't around, Girl acted as his assistant, calling to confirm appointments and writing down everyone's height and weight in their charts. Dad, as the visiting doctor, was treated as royalty, and the hospital staff and parents of his patients treated her with respect. No one questioned a ten-year-old medical assistant—Girl was Dr. Lillibridge's daughter, so therefore cut from a different cloth than the village children.

Brother and Girl went forward to haul up the anchor. They inserted the metal rod into its slot and took turns pushing the lever back and forth to run the manual winch. It was hard work and the weight of the metal, spade-like anchor tired out their arms quickly, so it forced Brother and Girl to cooperate.

They were both skinny kids, neither of them close to one hundred pounds, so they didn't have enough mass to be able to throw their weight into it, but summers on the boat were making the children wiry. Living onboard forced a transient truce between them, their constant competition held mostly at bay until they reached land, though they could never eradicate it entirely. After they weighed anchor and entered the open water, Dad cut the engine. Brother and Girl stood on the roof of the cabin by the mast. They unzipped the blue sail bag and freed the mainsail.

"Okay, hoist the mainsail!" Dad called, and Brother loosed the halyard from the cleat on the blond varnished mast. He and Girl alternated pulling on the line hand over hand to raise the sail, then Girl tied it off in a locking figure eight on the cleat. Dad adjusted tension on the lines with the cockpit winch, and they were underway. The boat was silent now, cutting through the water at ten knots. It heeled to the right, so the starboard gunwale was only a foot from the water, the port side rising like a wall. It was fun to climb around on the tilted deck, and especially to go below where navigating the cabin was like a crazy carnival house. Outside you always had to be ready for Father to yell *Ready about! Hard a lee!* Which meant the boom was coming across the deck at head level as they tacked back and forth on alternating diagonal paths across the water. The old joke—Why do they call it a boom? Because that's the sound it makes when it hits your head!—was true.

They were never entirely out of sight of land, but the horizon showed mountains and glaciers, not cities or even fishing villages. They skittered around islands too small to merit human habitation, but large enough to contain hundreds of untold adventures. Every evening they would choose a different harbor to anchor in overnight. The beaches were composed of small, gravelly rocks that hurt your feet, and the islands themselves seemed soilless, built on large stones that were less boulder than mountaintops poking up from the ocean floor. The island foundation was visible around the beaches with rock walls rising twenty feet high or more like exposed bones of a mammoth creature big enough for the whole world to reside on its back. The boulders begged to be climbed and always had gentle paths covered in soft moss that were easy to traverse with sneakers or bare feet. The woods covering the solid rock were lush green—pine and spruce evergreens, but smaller and stunted from living so close to the Arctic Circle. Tiny fairy pools formed in depressions on the rock high above sea level, fed with rainwater and rimmed with tiny saplings as big as Girl's hand. Girl was sure there was magic there just beyond the periphery, and if she could stay long enough she could join it and learn its secrets. The beauty of this place was that there were no other people there, and the islands were rarely marked with names on the nautical map, so they could claim these islands as their own and call them whatever they wished. The naming made them theirs more authentically than legal titles and without the need of lenders or mortgages. The small harbors were always good for a dog-faced seal or a few otters, and black-and-white puffins bobbed on the waves everywhere they went.

Girl played her wooden recorder on the foredeck for the orcas and blue whales to hear. She didn't think they minded her lack of musical training, but they never answered back, either. Every day or two they would spot a bald eagle flying overhead, but they never meant as much to Girl as the furry sea creatures she longed to pet. Eagles were good for bragging about, as grown-ups seemed to be in awe of them, and Girl recognized their ability to enhance a story, so she always included them when asked about Alaska—but the truth was that they did not evoke that "untouched wilderness" feeling as much as an orca breeching or otter floating by on its back, a clam held in its furry paws. Grown-ups always asked her to describe Alaska to them, and Girl developed a scripted response that included wild animal sightings and the size of fish she caught, which was all grown-ups really cared about. Girl couldn't tell them how it felt to be in Alaska, because she didn't really have words for it. It didn't occur to her that everyone didn't get to do stuff like this, or that one day she would look back on this time with longing. When Girl returned to the boat docks at Seward fifteen years later, the harbor was filled with cruise ships and the souvenir shops had sprung up shoulder to shoulder on the narrow village streets. Alaska stopped being the Last Frontier when Girl wasn't looking. By the time she returned and noticed, it was irrevocably inhabited and industrialized, but instead of producing cars or garments, the industry destroying the wilderness was tourism. All of that was yet to come, though.

Girl was reading a book in the sunshine, leaning back against the wall of the cabin while Father steered. Brother was reading too, on the other side of the cockpit, but he was reading a *Star Wars* book and hers was about John Paul Jones and old sea battles. The wind carried a whiff of ammonia.

"We must be near a sea lion island," Girl said.

"I think it's that rock," Father said, pointing to a tiny speck out in the distance. Father was farsighted and decades of scanning the waves had honed his vision to be considerably sharper than Girl's.

"How far away are they?"

"A few miles, I expect," Father said.

Pretty soon the wind brought the baritone barks of the animals to the *Ghost*, though they were still too far away to visually differentiate from the rock they occupied.

As they approached the island, Girl climbed around the sail to the foredeck. The stench of ammonia and animal feces was overpowering, but Girl liked sea lions anyway. They looked like big, huggable dogs. The creatures lay shoulder to shoulder, squirming on top of each other like a writhing heap of worms, but loud, barking worms that shat on each other with undignified abandon. Their rank smell made her glad when their island receded into the distance.

One night the waves broke hard against the sides of the *Ghost*, clouds thick and angry enough to block the light from the skies. Alaska summers were never dark, but Girl didn't notice the significance at the time. Girl lived most of the year in the predictable light patterns of New York, so she had forgotten than night didn't render you blind here. Years later, Girl realized that the darkness of the storm meant that it had been a big one.

Brother was below deck, sleeping, or trying to, even though Father had said they needed to alternate standing watch with him all night. They had a brass bosun's clock that chimed off the day into four-hour watches, but they had never used it to run shifts. Instead, they took turns at the helm based on tiredness or boredom. Now, though, Father said that they needed to stand watches all night through the storm. They were the only crew he had, and it didn't matter how young they were. He had trained the children from the kids who cried in frustration trying to fight down the sails into small, hardened sailors who could scuttle around the deck like a pirate's trained monkeys. They would rise to the challenge. Brother and Girl didn't like the idea of staying up all night, but Father said it was too rough to anchor and not safe for one person to pilot the boat all alone. Girl either volunteered to take the first shift or was ordered to. Father had softer expectations for Brother and he was always allowed to choose first when they divvied up chores or dinner.

Father had been raised in a house of women with a domineering mother and two older sisters. His father had been off fighting in World War II for much of his childhood, leaving Father the only male. Father had sired four children, but Brother was the boy he had longed for his whole life. It didn't matter that Girl was braver, or faster with the right answer, or willing to eat dog biscuits to amuse him. No matter how hard Girl tried, Girl could never be his second son. She didn't see then that Brother spent most of the year in a house with two lesbian parents and a competitive, bossy sister, and that maybe he needed to be cherished just for being who he was—a boy. Maybe Father was trying to save Brother from growing up just like he had. All Girl knew back then was that there was never enough time and attention from any of their parents to go around, and with her father Girl could never be good enough to merit his full affection, just because she was born female.

Taking first shift in the storm gave her Father's undivided attention, though, so Girl didn't mind. Girl sat curled up in the cockpit watching Father pilot the boat in his black survival suit, worn in case he went overboard into the glacier-filled sea. Girl wanted a suit of her own, but Father said they only came in grown-up sizes, and it wasn't like Girl was ever in danger of going overboard. The detachable autopilot was overwhelmed by the power of the storm, so he couldn't let go of the tiller even for a minute. Girl wore the life-jacket Father had apologetically handed her. They both knew Girl didn't need it, but it was officially the right thing to do when the wind whipped your hair in wet twig-like branches across cheeks red from the cold rain. Girl sat back under the protection of the canvas canopy of the dodger, cozy in the light streaming up from below decks. Girl was there to hold vigil. The rain and wind made talking impossible, and besides, Father had asked for company, not help, and Girl got to be the one he relied on. Under his black wool captain's cap the rain coursed down Father's cheeks and overflowed his beard, but he didn't bother to wipe his face. Although he later commended her for her lack of fear, Girl knew it wasn't about being afraid. It was that Girl got to be the chosen son. Girl got to be the strong one, the most-loved one, the one he could count on. Girl was a child not afforded the luxury of naiveté or innocence, and she knew that he had gotten in over his head with this storm and needed someone to help him muster the strength to get them all out. Years later, Father described that night on the *Ghost* as the most afraid he ever had been, but Girl never believed him. Father could do anything, and he would never have let the children come to harm.

When the storm passed by they found another inlet on a different island where they could drop anchor. Brother stood at the chart desk and fiddled with the knobs on the depth finder. He was adjusting the sensitivity of the sonar; if you turned the sensitivity up too much schools of fish would light up red on the black screen, rendering it useless, but if the sensitivity was too low they couldn't tell where the bottom really was. The screen blipped and flashed red dots and lines as Brother called out fathoms through the open door. They fought over who got to use the depth finder, like they fought over everything, but this time he won. Girl sat just outside the companionway, able to look down at the top of Brother's brown hair and smudgy glasses. Her job was to relay the numbers to Father as he slowly guided the boat into the cove. Father had first gone over the charts with them, pointing out submerged rocks and calculating the depth of the ocean floor based on tides. They always needed at least two fathoms or they would risk grounding. The *Ghost* glided past the tall gray rocks at the mouth of the harbor.

"Do you hear that?" Father asked.

"What?"

"Listen to the water on the rocks. It sounds like there's a hole in it, or a cave back there."

"I don't hear anything."

"We'll take the dinghy over later. I'll show you."

Father slowed the engine to an idle, and Brother and Girl scrambled around the boom to the foredeck to release the anchor. The metal, V-shaped anchor hung under the bowsprit, and they loved to watch it sink, the gray steel chain rushing through the water. Brother got to the foredeck first, so he pulled the lever this time, and Girl lay on her stomach with her head over the rail, watching. When the chain stopped its downward rush Brother called back, "Set!" and Father pushed the throttle forward, reversing the engine until the anchor snagged deep in the murky bottom. He cut the motor and they ran below, packing up their tin pot with the blackened bottom and tight-fitting lid that Father always placed right in the coals of their campfire, a box of Rice-A-Roni, plates, and flatware. The wooden-topped galley counter had a flush-set flat ring, and Girl flipped it open with one finger and pulled off the entire top to reveal the darkly wet, refrigerated hold below. The smell wafted up, invading her nose with pungent odor of closed-up Styrofoam, seawater, and old milk. Girl pulled her shirt over her nose as she rummaged around for the chicken. Brother flipped up the companionway ladder, unlatched the hidden door to the large dry storage bay, and pulled out the rectangular grill top Father used to cook over the campfire. It didn't take that long to assemble everything they needed to bring ashore, and soon Girl was pulling the yellow line to bring forward the dinghy they towed behind the *Ghost*. It was a twelve-foot wooden boat that Brother, Father, and Girl had made by hand the summer before in the garage of Father's condo, without a single power tool. Brother and Girl each had a skiff; Brother's was green and Girl's was painted lavender, and both boats had matching deep-blue trim to match the lettering on the *Ghost*. Father lowered himself in first and secured the oars in their locks, and then they handed him down the bags one by one. Brother and Girl leapt in beside him, and Girl cast off the bowline.

Father was a fast and powerful oarsman. Brother and Girl sat side by side in the rear of the boat facing Father, who braced his feet on the children's as he rowed backward. They cut quickly through the waves. Landing was the tricky part, and the surf was high today from the storm the night before. Girl always got nervous, but knew better than to say anything. Father hated nervousness almost as much as when they used the word *can't*. They could say *fuck*, but they couldn't say *can't*. Father always said, "If you two stop squabbling and just listen you can do it," but sometimes they cried because Father thought they were a lot more capable than they felt they were.

"Okay, this is going to be a little tricky. Brother and Girl, get in the bow and have the line ready. It'll take both of you to pull the dinghy up onshore," Father said.

They carefully maneuvered around Father, careful not to rock the flat-bottomed boat. "Ready?" he called, but as they prepared to leap off, the boat suddenly tipped to the side, seawater crashing in over them. Brother and Girl jumped out quickly; the surf was just barely over the top of Girl's black rubber rain boots that she wore sockless with her jeans rolled up. The force of the waves swamped the dinghy and Father rolled out into the shallow water. Brother and Girl grabbed the boat before the tide could carry it away as Father stood up in the water—it wasn't deep—but his clothes were soaked.

Brother and Girl rounded up driftwood while Father figured out which parts of their dinner were salvageable. The rocky beach was sandless, and the gray and brown pebbles hurt even through her boots. Girl found bleached wood branches the size of her forearm and gathered as many as she could carry. The grain of sea-worn driftwood was moiré taffeta beneath her fingers and she knew it would burn with a pale yellow flame. Father lay prone and motionless on the beach, his face inches from the burning tinder, his mustache and beard powdered with ashes. Girl started to run, chanting *please don't be dead, please don't be dead* over and over in her head. As Girl approached, he sat back on his haunches and fed driftwood into the fire, each piece gradually larger than the last. He had been coaxing flame from the tiny sparks with his breath. His patience meant he only ever needed one match from the Ziploc bag he kept in the breast pocket of his red-and-black flannel shirt, a skill he was inordinately proud of. Girl didn't let herself think about what would happen to her and Brother out here all alone if something happened to Father. Girl dropped her firewood next to him, and they were given permission to go play.

Brother and Girl scurried above the high-tide mark, exploring the island. They found a small grove of tiny evergreen trees, each only a foot high. Nearby was a stream widening to a small pool before it emptied into the ocean. They followed the stream inland, spawning salmon thick enough in the river to walk across. The fish were fighting their way upstream, missing scales and bits of flesh. The water here was so shallow that their slimy silver backs were out of the river, their top fins wriggling as they fought futilely to return to the place of their birth. The stream, salmon, and submerged rocks were all shining wet mercurial gray and indistinguishable from each other. It looked like the channel was boiling.

They ran back to the campfire, racing each other on their dirty-kneed, scrawny legs. Brother won. The extra year and extra few inches of leg he had on Girl always gave him the advantage. Girl dropped onto the driftwood log, breathing hard. Father was tending the fire in his bright red-and-blue-striped bikini underwear, his pants hanging off a branch to dry by the fire. His underwear never had a fly in front, like Brother's, and he always split the seam up the seat, leaving a gaping hole in line with his crack. He said it was because his farts were too big, but even Girl could see the fabric was straining to contain him—his pubic hair pouffed out the top.

"Father, there's a pool deep enough to swim in!" Girl said, before Brother could get a word in edgewise. "Maybe tomorrow I can bring shampoo down and wash my hair."

"And all these little trees. Like only this high." Brother bent over and held his hand about a foot off the ground. "Tons of 'em, like a nursery. Do you think someone planted them?"

"You'll have to show me the trees after dinner. Do you want to hear a limerick?" Father said to Brother, ignoring Girl completely. Brother stood up, his cutoff shorts high above his knees, and poked the fire with a stick. Girl was afraid of fire and never felt the urge to stir the flames. Father had the pot nestled in the coals with the lid on tight. He put the grill over the flames and laid the chicken on it to cook. He worked squatting on his haunches, each movement done with a conservation of energy. Watching him do anything— cook, sail, build boats, sew up wounds—was like watching a symphony played by a one-man band. He made everything look effortless. They never had stepmothers or friends accompany them on the boat, and it was the place where the tension left Father's face and his voice lost that impatient growl that was always simmering in the conversations of parents. Father loved jokes and limericks, and here there was no wife or girlfriend to groan about his perverted sense of humor.

"Nymphomaniacal Jill," Father began.

"What's nymphomaniacal mean?" Brother interrupted.

"A person who loves sex and can never get enough of it."

"Okay, go on," Brother said. Girl wondered if Father was a nymphomaniac, and how that was different from a *pervert,* her mom and sister's word for him. Girl wondered if it was inherited, but she didn't want to think about it too hard or ask questions.

"Nymphomaniacal Jill, tried dynamite for a thrill. They found her vagina in North Carolina and bits of her tits in Brazil!" They all howled with laughter. Girl knew Father wasn't supposed to tell the children dirty jokes, and it gave her a squirmy feeling, like she had a heap of worms in her stomach, when he said vagina. Girl didn't like to think of a woman so horny—Brother's favorite word—that she'd have sex with a hard stick of dynamite, and the limerick put a nasty image in her head that Girl couldn't get rid of. She wasn't menstruating yet, but Girl knew the words "bits of tits" described her body pretty well. Girl wondered about the nympho part of it— was Father nymphomaniacal? He was certainly obsessed with sex. Was Girl? *To hell with that*, Girl thought.

When Girl was eight she had asked Father what a blowjob was, in order to understand why everyone was laughing at a joke about African cannibal women. "It's when a man sucks another man's penis," he answered matter-of-factly, and Girl had blushed red with shame for asking the question. Later, Girl would wonder why he made oral sex only a gay thing, as the joke was about women giving blowjobs, not men.

"Daa-ud!" Girl complained now, dragging out the single syllable into two.

"Daa-ud!" he mocked her. "Here's another one. There once was a man from Nantucket, whose cock was so long he could suck it. He said with a grin as he wiped off his chin, if my ear was a cunt I would fuck it!" Girl repeated the limericks silently in her head so she could remember them to tell her friends back in New York. Dirty jokes were the currency of childhood, as long as Mother and Stepmother didn't overhear them.

Before they left the beach Father and Brother stood next to each other, peeing on the fire to extinguish it. Girl crouched in the bushes to relieve herself, wiping with a big leaf, which didn't work very well, but Father hadn't brought toilet paper for her. Girl didn't get her pants down quite all the way though, and peed a little on the back of the waistband. Girl watched their goose-pimply bottoms with envy. Girl wished she could pee on the fire or write her name with urine in the snow. No matter how hard she tried, Girl could never be entirely on equal footing with Brother and Father. Girl threw her used leaf into the bushes and pulled her pants up, trying to ignore the cold wet spot where she had missed her aim. There was no way to wash her jeans on the boat, and they were the only ones Girl had, so there was no use complaining.

On the trip back to the *Ghost*, Father detoured to explore the promontory at the entrance to the cove. Dad's hands reverse-pedaled the oars to keep the waves from smashing the boat against the sharp granite. Sure enough, the water had carved a tunnel through the outcrop, and they had to yell to hear each other over the roar and hiss of the sea smashing against and through the cave. They drifted a distance from the *Ghost*, so Father had to row a while to get the children alongside. He said that it was easier to work up a rhythm rowing if you sang, and they had a variety of songs he had taught them. That day he started in with her favorite.

"Be prepared. That's the Boy Scout marching song." Brother and Girl joined him as his oars dipped into the water to the beat. "Be prepared, as through life you march along. Don't solicit for your sister, that's not nice. Unless you get a good percentage of her price . . ."[1]

The next day they pulled into Cordova's harbor, called Orca Inlet. Brother and Girl pushed the white rubber bumpers over the sides of the boat in preparation for docking.

"I don't know if there will be someone there to throw a line to," Father said. "You two better be prepared to jump." Girl felt wiggly, and her heart beat

---

1. Lyrics to Tom Lehrer's "Be Prepared" from the album *Songs by Tom Lehrer* (1953).

faster. Jumping off made her nervous and excited at the same time. Girl liked how everyone looked at Brother and Girl when they did it—she was aware of how small they were compared to the *Ghost*, and was proud of their competence. Brother always worried about missing the dock and landing in the water, but Girl worried about not being strong enough to stop the boat, and what would happen if the *Ghost* smashed into the dock. Girl couldn't stand the idea of letting Father down like that, and besides, he would be furious. Father's anger had no trace of love below the surface.

"Okay, get ready," Father called. Brother and Girl climbed over the fence-like stays on the side of the boat and stood tightrope-style on the inch-wide strip of wood mounted below the gunwale, a line in one hand, a stay in the other so they didn't fall off. Girl liked the feeling of boldness, the water rushing by only a foot or so below her feet. Father slowed the engine as he got closer to the pier and Brother and Girl jumped. Father threw the boat in reverse and they pulled their lines as hard as they could. The boat stopped, and Girl tied off the white rope on a metal cleat anchored to the dock and then wound the excess line neatly around the bottom. Brother was doing the same on the other side. After Dad locked the companionway door to the cabin he joined the children on the dock and they walked to the hospital.

Cordova was a really small town at the southeastern end of Prince William Sound. It was filled with little square houses and had only two main streets and no stoplights. Brother and Girl had to move quickly to keep up with Dad's long strides. He was still wearing his black captain's cap and wool coat, but he had on a button-up shirt and tie underneath. At the hospital Brother went to play around on the physical therapy machines, but Girl had to work with Dad. Girl sat at a little table, called all his appointments for the day, confirmed that they were still coming, and reminded them of the time. Dad waited for no one. Most of the thousand residents of Cordova were fishermen, either on their own boats or on the giant floating canneries that went out for weeks at a time, harvesting salmon and packing it in tins for shipment. The patients Father saw were always brought in by women who were quiet and wore no makeup. Girl would record the children's height and weight on the chart, using the clanking medical scale where you had to move the weights along the slide at the top. Girl worried she wasn't doing it right. Once the patient and their mother went into the office with Father the door closed, and she didn't know what their complaints were. Dad was a double specialist—pediatrics and gastroenterology, a word Girl was proud of being able to pronounce. He was the only doctor in Alaska specializing in the digestive system of children, but it was unclear if the kids in Cordova were here for a regular checkup or something more complicated, because he saw both kinds of patients. The clinic was boring, but only lasted a few hours. Father, Brother, and Girl would then eat in the cafeteria when he was done, and afterward the children had to wait around for him to dictate all his notes before they could go back to the boat.

The hospital's staff cafeteria always had Jell-O with whipped cream on top, which Girl liked, and some sort of meat, which Girl didn't. Everyone here knew Dad, though, and people would come up to their table and chat with him, so he didn't notice how little Girl ate. Afterward they went to the closet-like dictation room where Dad dialed a phone and talked into it. Girl wasn't sure if he was talking to a person or a recording machine, because he never let her listen in. All Girl knew was that she had to wait forever. Forty-five minutes to a child is an eternity, so Girl put her ear to the door to work on her spy skills.

"The man lay on top of her, period, she said he smelled like sour milk, period. It hurt a lot she said, comma, but she didn't cry, period." Girl wasn't supposed to be listening in on her father when he dictated notes, but there was nothing else to do, and Brother was off somewhere doing something Girl was sure was more fun than what she was doing. They were all squished together when they were on the boat, and he needed time alone without his smelly sister. Girl knew which patient her father was talking about in the dictation room. Girl met her earlier in the day when she came in, and she seemed sweet, with reddish hair and freckles. "Note to file, colon, this is the second occurrence of stranger molestation this patient has experienced, period." Girl walked away. Girl knew the redheaded child wouldn't want her to hear this—it didn't seem fair to be listening to something that private, even though Girl didn't remember her name and would likely never see her again.

Girl found Brother fiddling with an EKG machine. "Dad's almost done," Girl said. They ran up the wheelchair ramp and jumped off the top a few times, then went back to the dictation room. Their father turned to the children with sparkling eyes, like he hadn't a care in the world, and they started walking back to the harbor. They'd sleep on the boat that night and take off first thing tomorrow morning. Girl couldn't stop thinking about what she overheard and how awful it would be to have a grown man force her body to open beneath him. It must have hurt. Girl didn't know how her father could distance himself from his work and smile and laugh when Girl couldn't escape the overheard words circling inside her head. Attachment disorder, she would later learn, was a valuable condition for a doctor to have.

thanksgiving road trip

Every Thanksgiving they drove eleven hours to Stepmother's parents' house in West Virginia—four people and one dog stuffed into a small station wagon. No matter where they went, the driving experience was always the same. The children and the dog always shared the back seat, the dog's tail slapping the face of one child as she tried to lick the other's face. Eventually they'd push the dog down to the footwell, and one of the siblings would place their hand flat on the seat in the middle. "Put your hand on my hand," they chanted over and over as they layered their hands one on top of the other. "Put your hand on my hand." The person on the bottom would slide their hand out and slap the top of the other person's hand, but not too hard, because the hand that got slapped was owned by the person whose hand was now in the bottom and whose turn it now was to retaliate. Their parents begged the children not to play this game, because it always ended in a midair slap fight, and the children always played it anyway. Girl got carsick when she read in the car, and the drive was long and boring.

Stepmother always drove, and Mother's job was to read the map. Whenever Stepmother came to a new town or highway intersection, Mother would hold the map six inches from her face, her arms spread wide so the windshield was blocked on the passenger's side.

"Judy! Judy!" Stepmother would yell. "Where am I supposed to turn? Left, did you say left?" Always loud, always angry. "Seventy-six? Judy, am I supposed to turn onto seventy-six?" She didn't ever ask politely, or quietly. She treated Mother, the person Girl loved most in the entire world, like she was an idiot, a servant, a child. She yelled and spluttered as Mother tried to read the map and mollify her at the same time.

"I don't know . . . I'm looking . . . I can't find it . . . wait . . . just pull over a minute . . ."

The silent daughter, the good child that never made any trouble, looked out the window with narrowed eyes. Girl squeezed her arms so tightly that her elbows hurt from trying to keep everything in. *Don't you talk to my mother like that,* she imagined saying. She didn't know why Mother let Stepmother treat her this way. Her fists ached with the desire to punch something. Who was she fooling? Hitting Stepmother would be as useless as trying to scream in dreams.

Stepmother had been adopted by Claude and Libby when she was two. Before that, she went from family to family in foster care. Multiple potential parents returned her to the system because she sang herself to sleep every night. This was why Stepmother was so afraid the people she loved would leave. "I have abandonment issues," Stepmother told her over and over. Claude and Libby went to the agency looking for a newborn boy, but left with a two-year-old girl because Baby Stepmother ran up to them and called them "Mama" and "Daddy," and Libby could not leave this precious creature behind. On the train ride home, Baby Stepmother went up to every woman and called her "Mama" and every man and called him "Daddy." Libby told Girl, "I felt like I had been swindled."

Claude was a Methodist minister, and Stepmother wanted to be one, too, if only she had been born a boy. Her father wouldn't let her use the good tools because she was a girl, or because she was reckless and refused to follow directions, depending on whom you asked. She was only allowed to play half-court basketball, because females had different rules for everything. Her mother beat her with a switch until she bled when she didn't practice piano. Stepmother swore that she would never hurt a child like that.

Stepmother had a sister, five years younger. Once her parents gave up on conceiving and adopted Baby Stepmother, her mother became fertile and gave birth to a sickly child. Stepmother chased her younger sister around with a butcher knife once, and another time she threw an axe at her sister's head. Their mother tried her best to keep the two girls apart as much as possible. Stepmother laughed and laughed when she told Girl and Brother these stories.

Stepmother didn't seem to like her parents very much, and Girl was intimidated by their stiff, formal demeanor. The grandparents didn't like that Stepmother was gay, but they still invited them for Thanksgiving every year, and bought Girl wonderful presents that were always exactly what Girl wanted: baby doll dresses, or plastic horses, or coral-colored nail polish, depending on the year. Grandmother also yelled at Stepmother for inexplicable things. "Did you squeeze this bread?" she asked Girl. Girl shook her head. "Your stepmother must be up to her old bread-squeezing tricks again!" Girl knew it was unlikely that Stepmother had snuck into the kitchen and squeezed the loaf of bread, but she liked seeing someone yell at Stepmother, so she nodded her head.

Every time they visited the grandparents, the family had to go to church on Sunday and listen to Grandfather preach. Girl hated church—it was always cold and her dress was always scratchy and it went on forever. The last time they visited, Grandmother pulled Stepmother aside.

"I hope you are happy. Your father is upstairs writing his resignation letter. He's quitting the church."

"Why is Daddy quitting?" Stepmother asked.

"Because you are wearing a wedding ring, and everyone knows you aren't married, and he doesn't want to explain to the congregation that you are married to a woman."

"Tell him not to quit the church, Mother. We'll leave before the service." They didn't go back for Thanksgiving for seven years. From then on, they had Thanksgiving with just the four of them around the dining room table, or at Coco's Carousel restaurant with a few friends. Someday, Girl told herself, she was going to marry someone with a big family and have Thanksgiving with cousins and aunts and uncles—so many people that they needed a kids' table in one room and more than one kind of pie.

seneca army depot

Mother was born in 1944 and grew up practicing duck-and-cover drills at school.

"There was a lot of talk in the neighborhood about building bomb shelters in your backyard," she told Girl.

"Did you build one?" Girl asked.

"My parents talked a lot about it, but decided not to. Their reasoning was that if you were in your bomb shelter and a neighbor came, you couldn't let them in, because they could bring radiation in with them or eat your food and then your family wouldn't have enough left to live on until it was safe again many months later. Some people were buying guns in case they had to shoot someone that tried to get into their bomb shelter. My father said that he could not refuse a neighbor, and if it came down to it, he'd rather they all died together than have to shoot a friend who tried to come in."

Girl and her family watched the news together every night, even though Girl thought it was boring. Brother and Girl played somewhat quietly with Barbie dolls and *Star Wars* figures on the living room rug. They liked to be near their parents, and their parents liked them to pay attention when important topics came on. In the summer of 1983 a group of fifty-four women set up a tent city they called a "peace encampment" outside of the Seneca Army Depot because it was rumored that the army stored nuclear weapons there. The women were arrested in a peaceful protest and garnered national attention. A group from the family's church, First Unitarian Universalist of Rochester, planned a trip to participate in the protest, so Mother and Stepmother decided their family would join them.

"Now, listen up, kids," Stepmother said. She was driving the family an hour south to Romulus, New York, where the base was located. "There will be soldiers there with guns. It might be a little scary. We aren't going to cross the line. It is only dangerous if you cross the line."

"What line?" Girl asked.

"There's a line painted on the pavement, dividing public property from the military base."

"Oh. Will people tie themselves to the fence again?" A few women had been arrested for tying themselves to the fence surrounding the base and refusing to leave. It sounded like an uncomfortable way to protest, but Girl kind of wanted to see someone do it so she understood how it worked. Did they use handcuffs or bandanas?

"I'm not sure," Stepmother answered. "Maybe. We'll see. But we won't tie ourselves to the fence, even if some of them do. We are just going to sing songs. Do you remember the words to 'We Shall Overcome'?"

"Yeah," Girl said, and went back to looking out the window while her parents started singing. Girl was in fourth grade, and dreaming about boys and what dog she might get someday was way more interesting than protests, unless people were going to tie themselves to fences, of course, but there was no guarantee of that this evening.

"Lock your door," Stepmother said. "This is a town full of rednecks. Look at all the American flags." They had exited the freeway and were driving through the town outside the base. Stepmother didn't trust people who flew American flags. She said that they were racists and homophobes. Girl wanted to defend the flag—they made her recite the pledge at school, after all, so she didn't see how flying it made you a redneck—but she didn't want to risk being wrong about it. She also didn't want to be beaten up for having gay parents.

Dark was just creeping into the sky when the family pulled into the grass field next to the peace encampment and parked. Kitsy was there, a woman from church Girl really liked. Kitsy had shoulder-length, chestnut-colored hair and an impish look to her face. She was overweight, like Girl's parents, but feminine and stylish, wearing long skirts and tall boots and many colored scarves. Kitsy liked children, and they gravitated to her. Kitsy had been to the peace encampment before, so she led the family over to the gathering and introduced them around.

There was a white line painted across the road to the base, as promised, and on the other side were soldiers wearing green fatigues and helmets, just like on *M*A*S*H* or *Hogan's Heroes*, two of Girl's favorite shows. No one was tied to the fence, but there were a few tattered ribbons from previous protests still waving in the evening breeze. Some of the women from the peace encampment had started a small campfire, and people were gathering around it. As night fell, the protesters became dark shapes with firelit faces, even their hair melting into obscurity, no longer people but only floating, glowing faces—a congregation of bald, singing ovals in smoldering hues of yellow and orange. Mother's glasses reflected the dancing tongues of fire, and Girl could no longer see her eyes. The air was cool and the grass was wet, and the sky so black, with lots of stars shining cold and distant on Girl. The voices, mostly female, sang "Where Have All the Flowers Gone?" "We Shall Overcome," and "Give Peace a Chance."

Stepmother sang protest and activist songs at coffeehouses and folk festivals, so Girl knew all of the songs already from listening to her practice over and over at home. Everyone said that Stepmother had a great voice. Girl recognized that her stepmother's singing was on key but thought that her inflection was hoity-toity and pretentious. It didn't seem natural, like when Mother sang. Girl was glad she was standing next to Mother, who had a deep voice for a woman—she was loud and strong and could find the lower octave all by herself. Girl could only sing on key if she stood close to someone else who could find the notes for her.

After a while Kitsy came up to talk to Girl. At nine years old, Girl was the youngest person there. Girl had hoped there would be more kids, but it was all various sizes and shapes of grown-ups, women outnumbering men thirty to one. A man would have to be very sure of himself to come here, Girl thought. She didn't wonder how Brother felt, though—it wasn't like he had a choice in the matter.

"Do you want to take a rose with me across the line to the MPs?" Kitsy asked.

Girl didn't know that MP stood for Military Police, to her it was a word that just meant army guy. *Emmpee.* It sounded like a rank, like corporal or private or something, but Girl didn't know what, and she didn't want to admit her ignorance by asking.

"Let me ask my mother," Girl told her. Kitsy followed her over to where Mother and Stepmother were standing. Kitsy explained her plan to cross the line, and how as the youngest child there, Girl could make the largest impact on the soldiers.

"Girl, do you want to go with Kitsy?" Mother asked. Girl nodded. "Okay, but when they tell you to cross the line, you have to do it right away. Just walk up, give them the flower, and come right back. They can shoot you if you don't cross the line when they tell you to."

Did Mother really warn her daughter that the soldiers might shoot her? Or did she say *arrest* and instead Girl remembered it as *shoot*? Was Mother merely trying to ensure that her daughter came right back? If she thought Girl might get shot, why did she let her cross the line? Mother was alive during the Kent State massacre and an active protester in the sixties and seventies. She knew sometimes things went wrong at peace rallies.

Kitsy held Girl's hand and they stepped across the white stripe on the pavement. It was only as wide as the yellow stripe down the middle of Girl's street back at home. They passed a tall fence topped with barbed wire. Behind it lay coils of razor wire almost as tall as Girl was. There were four men standing at the gate holding their rifles across their chests, one hand on the stock, the other hand on the barrel. They were tall, clean-shaven, and mean-looking. Girl didn't realize that they were young, too, not much older than teenagers, and likely as scared as she was. Her hands shook.

"Don't worry," Kitsy whispered. "I'll do all the talking. All you do is hand them the rose. I will say, 'we give you this rose as a sign of peace,' and then we will walk back over the line. Don't worry. They won't shoot a little girl. If they shoot anyone, it will be me."

Girl quavered a little, but she clutched Kitsy's hand and held her breath when they got close to the guardhouse. She was glad that she didn't have to talk. The drab green men loomed over Girl like evil trees from a fairy tale, except they had machine guns.

"Get back over the line!" one of them called, and Kitsy and Girl stopped walking.

"We just want to give you a rose," Kitsy said firmly, not sounding even a little bit scared. "Can we approach?"

The men talked among themselves for a few seconds, then one of them called out again, "Okay, but then you must turn and leave immediately." Girl couldn't tell if it was the same man who had spoken before. They all looked and sounded the same to her, with growling, angry voices.

The legs of Girl's size-nine-slim jeans whisked against each other as she continued her forward walk, the *tsk-tsk* louder in her ears than the crickets—or were they locusts? Girl could never remember. Her sneakers were the exact color of raspberry bubblegum, jarringly childlike against the dull, gray road. The floodlights stripped Girl's shadow and made it trail behind so she didn't even have that dark specter-child for comfort. She was glad Kitsy held her hand so tightly. There wasn't enough room between their palms to feel any dampness.

When they got within a few feet of the MPs, Kitsy nodded to Girl. It was too late to say, "This is too much for me." Girl didn't look back at the crowd of protesters, but she knew they were watching. She held the white, long-stem rose out to the closest soldier, glad she didn't have to speak, and proud that her arm didn't quiver.

"We give you this rose as a sign of peace," Kitsy said, just as she had planned. Later, Kitsy became a minister, and the profession suited her perfectly. She was meant to give roses to soldiers and hold the hands of scared children.

The MP took the stem from Girl's outstretched hand. "You have thirty seconds to get back across the line or we have orders to shoot," he said. He didn't smile or acknowledge the gift in any way. Girl's youth hadn't cracked his composure in the least—no *thank you*, or even a hint of movement at the edges of his mouth.

Kitsy and Girl turned and walked back across the line as quickly as they could and still appear dignified. If Kitsy hadn't held Girl's hand so firmly, Girl would have run, her bubblegum shoes slapping the pavement. She wouldn't have looked back until she found Mother, but Kitsy didn't let go and Girl didn't run. Girl wondered what she could have done differently to have made her brave, useless gesture matter to those olive-green, unsmiling men. If she had cried and let herself look like a scared child instead of trying so hard to be a perfect, small-scale adult, if she hadn't tied her shoes so tightly, and one had come undone, maybe it would have made a difference. Maybe one of the soldiers would have bent down to tie it.

The rest of the night was uneventful, just more singing of songs and holding candles. Girl waited until she was in the back seat of the car to cry in the dark, where no one could see her. The MP's face was so hard-looking as he took the rose, as if he would have been just fine with shooting Girl. Girl didn't say anything to Mother, though, because Girl had said she wanted to go with Kitsy, and had even been proud to be the one chosen. Girl looked out the window as they drove home, but instead of seeing the dark countryside roll by, she saw only orange faces of flame and stoic men holding guns.

the downhill slide

Girl had been given a diary for her birthday. It was brown fake leather with a tiny, gold lock and key. That was the crucial part of the diary—the lock. Here she could write all her secrets down in her messy, left-handed handwriting, her hair tickling the side of her face as she bent over her desk. Like many gifts, it was a slight disappointment—she wished it were pink or purple or a more girly color, but the gold lettering on the front made up for it. *My Diary*, it said in block letters, and when she ran her fingernail over the letters she could feel how they were slightly raised. Gold leaf, she decided, and that meant it was expensive, and everyone knew expensive was better. The edges of the pages were gold, too, and it had a red satin ribbon sewn in to mark your place.

She listed the boys she liked, turned the page, and wrote "Dirty Words" at the top of the next page, followed by a list of every bad word she knew: boobs, tits, shit, vulva. She wrote in her third-grade penmanship that she wished she was prettier, like the other girls at school. Her handwriting always looked like a boy's, but it wasn't her fault, she was left-handed, and she wrote with her elbow sticking straight out and her wrist curled into a half circle that made her hand ache and the other kids laugh at her. Still, she liked being left-handed. It made her special, and her long-dead uncle had been left-handed, and Brother was only right-handed like everyone else. All the teachers told her it meant she was creative. Girl didn't put much stock in that, though. She knew she wasn't creative—she couldn't draw or paint—she was just a little bit weird. She wasn't as weird as Brother, but she was odd enough not to watch the right TV shows or own the right clothes. She paused to think what else to write, but her hand hurt and writing was so boring and took forever so she closed her diary and locked it and went out to play.

The backyard was her favorite place. She had found a four-foot-long stick that was sharpened to a point at one end. Girl practiced throwing it from every position she could think of: standing, of course, but also kneeling, sitting, and even lying on her stomach in the grass. When she tired of throwing her spear, she'd climb the old, metal clothesline post that hadn't been used for hanging out wash since her family had moved in, maybe longer. She'd perch on the crossbar and practice looking at things. She wanted to earn the name "Eagle Eye," the name she called herself when Brother wasn't around to mock her for it. She tried to count the flowers in the garden at the other end of the yard, she scanned the grass for any interesting toy Brother might have forgotten about, and with the height of the pole she could see over the white picket fence into the Witch's yard next door. The Witch was a mean, old, nasty lady with grown-up kids and an above-ground pool in the back that she never, not even once, asked Girl if she wanted to swim in. The Witch wrapped her rose bushes in burlap every fall and her yard was filled with English ivy so she didn't have to mow. Girl's whole family called her the Witch, ever since she had come over to the fence and asked Stepmother, "Do you mind moving your weed garden to another spot in your yard? Your weed seeds are blowing into my yard." Stepmother had been so mad her face turned red but she didn't say anything back. Stepmother believed in respecting your elders, which was also why Girl had to say, "Thank you Stepmother, you're a good cook," after every meal, even though she never meant it, not the good cook part for sure but not the thank you either, because it was Girl's opinion that feeding the family was the role of the parents, and Girl knew Stepmother could be doing a better job. Food wasn't love or art or something to take pride in in her house. Dinner was hamburger on a piece of whole wheat bread. It was a can of Veg-All, and Girl swore that she would never eat a square vegetable when she grew up. It was spaghetti with Ragu, and Girl never actually tasted a meatball until she was in high school and had a boyfriend with more money than her family had. Dinner at Girl's house was bland and cheap and fast in a cold room on a Formica table, and she wasn't allowed to wear her winter coat at the table.

She heard her mother calling her for dinner, but she pretended not to. Stepmother was making "campfire stew," which was the grossest of all the things she made. Fried hamburger meat mixed in with rounded hunks of canned stewed tomatoes that looked like what Girl imagined a fertilized chicken egg would look like, if you cracked the wrong one open. Like a bloody egg sac. This was mixed in with Veg-All, like everything else. Sometimes Stepmother would give Girl a piece of whole wheat bread spread with margarine to dip into the stew, and that was better at least. But if they were low on bread, it was just the stew in her blue plastic bowl, the chunks of meat and vegetables sitting in a puddle of reddish-brown water. Mother called her again, and Girl could hear the edge to her voice, so she knew she'd pushed it as long as she was able. She wiped her dirty hands on the sides of her jeans and went inside.

"Stop making that noise with your spoon," Stepmother said.

"What noise?" Girl asked. She already knew not to chew with her mouth open, and to keep a napkin on her lap, although it always slid off onto the linoleum floor and she mostly just wiped the grease from her fingers on her pant leg. She wasn't yet old enough to be embarrassed about the permanent stains on the thighs of her jeans.

"You're clinking your teeth with the spoon!" she said. Girl tried to open her mouth wider. "Stop it! I told you once . . ."

"I can't eat without hitting my teeth with the spoon," Girl argued. The spoon was big and it hit her back teeth every time. She wasn't *trying* to do anything.

"Try harder," Stepmother said. "I can do it, and so can you." Girl's mother didn't say anything. Mother never said anything when Stepmother got in one of her moods, which was practically every night now. Girl tried as hard as she could to eat quietly, and kicked Brother under the table, but not hard. She didn't want to hurt him, she just wanted him to pay attention to what an asshole Stepmother was being again. He just smiled evilly at her, though, because he was glad it was Girl getting yelled at this time instead of him.

Stepmother blew her nose into her napkin and looked at it, then threw the napkin in her empty bowl. She rubbed her thumb and forefinger back and forth on her eyebrows and looked at her watch. It had a pale gold face and a brown leather band. She never liked anything girly. She was just counting the hours she had to hold herself together until the kids went to bed. Only an hour and a half left to go.

Girl didn't hate Stepmother, not then. But she knew something was different lately. When Stepmother laughed it had a franticness at the edge, but she didn't laugh much anymore. She used to play the piano, and Girl and Brother would try to act out whatever form their stepmother called out: hot air balloons, a seed turning to a flower, a lion, a mouse. Stepmother used to box with the children. She wrapped a towel around her forearm and let the children punch her arm as hard as they wanted to. She used to smile like she meant it. Now, though, she rarely smiled and everything enraged her. Girl tried her hardest to turn invisible, blend into the wall, and shrink inside her winter coat until her face was no longer visible.

At night, she often woke in the middle of the night in cold, urine-soaked sheets. "Such a baby," she thought to herself. Mother always bragged how Girl toilet-trained herself at eighteen months, because it was hot outside and Girl wanted to run around naked. "You have to wear a diaper until you pee on the potty," Mother had said, and Girl had promptly peed on the potty and spent the rest of the day running around without clothes. How had she gone from being advanced at bladder control to suddenly having accidents in fourth grade? She couldn't trust her body when it was asleep. Too mortified to tell Mother, Girl crept down the dark hall to the linen closet in search of a dry towel. She laid the towel over the wet spot and went back to sleep.

liz

It was the first day of sixth grade, and Girl was in Mr. Malley's homeroom. She was wearing her favorite skirt: a long, purple granny skirt printed with little flowers that had an eyelet ruffle at the bottom. Juli had taken her shopping last year, and Father had bought everything Juli had picked out. The skirt no longer reached her mid-calf, like it used to, but Girl figured that it worked as a knee-length one. By the time she got to school, though, she realized that she was wrong. She could hear the whispered comments and see the eye-rolls. Girl was a skinny-legged stork, and yes, they were right, it did look a little bit like her legs turned in, now that she looked closely. Her knees were indeed too big. Her outfit was, yes, just like they said, stupid and horribly out of style. It was the not-knowing, the foolish pride she felt, that most made her want to cry. She pushed up her big, golden-brown plastic glasses and tried to ignore the other girls, like Stepmother always told her to do. "Just don't respond and they'll get bored," Stepmother admonished any time she complained, but Stepmother underestimated the tenacity of sixth graders. Girl just stopped talking about it at home. It was pointless.

She had Mr. Malley for first period math, too, which was her least favorite subject. When he called roll he paused at her name.

"Lillibridge? Didn't I have your brother last year?" he asked.

"Yeah," Girl said. She hated following in Brother's footsteps at school, because all of his uncoolness rubbed off on her.

"Why don't I save us all a lot of time and just send you down to basic math now?" he asked. Everyone laughed. Girl was too busy not-crying to explain that she had never gotten less than a B in anything besides handwriting, and even that C made her so sad she wanted to close her eyes and never wake up. She was left-handed and she couldn't make her hand work the way they wanted it to. But she'd always gotten As and Bs in math, even though she hated it.

She looked around the room and noticed a new girl. Her school had had pretty much the same kids since fourth grade; new kids were practically unheard of. New Girl asked the teacher a lot of stupid questions about what supplies were acceptable, like could a Trapper Keeper work as a three-ring binder, for instance; things everyone else knew already from last year. The new girl wore glasses, like Girl. Unlike Girl, she was overweight. She was bigger than Michelle and nearly as big as Laura, who had so far been the biggest girls in school. The new girl's name was Liz.

Girl had always been a one-best-friend person. Sure, she had enough acquaintances to be able to find someone to sit next to at lunch or to fill up a birthday party, but since first grade it had been Girl and Gretchen. Velcro sisters. That was until last year, when they got into a fight and never talked to each other again. But Liz's notebook had brown horses on the front cover, and Girl was not horse-crazy.

"We're going to get you after school," Timmy said to Girl between classes. He was one of the popular kids, and even though he was short and freckled he was tough.

The popular kids, of whom Girl most certainly was not one, had had a party with kissing or sex or something. Someone told on them, and they all had to go see the guidance counselor one at a time and everyone said that the popular kids had to take off all their clothes and talk about their bodies and sex. The student elite were filled with a murderous rage for the snitch, and for some reason, they had decided that snitch was Girl. She never would have told, even if she had known—she wanted them to like her so damn badly. She would have done just about anything to get invited to a popular kid's party. Of course no one believed her, and she was going to get beaten up as soon as the last bell rang. It was a mile-and-a-half walk home, and Brother was now in junior high, so she would be on her own. She knew that she couldn't run that far.

Liz had overheard them, though.

"I'll walk home with you," she said. "No one is gonna mess with you when you are with me. If they try, I'll sit on them."

Girl looked at her, confused. Was she making fun of herself?

"Hey, I know what they say about me," Liz explained. "I just turn it around on them before they get a chance." Girl had never met someone so confident before, so accepting of who they were.

As it turned out, no bullies appeared on the walk home that day or any other, but still, Liz became Girl's best friend. Liz and her mother lived with her grandparents. She didn't have a father around or a regular family, either. Girl waited for Liz on her screened-in porch every morning before school—she was not invited in, and never saw Liz's room. Liz spent the night at Girl's house nearly every weekend, and after a few months her mother found an apartment just five blocks from Girl's house, where Girl could spend the night as often as she liked.

Liz wasn't boy-crazy, like Girl was. Even though her hair was way cooler than Girl's—two-tone blond on top, brown in the back, and perfectly straight—without weird cowlicks like Girl's—Liz wasn't obsessed with fitting in and wearing makeup. Liz loved horses. She taught Girl to draw a pretty decent horse, and they both collected Breyer models of the different breeds. Sooner or later, Girl gave in and went to the stables. She had to—it was where her best friend was. Before she knew it, they were both spending all their free time mucking out other people's stalls in hopes of a chance to ride.

She and Liz remained friends for years, telling each other secrets, having crushes on boys, riding horses and bikes, and swimming. They had their first kisses standing next to each other with a pair of boys they met at Seabreeze Amusement Park. They smoked their first cigarettes together. Girl had a tendency to be gossipy about her friends, but it was different with Liz. Liz was the only friend whose secrets she kept.

junior high

gilli

L iz got a horse first. She volunteered at the stable for so long that the stable manager gave her Gizmo, a sturdy, chestnut-colored Haflinger pony with a blond mane and tail. Gizmo wasn't working out for lessons, and instead of selling him outright, the manager gave him to Liz in trade for labor. Girl was so jealous she didn't talk to Liz for a week, but she couldn't stay mad that long, particularly when she knew she was just being stupid. Girl knew that Liz had worked hard for years at the stable, and she also knew that Liz's family could never afford a horse otherwise—working for one was her only option, and she knew Liz needed this horse more than anything else in the world. Seventh grade had been hard on both of them. They had started junior high and didn't have a single class together, not even lunch. Girl went from being called "Larva" and "Looney Tunes" back in middle school to being called nothing at all—she would speak to girls and they wouldn't even respond. It was as if her mouth moved and no sounds came out. Girl couldn't stand the silence, so she looked for the girls that she knew would never reject her—the geeks and misfits—and sat next to them. But Liz just stopped going to school.

Girl was pissed when Liz stopped going to school, because she would have been more than happy to skip school with her. She wasn't against being bad, she just wasn't bold enough to be bad on her own. Girl just prayed to get hit by a car as she walked to junior high each day. She figured if they hit you hard enough, you probably wouldn't even feel the pain.

Liz and Girl both walked paper routes and babysat kids and saved every dollar they could. Every chance they got they rode the mile and a half to the stables on their ten-speeds. Away from school and other preteens, they were happy.

Girl's father had said that he was going to buy her and Brother gliders. He had a two-seater airplane and a head full of dreams he couldn't deliver on. Girl had already told everyone how they were going to sail around the world in two years with Father, and when the two years never came, she had finally admitted what all her friends already knew—it was never going to happen. For some reason, though, she was sure that this time, he really was going to buy the ultra-light planes for her and Brother. Girl carefully read the article Father had sent from the Airplane Owners and Pilots Association's magazine. The gliders were four thousand dollars each. She spent a month carefully crafting a letter to Father, breaking down all the costs of buying a horse and boarding it, researching vet expenses and local stables. She wrote a persuasive essay, like she was learning to do in English class, explaining how it would be cheaper if Father bought her a horse than a plane. She asked him for two thousand dollars: one thousand to purchase a horse and one thousand to cover the first year's board. She had saved one thousand dollars on her own, and she figured if she kept babysitting she would be okay for the first two years. Surprisingly, her father agreed.

Aunt Kiki found Girl a free horse. Her favorite waitress at the pizza place was going to college and had a pony named Gilli that she loved too much to sell, but was willing to give away to someone who would love him and let her visit. Mother found a stable that was a little further away but cheaper than the current stable they haunted—the only hitch was that Girl had to muck out her own stall, no matter what. Liz traded Gizmo for a tall, bay Morgan horse named Bubba, and soon they both had horses at Cold Stream Stables. They rode their bikes two-and-a-half miles each way, unless Liz's mother felt like driving them. She was a teacher and had the summer off. Girl's parents worked full-time, but they wouldn't even drive her on the weekends. Liz and Girl mucked out their own stalls and leveled the manure pile to reduce their boarding fees. Girl was not allowed to ride in the lower rink, so Liz didn't either. The lower rink was set in the woods, back where no one could see them, and it had jumps. The stables had forty acres of trails, too, but Girl wasn't allowed to go on trails so they didn't do that either, even though there was no way Stepmother would have found out if they disobeyed. There were only a few other horses in the barn, and most days it was just Liz and Girl and brown bags of peanut butter sandwiches. If they got too hungry, they ate the horses' molasses-covered oats, called "sweet feed."

They were happy enough riding in circles in the sand ring, brushing and washing their horses, and talking about boys and horse shows and the obvious crush Liz's mother had on the stable manager. They were both in love with the old sixties band called the Monkees, who were on a twenty-year revival tour. When the Monkees came to Rochester, Liz's mother helped Girl form a lie to her parents so she could go, too. Liz snuck a camera down her pants and although the men standing next to them offered them beer, they both declined. That summer, they both started getting noticed by boys more often. Liz's mother had smiled and told Girl, "You think I'm happy for her that boys like her, but I'm happy because she's going to be someone else's responsibility soon."

That fall Gilli got sick with an upper respiratory infection. The vet had to come every day and give him fifty-dollar shots. Girl's savings were dwindling, and her two-dollar-an-hour babysitting job wasn't keeping up. Winter was coming, and she didn't know how she was going to get to the stable when there was too much snow to ride her bike. Liz's mother, who had once been so involved, even driving Girl to the doctor when she was hit by a car on the way to the stable once, had suddenly and inexplicably become unreliable, sometimes driving, sometimes refusing. Her substitute teaching job ended and she couldn't find another one, and she went to work at K-Mart full-time. She put Liz on a PINS (People In Need of Supervision) petition requiring Liz to go to probation. Girl couldn't figure this out at all, because Liz was smart and nice and not violent that she had ever seen. Liz's mother seemed to just wear out of parenting, and sent Liz to live in a group home. Girl only saw her every few weeks.

Girl felt the pressure of bills and impending snow and it was too heavy to bear alone. Mother and Stepmother had no suggestions. Responsibility pressed down on Girl and she just wanted to sleep all the time. Girl gave the horse back to the waitress. She didn't tell anyone what it cost her—the black sadness that hung on her body like fog was invisible to everyone else.

"Well, at least you had a horse for a summer," Stepmother said, as if that was any consolation. Girl never heard what happened to Gilli, but she doubted that he ever got well.

notes from the fourth wall
this is what you hear
when you have lesbian parents

You hear your parents tell you over and over again how you must not tell anyone. You hear how your stepmother lost her job at the YWCA because she was gay. You hear about Stonewall and Harvey Milk and all the unnamed men and women beaten and sometimes killed by gay bashers. You are told how if your parents lose their jobs, you will lose the house and you don't want to be homeless. You don't, however, hear the word *lesbian*. *Gay* is the word your mother prefers, as it sounds more neutral, less sexualized. Lesbian is a word she will claim much later.

You hear a rock hit your living room window one day, and the whole family goes outside to look at the golf-ball-sized hole in the glass. Your stepmother cries, "They threw a rock through our window because we are gay!" But you didn't hear any name-calling, and you didn't see any note, nor did you see anyone running away. You live on a busy street and think it was just as likely that a truck kicked up a rock as that someone threw it intentionally. This assumption of harassment doesn't sit quite right with you, but you are quick to use this story as an example of how you were persecuted, even though you were never really sure if it was true. It was only one way to look at the hole in the window.

In eighth grade you no longer had to keep the secret—somehow the students at school found out, and the story was everywhere. Unfortunately, your name starts with "L" so "lesbian" pairs up with it quite nicely. You are called Lara the Lesbian for the rest of the year. "Lez," "Lesbo," and (inexplicably) "Fag" are yelled at you in the halls between classes. Even a few people you thought were your friends write, "To Lara the Les" in your yearbook. You get into a fight with one of your closest friends, and she gets the last shot in, looking at you with hard eyes and saying, "Maybe you really are a lesbian like your mother." Years later, you will forget the reason you were so mad at each other, but her parting words still echo clearly in the cavity of your chest.

You are asked, "But don't you have a father?" over and over. Back in the seventies and eighties, artificial insemination was not an option for gays and lesbians. The first test-tube baby was not born until 1978, so it was a legitimate question. But your father happened to move across the continent and not all of the kids at school believed that he even existed.

"But who is your real mother?" This question infuriates your mother. She and your stepmother want to be viewed as equal parents. But they can't erase your father, and you don't want them to, because not only do you love him, he is your one connection to the straight world. He is the one parent you can talk about without hedging pronouns, and he looks really good on paper. Besides that, you want to be very clear to all interested parties who you got your DNA from. Any ambiguity as to who your mother is diminishes her importance to you.

Teenaged boys will ask to look in your windows, even though you assure them that nobody wants to see your parents naked. You compare your step-mother to the androgynous Pat on *Saturday Night Live*, and it is an accurate description, even down to their shared first name. Your Pat loves the skit and tries to mimic the character as much as possible.

In high school, every single straight male you meet asks, "Did you ever think you were a lesbian?" or some other permutation of that sentiment. You spend your teen years on a quest to prove your heterosexuality. It sounded like, "Look, I have a boyfriend, so I can prove I'm not gay." Of course you don't tell anyone about the tingling rush you feel when you look at the supermodels on *Cosmopolitan* magazine's covers in the checkout line. You push any thought of women as sexy deep down inside, as deep as you possibly can. At night, you are afraid that you might wake up and find that you have turned into a lesbian in your sleep, and then you would have to live this sad, furtive life forever. You know that your stepmother knew she was gay since she was twelve, and you were relieved when you passed that age and still liked boys, but you also knew that your mother didn't turn gay until she was in college and became involved in the feminist movement. College was still a few years away but you refused to become a feminist, just to be on the safe side. You don't want to be the kind of feminist you see—unshaven, man-clothed, angry all the time. You want to be Mrs. Brady, Mrs. Anybody, and you want, more than anything, to be beautiful, sexy, a head-turner.

But you also don't see why anyone would think girls aren't as good as boys. Of course girls can be anything they want. Of course they are just as smart. Why can't they be anything they want and still shave their legs and wear high heels and stay at home with their children? You want, more than anything, for your mother to stay at home, but she works full-time and that's not something that is ever going to happen in your lifetime. When you tell your stepmother that you want to stay home and have children, she follows you into the front yard, yelling, "You will not be a housewife! You will be a business woman!" You jump over the hedge at the side of the yard and take off running for high school. You don't know what a business woman does exactly, but it sounds boring. You only know how much you yearned for your mother when you were small. You want more than anything to raise children who don't have mother-sized holes in their chests.

You hear your stepmother berate your brother over and over, like a broken record. "If I had been born a man, I could have been a minister, or a doctor. If I had been born a man I would be so much more successful. White men have everything—all the power, all the money, all the good jobs. Look at you, you were born a boy, you were given every opportunity from birth and you just squander it. You'll never amount to anything." So many words tell you that men are the ruling class, and you want to hitch yourself to a rising star, so you don't have to rise yourself. You're not sure you are as smart as your mother thinks you are.

If you have to choose between being a man-hater, an abuser, and being soft, feminine, gentle—if those are the only options you think you have, you will teach yourself to be submissive, you will make yourself as sexy-beautiful as you can, and you will even vote Republican. You will look for a strong man to defend you against everything that scares you.

the memorial day parade

The seventh-and-eighth-grade band at Dake Junior High was marching in the Memorial Day parade. Of the dozen percussionists, only eight could play snare drum, so Girl made sure to audition on the first day to secure a spot. No way was she playing bass drum or cymbals if she could help it. Snares were the lifeblood of the band, repeating their cadence over and over while everyone else marched in place, the only instrument that never rested. She might let the boys intimidate her into playing triangle and bells during daily band practice, but she was claiming her spot on snare for the parade. Mr. Bell, the conductor, let her pass, even though she wasn't able to hit the emphasis right on the sixteenth notes. She practiced every night, but she just didn't quite have the coordination down to really nail the accent notes. DA-da-da-DA-da-da-DA-da-DAH-DAH she chanted as she played, trying to get it down. The band got to miss afternoon classes the week before the parade to march around the neighborhood, learning to walk in step. She marched next to James—the coolest boy in eighth grade—not that he spoke to her or even once made eye contact. Girl was sure that he wouldn't have looked at her even if she was an eighth grader—not with her braces and glasses and bad jeans. James was kind of chubby and didn't follow clothing trends, preferring to wear button-down shirts over his jeans. But James's father was a famous jazz drummer who died of a drug overdose, and just about every girl in school wanted to tousle his chestnut curls and stroke that baby doll face. The boys said that sometimes, when he practiced, James made all the teenaged hang-arounds leave because he was channeling his father, playing long into the night in a fit of rage and sorrow.

Memorial Day morning Girl woke up lazily, then remembered the parade with a jolt, and grabbed the alarm clock that she had forgotten to set. She had to be there in fifteen minutes—fuck. Her parents were still asleep—no one had bothered to make sure she got up in time to shower, but she was twelve, after all, she was supposed to know how to set an alarm clock. Girl ran a brush through her hair, but she didn't have time to tame the messy sleep-swirls out of it. Mr. Bell said if you were even a minute late they would leave you behind. She pulled her navy blue, hooded sweatshirt with the school insignia on it over her head and hoped it would at least cover the cowlicks at the nape of her neck. Her big glasses were covered in fingerprints, but she didn't have time for makeup, let alone washing them off. She slid her lavender drumsticks into the back pocket of her jeans and ran for Irondequoit Plaza, where the parade was lining up. She made it with five minutes to spare—luckily not the last one to arrive. When the drum line stepped off right-left-right she no longer cared if her hair was unruly or if her pimples were showing. Her sticks bounced on the drum head, and she was part of the music that had always made her cry.

scar tissue

Girl had an inch-long scar on the right side of her abdomen, nearly parallel to her navel. It took five stitches to close it, not as impressive as the seventeen Brother got in his hand when he was seven and accidentally put his hand through a window pane. (Girl had intentionally slammed the playroom door, which always stuck and required a lot of force to open. Brother shoved the glass door as hard as he could so that he could resume trying to kill his sister, and his hand went through the glass.) But five stitches were more respectable than the one stitch he got in his finger when he was eight. (That time, Girl slammed the door on his actual finger. She supposed she should feel bad about these injuries, but in her opinion, he shouldn't have been chasing her in the first place.)

One morning, Girl opened the brown, vintage 1940s cabinet in their kitchen to get the peanut butter out so she could make her lunch for school. The handle was a bronze, round knob with a sort of four-pointed star behind it. When she opened the cabinet, a ceramic pitcher fell from the top shelf, hit the counter, and shattered, sending a shard into her stomach. Stepmother was in the kitchen, getting ready for work. Brother was there too, which was a lot of bodies for the small space, but that's how it worked every morning. Their kitchen table was tucked in the corner and pushed close to the wall. There were only a few feet left to walk around the other two sides. Girl turned around to face the middle of the room as she pulled the shard from her stomach. Blood flowed freely from the wound, and although she thought she should cry, she froze. Girl had just wanted to make a sandwich, and it had happened so fast. But Stepmother started to cry.

"I'm so sorry, I'm so sorry," Stepmother repeated as she cried. "I knew when I put that pitcher in there that it was going to fall, and I just closed the door anyway. It's all my fault. I'll take you to the doctor—you're going to need stitches."

Girl was afraid of stitches. She had only had them twice before, both times before she was in kindergarten, and both times in her face. Once she had fallen off the ladder of a backyard swing set at daycare, the rusty wing-nut rising toward her face and gouging her above her eye. The second time, also at daycare, Girl had stepped on a coloring book on the floor, skated across the hardwood, and face-planted into an old iron radiator. She remembered the feel of flying, but not the landing. She did remember being strapped to a blue "buddy board" in the hospital. She kept tearing at the stitches, pulling them out as fast as the doctor tied them, so they Velcroed her arms to her sides. She had tried to bite, but a nurse held her head. Girl still remembered watching her mother walk out the door, ignoring her screams. But despite those two incidents, Girl wasn't an accident-prone child, like Brother, and she didn't get hurt all that often.

"Can I bring my Pound Puppy?" Girl asked. She knew that at twelve years old she was too old for stuffed animals and dolls. She was on the cusp between child and teen, aware of how she lagged her peers in small social ways. She figured Stepmother would say, "You're too old for stuffed animals," but she had to ask. She needed something to hold against her body when she was afraid—something that wasn't her stepmother.

"Of course you can," Stepmother said, still crying. They drove to her pediatrician, and Girl got five black stitches. It hurt. A lot. Watching that curved needle poke through her skin gave Girl the heebie-jeebies, so she held her Pound Puppy and tried not to look, but she couldn't help it. Afterward, Stepmother dropped Girl off at school and went to work. The cut wasn't bad, but Stepmother's reaction was. Her guilty tears ran down her face, her words spilled over Girl, *sorry, sorry, sorry,* as they pulled in the school parking lot. Girl didn't think it was her stepmother's fault. Girl didn't understand why Stepmother was so sure that it was.

Stepmother was all creamy skin over thick body meat. She was a mountain of a woman, soft, but not snuggly, like her mother. There was something stiff under her softness, the way she kept her spine straight, or how she turned her face away when Girl went to kiss her, so Girl only got her cheek, not her lips. But this time, she was all tears and love and this weird, inexplicable shame. Girl did not know what to do with this emotion-leaking parent. It was like Stepmother had been switched by aliens. Girl didn't know how close the sadness and the rage lived inside Stepmother, or how they both flowed from the same place. Most days, she only saw the rage.

bravery

It takes a certain kind of bravery to step in front of a moving train, and once your foot leaves the sidewalk, the rush of terror makes the very air lighter, less oxygenated, giving nothing of substance.

Mother only had two rules for Stepmother: spanking the children only on the bottom, and no swearing at them. Of course, as soon as Stepmother started yelling, Mother always left, slamming the side door behind her, peeling out of the driveway, leaving the children alone. Although Stepmother mostly kept to the rules, there were a few exceptions. When she called Brother an asshole, Girl stepped out in front of the train.

"Don't you swear at my brother," she yelled, running out from behind the living room chair where she had been hiding, standing in between Stepmother and Brother. Stepmother's hand was still raised from striking him. Stepmother turned and looked at Girl, her face contorted, eyes narrowed. Rage turned her pale skin the color of watermelon flesh. Uh-oh. Girl was suddenly less brave than she thought she was.

"Run!" she called to Brother.

The children ran up the stairs as one four-legged animal, feet pounding the wood floor, down the hall to Girl's bedroom—Brother didn't have a lock on his door. Girl slammed the door and flipped the arm of her little hook-and-eye latch into its metal ring. Stepmother was only a moment behind the children, her feet already thumping across the hall. The door shook as Stepmother threw her shoulder into it.

"Open this door!" she ordered, but even if Girl was foolish she wasn't pure stupid. Stepmother hit the door again, and the door gave just a little, the metal lock gouging a line into the wood. She tried a third time, the lock rattling, the doorknob turning uselessly. Thank God the lock held. Stepmother gave up and went downstairs. Girl and Brother didn't come out until Mother knocked on the door.

"I told her she is not allowed to swear at you," Mother said, as if that made everything all right. As if that evaporated the fear out of Girl's bones. After that, Girl stayed on the curb when the train was coming. She wasn't as brave as she wanted to be. When Stepmother degraded Brother—"You'll never amount to anything"—or screamed at Mother for not knowing what road they should take, Girl pushed her lips together until they were hard paraffin wax, safely keeping her voice inside, and wished she were braver.

a poorly thrown punch

Stepmother punched Girl's arm, closer to her shoulder than to her elbow. Even in the moment, Girl thought it was a stupid place to hit someone, and Stepmother did it like someone in a cartoon—she was as red-faced as a villain on *Looney Tunes*. Girl wouldn't have been surprised if a thermometer popped out of the top of her head. Stepmother raised her ham-hock arm like Popeye, her little fist pulled back. Time froze when she cocked her arm. Stepmother wore two rings on her right hand: her gold college ring, and a second ring with a weird, brown, rectangular stone. Luckily, neither of her rings were sharp or scratchy.

Girl didn't understand the fight, even when it was happening. She wasn't trying to be disobedient. She had been responsible for doing her own laundry since fifth grade, but on this occasion, Girl went to the basement and the dryer was filled with Stepmother's clothes. They were cold—the dryer had been finished for at least a day or two. *No big deal*, Girl thought, and found an empty laundry basket. She tossed Stepmother's blouses and white cotton underpants in a basket so Girl could continue her wash. It was how laundry was always done—if Girl neglected to get her clothes before someone else needed the dryer, that person would simply pile them in a basket or on the folding table. When that got full, they'd use the top of the dryer.

When Girl carried her laundry upstairs Stepmother's demeanor changed suddenly.

"Where are my clothes?" she accused Girl and stormed down the basement stairs. "Get down here!" she yelled up from the basement, and Girl complied.

"You took my clothes out of the dryer and threw them in a basket! Now they will be all wrinkled!" Stepmother seethed. Girl was confused. It wasn't like she threw them on the floor or something. This was what Girl had been taught to do with laundry.

"You should have hung up my shirts. You need to iron them, now."

"I put them in a basket, like I was supposed to," Girl said, confused but indignant.

"When the clothes are in the dryer they are surrounded by a puff of air that keeps them from wrinkling. They were fine in the dryer, but once you take them out of the dryer they wrinkle!"

"Balled up in the dryer isn't any different than balled up in a basket," Girl replied. She had been doing laundry for a few years now, and Girl knew that they got plenty wrinkled in the dryer. They went around and around like this for nearly an hour and Girl still couldn't understand what she had done wrong. Stepmother couldn't understand why Girl was such a lazy and difficult child.

"I love you, Stepmother," Girl finally said, trying to get by Stepmother's anger and reach that part of her that wasn't consumed with hatred for Girl and just *be rational*, Mother's mantra.

"Yeah, well, you need to iron my clothes!" Stepmother said, and Girl started to cry.

"Don't you cry over this! Crying won't get you out of your responsibilities!"

"I'm crying because I said I love you and you didn't say it back."

Stepmother punched her in the arm. Girl saw her fist ball up, and she instinctively moved a little bit to avoid her blow. There had been rules before. Spanking only on the bottom. Now there were no rules. Stepmother had never punched anyone before, not even Brother. But when she hit her, Girl had won. She now had proof of how out of control Stepmother was, a story Girl could hold up to match Brother's. All the years of terror, and all Girl had was this one poorly thrown punch. Stepmother had meant to hurt her more, but Girl had turned at the last minute, or she had aimed badly. Girl knew she hadn't hit her hard enough to bruise, and that scared her more. If Stepmother knew it didn't really hurt, she might hit her again. Stepmother never stopped hitting Brother until he cried. Girl made damn sure she cried right away.

Brother jumped to her defense. "Don't you hit my sister!" he yelled, and Girl exploded with love for him. Brother had promised that if Stepmother ever hit Girl again, he would stand up for her, but Girl hadn't thought he was brave enough. She knew how hard it was to enter a fight against Stepmother.

"You stay out of this!" Stepmother yelled at him, and Brother backed down. Still, he had tried. The angry woman's attention switched back to Girl for more yelling about wrinkles and laundry and what an *ungrateful child* Girl was who *did precious little around here*. Girl begged Mother to help. "I told Stepmother

I loved her and she wouldn't say it back. I don't care about the laundry," Girl said. "I just don't know why she doesn't love me anymore." Finally, Mother got involved, yelling for Stepmother to calm down.

"Honey, she's not crying over the laundry! She's crying because you didn't say *I love you back*!" It took Mother almost twenty minutes to get the hate to leave Stepmother's eyes. Girl was so glad that this time Mother didn't leave when the fight started. For once she stayed and interfered, and she was the only one who could ever get Stepmother to see reason. Eventually Stepmother calmed down. Mother got her to admit that putting clothes in a laundry basket was what Girl had been told to do. The fight sizzled out and everyone cried and said they were sorry and said they loved each other very much. Mother never mentioned the punch, as if it never happened. Stepmother opened a can of generic beer—white with only a black barcode and black letters that spelled BEER—and passed it around the table to Brother and Girl. "Nerd beer," Girl called it. She took a sip when it was her turn, even though it was warm and bitter. It seemed necessary to Stepmother.

Stepmother rarely hit Girl, that's what was so weird about it. She didn't even yell at her that often. It was always Brother that was her target. He was Girl's very own flesh, more so than anyone else in the world. He was the only one who shared all of her childhood—the Alaska part as well as the New York part. He was the only one who knew what school was like for children who didn't make friends easily and wore the wrong clothes and liked the wrong TV shows and had the wrong kind of parents. Stepmother would hit Brother and Girl would watch silently in the corner, wishing she could take it for him, wishing he would just do enough to get by and not provoke her. The crack of Stepmother's hand across Brother's body opened a wound inside her own chest, a chasm filled with hate. Good girls don't get mad, though, so Girl learned instead to turn her rage inward toward herself, she learned to call the rage *fear*, and after a while, she no longer knew the difference.

notes from the fourth wall
this is the explanation you hear when your parent is diagnosed with a mental illness

A vacuum, where everything you did was not good enough to keep the family stable, where you were constantly off-balance, waiting for the other shoe to drop, trying to be who your parents wanted, crossing your fingers, *please don't let her notice me*. Nothing made sense and you were supposed to pretend everything was okay. The void was filled with your sweaty fear and stubborn rage. But you did not speak of it.

Your parents' sexuality complicated things. Everyone treated you as a fascinating specimen under a microscope, asking probing questions about being raised by lesbians. You knew gayness was something that must be hidden and lied about and you had been given no other words for what was wrong in your family, so lesbian was the only word left to explain why you never felt safe in your house. Especially when your stepmother's particular brand of lesbianism was of the man-hating variety, when the rage spewed over the dinner table was often directed at men in general, your brother in particular. It was an easy out, but you knew it wasn't quite right. Red wool socks are both colorful and scratchy, but the red and the scratch are independent of each other. Other red things are not scratchy; other scratchy things are not red. But as a child you did go through a lesbian-hating phase, though it only lasted a few months, because you only had one word for the two conditions that defined your stepmother. You knew there was something more to what was wrong at home than just same-sex union, but it gave you a target for your impotent rage.

If you write this the wrong way, how will people look at Babs Walker? Your mother's friend, the one who untied your sneakers to tickle your feet back when you were three or four, who didn't know that you couldn't tie your own shoes yet and were sensitive about it. The one who you refused to speak to for two solid years? And how many years did she keep coming over even though you were a total snot? She kept drinking coffee in the kitchen with your mother until one day you let your guard down and forgot that you were punishing her for untying your shoes and instead let her pull you onto her lap and everyone laughed about that resentment you held for so long. Babs painted her house the exact raspberry color of Bubblicious bubble gum, and she gave you your very own paintbrush and bucket even though you were too small to do anything resembling a decent job.

You picture Shirley and Betty giving you little presents every Christmas Eve, and letting you and your brother watch TV in their bedroom as you stayed up for the eleven o'clock service at church. They had cats and lots of books and a big garden. You remember Marty, who always made you feel like what you had to say was important, and who was always smiling. You don't want your words used against them. You want to show the world how sweet and normal they were.

You remember them and all the other nice lesbian couples who weren't weird or different or scary and how your stepmother's mental illness drove them all away. You don't blame them, but the problem with having a family made up of friends is that once they decided to leave, you didn't run into them at weddings and funerals. Once they left, you never saw them again.

flying to new york

When Girl and Brother left Alaska at the end of the summer, they took the red-eye flight at midnight. Father took tongue depressors and a black pen out of the camera/medical bag he called his purse and made stick-puppets for the children to play with while they waited to board the plane. He pulled out rubber gloves and blew them up into balloons with fingers. He turned one into a chicken, the other into a weird head with only one ear. The children pushed and shoved each other to get closest to Father. Girl scratched her cheeks against his rough wool coat as she tried to fill her lungs with his scent.

Father walked the children onto the plane, just like Mother did back in New York, and let them take their balloon-hands on the plane with them, even though they were big and didn't fit under the seat in front of them. When Father walked down the aisle and off the plane, the children started to cry. He never looked back.

Brother cried all the way to Seattle, and sometimes on the next flight, too. Sometimes he cried all the way back to Rochester. Off and on, of course. He'd cry himself to sleep, wake up and cry some more. Girl cried for the first hour, but after that she just sat quiet in her sadness, letting the sorrow fall down inside her chest like rain down a window.

When Girl was twelve, she stopped crying when Father walked off the plane. When she stopped crying, Brother started yelling.

"You don't love him at all!" he raged.

"I do, too!" she answered. But she looked at her brother as a naïve boy who didn't know the first thing about love and parents who didn't look back when they walked off the plane. When she saw Rochester below the plane window, little houses down below like on *Mister Rogers' Neighborhood*, she felt all mixed up: the warm, glowy love of her mother balanced by Stepmother who was always mad all the time, and the town where the kids at school mocked her and Girl never had a warm enough sweater.

a series of awkward conversations

phone call, 1985

Girl never understood why her father moved so far away. Juli lived in Seattle, and Girl and Brother lived in Rochester, New York. It was like Father was trying to get as far from all of his children as he possibly could. When Girl was twelve, in the seventh grade, he finally offered an explanation.

"Now that you are older, I thought you should know why I had to leave Rochester," Father said when he called one day.

Girl had been practicing piano in the dining room, and now she sat straddling the dark wood bench. She twisted the yellow telephone cord around her fingers as they talked.

"Well, do you know the class 'About Your Sexuality' at church?"

"Yeah. Brother took it this year. I take it next year." The sex-ed class was offered to eighth graders only and Girl was dying to take it, but she had to wait one more year. Brother got to do everything first.

"Well, I was teaching it back then. And this other doctor, Dr. Wu, had it out for me. He was from Japan, and for some reason he just hated me."

"The one you said always called you Crinton Rirribridge?" Girl wiggled on the piano bench, rocking it back and forth like she was riding a horse, making it squeak.

"Girl!" Stepmother called from the living room. "Stop doing that to the bench! You are going to break it!"

Girl blew her bangs out of her eyes. Girl hated her perm. It was supposed to be cascading ringlets, but the end result was more poodle. She was trying to grow it out and her bangs were almost to her nose. Girl got off the bench and crawled under the dining room table where Stepmother couldn't see her. She unwound the phone cord from her fingers so she could make circles with her hand on the pink rug to ball up the dog hair. Girl was supposed to refer to the rug as mauve, not pink. Stepmother hated pink, but a decorator had talked her into mauve—the "it" color of 1985. Girl liked pink though, and she defiantly refused to call it mauve. Girl pulled the spiral telephone cord a little too hard and the phone crashed down off the table above her.

"Girl!" Stepmother was yelling again, but Girl pretended she couldn't hear her.

"Father? Are you still there?"

"Anyway," he went on like nothing had happened, "Dr. Wu went through my desk drawers when I wasn't there. He found some movies I was using to teach the class."

"Uh-huh." Girl lay on her back and put her feet on the underneath of the tabletop above her—she sucked at sitting still. The carpet smelled like dog. Girl didn't know why one dog smelled more than two cats, but it did.

"He said it was pornography and he brought me up on charges. Man, I hate him. I have no idea why he hated me so much. Maybe he was envious, because I was such a good doctor and all the patients loved me."

"I don't get it. How could a doctor think educational movies were dirty?" Girl rolled over to her stomach and blew her hair out of her eyes again.

"I don't know, Girl, he just had to make up something to get rid of me."

Whatever, Girl thought, though she didn't dare to say it aloud. This was stupid, and Girl didn't know why he wanted to talk about it. It wasn't the truth. It didn't help anything.

"I gotta go. I gotta help Mother make dinner." Mother wasn't actually calling her, but Girl was tired of the pretense of talking.

"I so love you, Girl." Father was always overly affectionate on the phone, maybe to make up for only calling every couple of months. It made her stomach ball up inside. His words didn't mean anything.

"Love ya, too." Girl pulled on the phone cord to bring the base of the phone close enough to hang up. Girl left the phone under the table and went in the kitchen to find her mother. Let the next person follow the cord when the phone rang. Girl didn't care, though she would catch hell if the call was for Stepmother.

"Off the phone, honey?" Mother asked.

"Yeah." Girl sat down at the table and fiddled with the salt and pepper shakers, just moving them around.

"What did your father say?"

"He told me some stupid story about why he left Rochester. It was dumb, it didn't make any sense."

"I never knew why your father got in trouble," her mother said. Girl watched her mother's hands chopping carrots. Her hands were big, her fingernails bitten back. Her engagement ring had a little gold hook that wrapped over the top of her wedding band. Girl knew her mother hated her hands. They looked strong, just like Girl's.

"My cousin Iris used to work for him back then, in the pediatric clinic. She might know what happened."

Girl sat at the wood-grained Formica table fiddling with the napkin holder. The paper napkins were always falling out. She took out the stack and lined up all the dimpled paper edges.

"Why did he have to move so far away?" Girl asked. She might have been twelve, but her voice sounded young and whiney even to herself.

"Well, after he left the hospital, he tried to go into private practice. You could ask his old partner, Dr. B, if you want. I could look her up. I always liked her. She was one woman that I knew for sure never slept with your father. She has horses, I bet she'd take you riding."

"That's okay." Girl folded the stack of napkins and slid them back into the plastic holder in the middle of the table. Girl didn't want to ask anyone about it, not cousin Iris, who Girl barely knew, and not some other pediatrician, even if she had horses.

"Anyway, no one would refer patients to him. He really didn't have a choice, honey. There was no way he could make it here without referrals."

Rochester wasn't that big of a city: four hospitals, a couple colleges, and the world headquarters of both Kodak and Xerox. It wasn't a small town, but it wasn't big enough for a professional sports team, either.

"But why did he have to go so far?"

"I don't know, honey. I wish he hadn't. Before he left you used to go see him every other weekend. Do you remember?" Girl shook her head. "You would have been so much better off if he stayed. Your father is a truly brilliant doctor. He could have been a leader in the field, if it wasn't for all his women problems. When I was with him he was on the verge of making an international name for himself—even traveling to speak in Argentina—but he couldn't keep his pants zipped. Whatever trouble he caused in Rochester was bigger than just an average affair or jealous coworker. It ruined him here. It was too bad, really."

Mother scraped the carrots off the cutting board with the side of her knife and deftly chopped the celery. Her hands rocked the knife smoothly and it sounded like tiny people knocking on the door. Girl watched the short black hairs at the back of her mother's head tremble as she cut.

"Did I tell you about the time he fooled around with my cousin's wife?"

"No." Girl took off her big, plastic-framed glasses and polished them on her shirt. Mother and Girl had the exact same frames—golden-brown on the sides fading to clear by the nosepiece.

"Hey, will you peel me a couple of potatoes?" Mother asked.

"Sure."

"When my cousin found out that your dad was sleeping with his wife, my cousin said that he was going to shoot your father. We both had to go into hiding a few days. Then there was the time, after he left, when some woman was throwing rocks through the windows on Mulberry Street."

"I thought you left him?" Mother was the only woman to ever leave her father, and Girl was proud of that. The rest of his wives put up with his shit until he got tired of them and moved on.

"Well, not exactly. I kicked him out. But that house had been his before I married him. He had lived there when he was married to Sharon and Juli was little. I moved out as quick as I could. It never felt like my house."

Girl stood over the garbage can peeling a potato with the old rusty peeler. She dropped the potato in the garbage by mistake and reached in quick before Mother noticed.

"It's okay. We can just rinse it off." Mother put her hand out for the potato. "Anyway, one night this woman was in front of our house in the middle of the road throwing rocks and screaming at your father. I tried to tell her that he wasn't there, but she didn't believe me. She seemed to think he was hiding. So I had to call the police."

"God, Mother!" Girl handed her another potato.

"Anyway, you should really talk to Dr. B. I bet she'd love to go riding with you."

Juli had heard that their father slept with all the nurses in the hospital, and even with a sixteen-year-old patient once, but Girl wasn't going to ask Mother about that. It was too embarrassing. Besides, if it was true, Girl didn't want to know.

"Someone told me that Father slept with the mother of one of his patients."

"Wouldn't surprise me. Pediatricians aren't supposed to do that, but I'm sure he did once or twice."

"Well, they said the woman tried to kill herself. Ended up in the psych ward." This seemed the most likely reason for his exile in Girl's mind.

"I never heard that. What did your dad say about it?"

"I didn't ask him."

car trip, circa 1985

"My mother didn't want a boy," Father said, looking out the front window of his yellow Subaru. It was just the two of them on the two-hour drive from Anchorage, where Father lived, to Seward, where he kept his sailboat. Girl would start eighth grade in the fall.

"My mother already had two girls, Jean and Anne. She said my dad got her drunk and raped her because he wanted another child—he always wanted a boy. When Mother found out I was male she wanted to drown me but my dad wouldn't let her. Then he went off to war and left me alone with her."

The sky out the window wasn't very blue. The road from Anchorage to Seward curved around the end of Cook Inlet; the view out the window was gray-brown silt and boulders; the water had receded before cleaning up its mess. Girl knew she was supposed to appreciate the sparkle of the water and the great expanse of wilderness unsullied by human habitation, but all Girl saw looked cold and bleak.

"Never walk out on that mud," Father said, "you'll sink in right up to your waist. Some fool always tries to drive out there every year and gets stuck. Look, there's a pod of belugas."

Girl looked out the window, but all she saw were whitecaps on the ocean. No matter how often he pointed, Girl never saw the whales he was so fond of.

"Uh-huh. Pretty," Girl said, because she had to say something.

"Did I ever tell you about my dog?"

"No."

"Well, you know where I grew up in Olympia, Washington. The closest kid was five miles away."

"The boy who lit his model planes on fire and threw them out the window?"

"Right. I didn't like him very much. He was kind of weird. I was happy it was too far to go over there often. So my best friend was my dog, Pooh!"

"Like Winnie-the-Pooh?" Girl asked.

"Right. And because he was all white and had a big brown spot on his rump." Father's eyes sparkled as he looked at Girl. He turned his whole head, ignoring the road like it didn't need watching. It made Girl crazy but he always did it.

"What kind of dog was he?"

"Terrier-like. Medium size. Wiry hair."

"Okay." Girl wound a strand of hair around her finger and loosened it again.

"Anyway, Pooh and I had a *wonderful* time exploring the woods! We'd mosey along through the woods. World War II had just ended, so I'd pretend we were spies, reconnoitering, going on missions. Chasing rabbits. We'd stay out all day until Mother rang the dinner bell." Father's mother had an unusual dinner bell in the dining room. She would hit a descending series of bells and end with a giant gong that resonated throughout the whole house with a deep note that you could feel vibrate in your whole body, like a timpani drum. When Grandma Mary was feeling kind she'd sometimes let Girl ring it, but only once per day. The gong looked like a black iron kettle and she hit it with what looked like a tiny wooden baseball bat, maybe eight inches long.

"What happened to Pooh?"

"He barked a lot, and he woke my father up every morning. Dad said I had to train Pooh not to bark, that if he woke him up one more time he was going to shoot him. But they wouldn't let him sleep inside, so there wasn't anything I could do. One morning the dog started barking, and I heard the gun go off from my bed."

Girl had stayed once in Dad's old room at Grandma Mary's. It still had his old bunk bed and model airplanes hung from the ceiling. He had a little brown desk in front of a window that looked out on Puget Sound. From their house you could only see ocean and forest; there wasn't another house anywhere nearby. It should have been a great place to explore, but Grandma Mary didn't seem to like kids very much, and Girl didn't like visiting her. The house seemed to breathe disapproval and discourage laughter. Girl noticed that her father had the smallest room in the house.

"He didn't really shoot him, though, did he?" No father would do that to their kid, Girl thought. Father passed a car lazily. He always set his cruise control for fifty-seven miles per hour, just two miles over the speed limit. He had done extensive calculations and decided this was the optimal speed to drive on the highway for gas conservation and motor efficiency. This stretch of the trip consisted of miles and miles of highway with the inlet on one side and mountains rising up on the other.

"I thought he was just trying to scare me, but I ran down the back stairs as fast as I could, just to be sure. It seemed to take forever to get outside, but I wasn't allowed to use the front stairs, so I had to go around." Father's mother had inherited a million dollars in the Depression. The first thing she did was build a huge house on ten acres of beachfront property on Puget Sound. Girl had counted seventeen rooms the last time she was there, if she included the maid's quarters in the basement. Girl always loved the spiral staircase at the front of the house, but kids had to use the "children's stairs" closer to the kitchen, even the grandkids like Girl. Grandma was inflexible in her rules and had a way of reprimanding children without raising her voice that was scarier than if she had yelled. It was like she had no warmth inside her at all.

Girl was chewing on her hair as her father talked. She knew she should stop that, but it was a nervous habit. She mindlessly twisted a lock of hair between her fingers, then absentmindedly rubbed it across her lips. Next thing Girl knew she was sucking on it and chewing it. Girl wiped the broken hairs off her tongue and rubbed them on her jeans.

"I got outside and there was Pooh, lying on his side. Dad shot him through the heart. Dad looked at me and didn't say anything. He just went back in the house. I was hugging my dog and crying and he just walked away. He killed my best friend. I took a shovel and dug a hole. I took off my pajama top and wrapped him up in it as best I could. Tears were streaming down my face. It took a long time to fill that hole back up, and all I could think about was revenge."

Girl was chewing her hair again, her body tense. This anxious oral fixation would morph into smoking in a few years. Girl wished she didn't have to wear a seatbelt. There was something about being alone with her father that made her want to be able to escape quickly, but he always made her buckle up in the car. Father had taken Girl and Brother to Washington, DC, to lobby for seatbelt laws the year before, and he'd pull over and stop the car if he saw that Girl was unbuckled. She looked at the car door and unlocked it. She didn't know why, but being alone with Father scared her, even in a moving vehicle.

"After I buried him I went to my room and went through my closet and found some old clothes." Father went on. "I sewed them together like a scarecrow. I even sewed a head from my winter hat. I went outside and got straw and grass and leaves and stuffed it, so it was a life-sized doll of me. Do you remember that big window in Grandma Mary's bedroom?" Girl nodded, even though she didn't. Girl knew that Grandma's room was on the second floor, and the house was on a slope, high up from Puget Sound. She imagined that her grandmother could see the ocean over the top of the pine trees. Kids weren't allowed in there, so Girl had only peeped in once or twice from the hall.

"Well, every morning as soon as my dad woke up, he'd open the curtains and watch the sunrise over the water. So I crawled on the roof and dangled the scarecrow down so it looked like I had hung myself."

"Wow," Girl said. She wasn't sure how to respond. She wasn't even sure how a kid could get on the roof.

"I did it over and over, every morning. Got him every time."

Girl closed her eyes and laid her head back on the tweedy brown headrest. Her windbreaker was zipped up, and she buried her hands in her pockets, tunneling into herself for comfort. Grandma Mary's house didn't look like much from the front. It was white, with a dark red door. It didn't look big at all, because it was built into a hill. The back of the house, which faced the ocean, was four stories tall, so the basement was really at ground level. There were four separate doors to the outside, besides the attached garage. The main door and the private entrance to Grandpa Doctor's medical clinic both faced the driveway. Girl's grandfather had died before she was born, but his office was kept like a dusty shrine filled with ghosts. Girl wouldn't have been surprised if she heard lingering screams of forgotten patients. No one was allowed in there, but Girl didn't want to go in anyway. She ran by the door as fast as she could, even though she was twelve and old enough not to believe in ghosts. With her eyes closed now, Girl could picture dark gray specters in a foreboding swirl around the ceiling of the exam room as Grandpa Doctor loaded the pistol he brought home from the war. She pictured her father running out the front door, the tall trees softly releasing leftover drizzle in the way trees around Seattle always seemed to start their day. But that wasn't right. The front door faced the driveway. If Grandpa Doctor was going to shoot a dog, he wouldn't do it out front where anyone could see.

The dog would have been in the backyard. If someone walked out the workshop door at ground level, below the kitchen balcony and dumbwaiter, there was a huge lawn leading down to the beach. That's where Girl would go, if Girl were a dog. The dog probably chased the seagulls in the sand, his little white paws gritty and his head looking up at the clouds of birds he raised with his shrill barks. Girl saw him clearly, his tongue hanging out one side, the edges of his mouth curling up in doggy bliss as his ears flopped behind him, his wiry fur parted by the wind. A young dog could run a big circle from the beach to the house and back, bits of grass kicking up behind him, dirt and sand clinging to his toenails. Grandpa Doctor's bedroom window was on the third floor from the back of the house, but a piercing yap would carry from far out—there was so much clear open air and no city noises. Terriers like to bark—even Girl knew that.

Pooh laid very still in the grass behind Girl's closed eyelids, white fur sticky with red Jell-O-like goo. His front paw gave a reactive twitch as his brain stopped firing.

Girl's dog at Mother and Stepmother's house, Wimpy, had died that year of cancer. When Wimpy took her last breath, her whole body arched up, her head and tail reaching toward each other to form a circle with her prone body. Mother, Stepmother, Girl, and Brother sat around the dying dog and cried. When Wimpy's body arched up, Girl thought she was trying to lick her and had reached out to touch the dog's black muzzle. "Don't touch her," Stepmother yelled. The dog had been Stepmother's before they formed a family. Girl wondered if a dog that had been shot made the same death arch or if it fell where it stood and lay there twitching. Mother had explained that the paws still moved as the energy left the brain. It didn't mean the dog was dreaming of running. All the doggy dreams were already gone.

Would there have been splatter? Did he shoot him at point-blank range? Did her grandfather call him, and did Pooh run up happily, expecting a good ear scratching, just to have a cold muzzle pressed into his fur? Where would her father have buried him? The beach would be easiest to dig up. They had a handyman who lived in a cabin down by the water, part of the permanent house staff. Maybe he had helped Father dig the grave. Girl had dug holes lots of times before. Digging in grass meant first you had to stand on the shovel and sort of jump on it to bite through the plant fibers, then cut out a big square of lawn and set it aside. You had to push through rocks and tree roots, pinkish-white worms wriggling in brown soil. Sand was easier to dig up—as your shovel bit deeper the darker wet sand gave way easily, the bottom of the hole softening with water. But beaches were impermanent. The tide might unbury the dog, letting birds pick through the sand and hair to get at the soft bits. Girl wouldn't risk the beach, if it were her dog. Girl would choose the grass, even though it would take longer. She wasn't about to ask her father what he chose, though. Father always said that it wasn't lying if it made the story better. Girl didn't want a better story—she wanted a true one.

conversation with wife #5, stepmother #2, circa 1986

Father had separated from #Five the summer before Girl turned fourteen. He had fallen in love with the new youth minister at church. #Five was Girl's second stepmother and Girl had never liked her much. #Five was ugly and mean. She was tall with short, permed hair and dark, snaggly teeth. Girl never knew what her father saw in #Five. The house they lived in had been #Five's house before they married, so Father was the one moving out. Girl had never liked the neighborhood of tiny, charmless houses. The fact that Father hadn't lived in that part of the city before they married, even though it was walking distance to both his office at the hospital and the airstrip where he kept his plane, told Girl that it must be an inferior neighborhood. Girl was glad he was moving, even though it was unfair that she had to spend her vacation helping him pack. At thirteen years old, Girl had better things to do.

Girl was taping up boxes of books in her father's study when #Five walked in and sat in his wheeled office chair. It was wood and didn't have a cushion. She didn't spin, not even a little. Girl would have spun or at least rocked from side to side. Who sits in a rolly chair and doesn't wiggle at all?

"There's something you should know about your dad. I think you are old enough," #Five said. Girl didn't know why #Five thought they needed to have this bonding talk now, the day before the moving van came. No matter what she said, it wasn't going to make Girl like her all of a sudden.

"When your dad was little, maybe six or eight, he crawled into bed with his sister, Anne. She was just a few years older, and they were touching each other, the kind of experimenting all kids do. It didn't mean anything—just natural curiosity."

"Uh-huh," Girl replied. She remembered a version of *I'll show you mine if you show me yours* with her own brother, when Girl was five or six, but Girl would never tell #Five about that. The memory made her squirm.

"They say that experimentation is natural at a certain age," Girl replied. It was what the book about puberty and sex that Mother had given her said, anyway. Girl put more books into a box so she wouldn't have to look at #Five.

"Well, anyway, Grandpa Doctor walked in and caught them. He figured your dad was too young to be held responsible, but Anne should have known better. So he made Anne strip and whipped her, and made your dad watch. So now, the closer he gets to a woman emotionally, the further he runs from them physically. This all came out in therapy."

"Oh."

#Five looked at her expectantly, but Girl didn't know what to say. She wished #Five would just go away.

"Well, anyway, it's not his fault. Just thought you should know," #Five said as she walked out of the room. Girl never told her father what #Five had said, and Girl never saw #Five again.

Brother and Girl helped Father move from his ex-wife's small ranch house to a bottom-floor unit in the apartment building he owned. It had brown carpeting, white walls, and a large stone mantel that ran the length of the living room. The kitchen had an almost-modern counter that did double duty for kitchen prep and eating space. The apartment was large and utilitarian, identical to all the other one-bedroom units. The four-plex itself was one of a half-dozen buildings set off the main cul-de-sac in groups of twos or threes—a development well thought out but then abandoned, the individual buildings sold off to various investors. #Five, her father's newest ex-wife, was a realtor. Owning rental property had been her idea. It was 1987, and the Anchorage real estate market was hot, or was going to be hot, or might be hot someday. Girl thought the place was depressing, and like all of Father's places, didn't have room for both children.

photographs

Mother didn't have a lot of rules for the children. She didn't like to hear dirty jokes, but she didn't mind the children telling them to each other. Mother didn't swear, but she didn't complain when the children did—other than *motherfucker*. That word was banned. She didn't mind them kissing people in the back seat while she drove. She didn't think clothing was necessary around the house, though they had stopped going nude camping the year after Girl started "developing."

"Why aren't we going to Sabra's Pond this year?" Girl had asked.

"Well, since Michael took over, it's gotten over-commercialized. People with cameras hiding in the bushes, planes circling overhead," Mother said.

"I wish he hadn't put that ad out," Stepmother added. "It's not a safe place anymore."

But there was more to it than that—Mother thought puberty might make it awkward for the children. As it was, they went one summer too long. The last year, Girl's breasts were starting to appear, and she was growing hair between her legs. Girl struck up a friendship with a twenty-eight-year-old man, eating breakfast alone with him in the woods, something expressly forbidden, but how was Mother supposed to make Girl feel safe and warn her of the dangers of adult men at the same time? He came into their campsite at night, after everyone was asleep, and left presents for Girl to find when she woke: pretty rocks, which were all right, and a vial of perfume, which somehow wasn't. It was easier to just stop going.

The one rule Mother expressed loudly was "no naked photographs." Once, at Sabra's Pond, Girl and her friend Stephanie were singing a song down at the beach. Well, actually, Stephanie, a year younger than Girl, was singing, but she was shy and hid behind Girl, who stood in front and lip-synced. One of the adults grabbed a camera, but was stopped by someone before they could depress the shutter.

"Judy doesn't allow photographs of the children," they explained. Mother didn't want Girl to have anything in her past that could affect her future.

Girl was thirteen when it happened, a few months shy of fourteen. She had kissed her first boy at an amusement park—both of them in their long Hawaiian shorts called jams—one month before she turned thirteen, and during the next year she kissed a few more, but no hands had gone over her shirt or under it. The kids at church were all kissing each other in the woods, more a game than any real intention. Girl would kiss just about anyone to see what it was like, but when one of the boys tried to get her to kiss her brother, "just so you can say you have kissed everyone at church," she refused. Kissing his best friend had been weird enough.

One day, the family was over at Mother's best friend's house. The grown-ups were talking downstairs, and Brother and Girl were upstairs with Jim, Mother's best friend's son. He was the only kid they knew who had a lesbian mother, and it was always a little more relaxed around him, like a cousin, only not exactly. Jim was one year older than Brother, two years older than Girl, which would have been enough to make him their natural leader, but more than just age, Jim was a genius. He had skipped a grade or two already and had his own personal computer. The children played B-52 Bomber on his Amiga, and there was a virtual therapist program called Eliza that Girl particularly liked. When you typed "shut up" to Eliza, she replied "OK" and closed the program.

Jim also had a real camera, not just a point-and-shoot, and his own dark-room.

"We should take pictures of Girl," he said. "You know, like if you want to do *Playboy* one day." He brushed his dark chestnut hair to the side, his brown eyes bright behind his wire-rimmed glasses. Girl had a kind of half-crush on him, but he never said or did anything to indicate he felt the same.

"With your tits you should definitely do *Playboy* as soon as you're old enough," Brother agreed. "Then we wouldn't have to get jobs."

Girl wasn't so sure. She thought, yeah, if times got tough, it would be good to know that she had something to fall back on, but if she did *Playboy*, she'd keep the money for herself. She wondered how much they paid.

"They wouldn't even know you aren't eighteen now," Jim added.

"Did you see the pictures of Madonna? She was fourteen and they printed 'em," Brother said.

"She was not," Girl argued. "That would be against the law."

"It wouldn't be against the law if she *said* she was eighteen. Her tits were tiny. No way she was eighteen," Brother said. He was sprawled on Jim's bed, lying haphazardly on top of the dark blue rumpled sheets. Girl wanted to see the topless pictures of Madonna, but didn't say anything.

"But what if I want to run for president some day?" Girl asked, kind of joking. She didn't actually want to be president, but that was what Stepmother was always saying.

"I'll give you all the negatives," Jim said.

"How do I know you won't print a copy for yourself?"

"How long have you known me? I would never do that to you," Jim said. Girl didn't know how not to believe him. His mother was her mother's best friend. She had known him since before she had known words.

"It's important for you to get comfortable with nude photos," Brother said. "You really need to always have that option with your tits. You'd be a star for sure, but only if you get comfortable with the idea now."

"Okay," Girl said. "But I'm only doing it if I can wear sunglasses and Brother's fedora." The hat was the coolest thing either of them owned, and although they sort of shared it, the way they shared Girl's *Doonesbury* T-shirt, it was officially Brother's property.

"Let's go," Jim said.

Girl took off her shirt and bra, but left her acid-washed jeans on. No way was she taking them off. She pulled the black fedora over her permed hair—the real reason she wanted the hat, to disguise her latest perm misadventure—and put on a pair of "Risky Business" sunglasses. She felt like a model, and when she saw the pictures the next time they visited, the 8 x 10 black-and-whites looked arty, not pornographic.

"Where are the negatives?" Girl asked Jim.

"They're in a pile around here somewhere," Jim said. "I'll have them for you next time. Let's do another, but this time, you should take off your jeans. And I'll shoot in color."

Girl was wearing her only matching set of bra and panties that day, or she would have said no. She did want pictures that looked more like *Playboy* than something you'd see in an art museum, so she stepped out of her jeans and pulled her shirt over her head. This time, she refrained from wearing the hat and glasses.

Jim snapped away from multiple angles, while Brother encouraged her. "You look great, Girl. These are gonna be so hot." Girl could see Jim's erection through his jeans, but didn't comment on it. It was power, to be able to make a man hard without even touching him, so when he lay on the floor and asked her to straddle him, so he could shoot from below, she agreed, even though it made her squirm inside. That last picture was too far.

She called him on the phone a few days later.

"How did they turn out?" she asked.

"Oh, it's a funny story," he said. "It turns out, there wasn't any film in the camera. We'll have to shoot them again the next time you come over."

Girl's lungs tightened. No film? Really? How was that even possible? Would the camera still advance if there was no film? Wouldn't he have known? She didn't say anything, though, because she didn't want to believe it had all been a hoax, or worse—that pictures of her existed that she had never seen.

"What about the other negatives?"

"I still can't find them."

"Well look, okay?"

"Okay, okay," he said, but the negatives never showed up. Girl wished more than anything that she had never agreed to that second shoot, and she really, really wished that she hadn't let him take a photo between her legs from the ground up, even if she was wearing panties.

high school

girl turns fourteen

For Girl's fourteenth birthday, she didn't invite any of her school friends, just the half-dozen kids that made up the church group, who ranged in age from thirteen to sixteen. It was a last-minute party, thrown together that Sunday, so the guests were only given two hours' notice. Girl just wanted to have fun, and the day was sunny. All the kids ran through Durand Eastman Park, running up and down the paths in the woods and winding up on the beach. Even though it was September, it was actually warm enough to swim, and Girl, Brother, Karl, and Dave all swam in their clothes. The good girls stayed on the beach but not in a condescending way, more like an "I'm wearing nice clothes" way.

Running through the woods sopping wet, Girl and Karl found themselves alone for a minute, and soon they were kissing and fighting to get their hands under wet jeans while no one was around. Later, Girl was alone on a different path with Dave, and it was his mouth and body she was tangled with. That was just how they were at church—Brother had kissed all the girls, even the good girls, at least once. They were all still virgins and no one took anything that far or thought it meant anything. It was a hobby, like skateboarding, only one that everyone could participate in, not just the boys.

Mother had taken Girl to the grocery store to order a cake for the party. Girl always hated ordering her own cake—picking out the picture and even choosing the writing. It felt like buying herself a birthday card. She just wanted someone to surprise her. She picked up the book of cake decorations and pointed to the most ridiculous one she saw: a red lobster.

"And what do you want on the cake?" the baker asked Mother. Mother looked at Girl expectantly. *How hard would it be for Mother to pick the words?* Girl thought. She felt so stupid telling the woman "Happy Birthday Girl" every year. Fuck that noise. Not this year. Fuck 'em all.

"I want it to say 'Happy 47th Wedding Anniversary Joe and Mabel,'" she said.

"Really?" the baker asked.

"Really," Girl said. She knew that her friends would get it. They would see how funny it was.

She opened her presents, touched that somehow between church and the unexpected party the girls had found a way to get her something and even wrap it. She hadn't been expecting anything. For once, she wasn't concerned with getting gifts. When it was time to eat the cake, some of the kids laughed and others thought she bought it on the sale rack, but Girl didn't care. Brother knew exactly what she meant. Brother knew her better than anyone else.

Girl didn't have any photographs from her little kid birthdays. No first birthday picture with cake smashed all over her face like her friends had. So she decided to reenact it. She held her hands behind her back and face-planted into her piece—not the whole thing, that would be gross. The boys laughed, the girls looked embarrassed. Fuck it, it was her birthday, the best one ever.

quicksand

Mother said that the infection began with a herpes outbreak in her mouth, the worst she had ever had. Mother woke up after midnight to find her left eye was red, more painful that anything she had ever experienced before. Girl was small—three? Four? Brother was a year older. The doctors removed Mother's cornea that night, replacing it with one someone had donated by checking the organ donor box on their driver's license, their eyes harvested at death and the corneas frozen away until someone needed them.

"If kids ask you what's wrong with my eye, whatever you do, don't tell them I had herpes," Mother instructed as she drove Brother and Girl to their first day of school—kindergarten for Girl, first grade for Brother.

"What am I supposed to tell them?" Girl asked.

"I don't know, but don't tell them that."

"Why not? You did have herpes," Brother said.

"But there's a bad kind of herpes, and I didn't have that kind. I had a different kind, and people might not understand."

"What's wrong with your mother's eye?" asked every kid who ever saw Mother.

"Um, she had an infection," Girl said.

"What happened?"

"I don't know," Girl answered. It satisfied nobody.

Mother went on to have three more transplants before she lost her eye entirely. For Girl's entire childhood, her mother's left eye was red, goopy, half-closed, swollen. A few times a year, the transplant would "reject" and Mother had to get shots in her eye. Girl could not think of anything worse than having her eye clamped open, watching the needle get closer and closer . . . she clenched her eyes shut just thinking about it. If the shots didn't work, Mother went back in the hospital.

When Girl was thirteen, Mother awoke from her latest eye surgery unable to move her arms. The doctors ran test after test, but their final diagnosis was that it was a stress reaction—psychosomatic. Mother had always told the children that the surgeries were no big deal—she had held in her terror for too long.

After a few days, Mother was able to move her arms, but not properly. If Girl held up a finger for her to touch, her arm moved in a horizontal Z through the air. Her hands were numb and unable to grip coins, a pencil, a fork.

"We're gonna need you to stay home with Mother this summer," Stepmother said. "You are both going to have to help out more. Grocery shopping, cooking dinner. You're going to have to pick up the slack."

"But—" Girl started to object, but Stepmother cut her off.

"We are a family. We all have to contribute. It won't hurt you to stay around the house."

Mother was the person Girl loved most in the world, but Girl couldn't figure out how to make her okay again. The details Girl could manage: buying groceries, answering the phone, cooking dinner. Girl did not know how to comfort her, and the thought of failing her made her want to run down their tree-lined street, run till her nose ran from the wind and her legs ached, run until she was a less selfish daughter.

Girl was afraid, not just of the loss of summer—riding bikes and horses and swimming—but this feeling that Girl would lose herself into her mother. Girl knew she had been waiting all her life to take care of someone. She had watched Mother for as long as she could remember—trying to learn how to give up everything of yourself for other people. Girl knew she wanted to do this someday, and she knew she did not want to do it at thirteen. Girl had a feeling that if she stayed home with Mother, she would never leave again, and she would morph into a smaller version of her mother, forced to wait on everyone and not talk back.

Girl had been trying hard to learn this mothering business. When Girl was cold she said she was warm enough. Girl tried to always make her vote for "whatever you want to do." Girl tried to swallow every opinion and complaint whole without choking on it. But she was young. She wanted to run as fast as she could and swim and laugh with her friends. She wanted to jump up onto her pony's bare back and feel his sweaty sides beneath her naked calves. She did not want to do chores and walk to the grocery store with their green folding grocery cart like a homeless person. She hated using coupons. She felt no satisfaction in helping take care of the family while her mother couldn't. More than that, Girl resented it. She knew she only had a few more years before this would be the rest of her life. She did not want that life quite yet. Becoming Mother's caretaker meant Girl would be fully subsumed by the woman she was destined to become. Her future was waiting to devour her. She just wanted one last summer.

Girl had been hungry for as long as she could remember. Her chest cavity was filled with hunger pains from the empty walls rubbing together. No matter what Mother did, it wasn't enough to ever fill the hollowness. Beneath her sternum, a burning ache—a craving—left her concave. Yearning, futile appetite for love . . . what did that even mean? This feeling that she was broken, missing a piece, when did it begin? When Girl was born? When her father moved to Alaska when she was four? When Girl watched her first Disney movie with a handsome prince who swooped in and surrounded the princess with dancing hearts and singing bluebirds and blaring theme music? All she knew was that there was this quicksand inside her that devoured everything and was still gaping.

Is it any wonder, then, that the first time she found a boy who wanted to touch her under her clothes she fell head over heels in love? Even though Mother was sick, Girl was still allowed to visit Father for three weeks. Jack was the son of Father's office manager, and a few years older than Girl. His face was scarred with acne and his body was heading toward plump, but not there yet. He wore his hair in a sort of spikey, side-swept style kept in place with a lot of gel. His clothes were preppy and he talked a lot about all the cool parties he went to and how pretty his girlfriends were.

One day that summer he decided to kiss Girl. That was all she needed to fall in love, and her returning kiss was all the permission he needed. Quickly he was under her shirt, unbuttoning her jeans, and shoving rough fingers painfully into her. He told her to go underwear free, because the little girl panties her mother insisted on buying her were far too uncool for him to look at, and she gave them up, even though her jeans chafed. He didn't wear underwear either. In the past year she had thought long and carefully about how much time she would need to go to the next "base" of sexual play, but Jack convinced her to throw the timeline out the window. Jack taught her how to touch a boy and talked her into oral sex, something she wasn't sure she wanted to do. He held his hand on the back of her head and pushed it rhythmically up and down. He made it clear that Girl wasn't cool enough to be his actual girlfriend, though, and Girl's *I love you*s went unanswered.

It was summer and the Alaskan sun did not set. Perhaps if the night had darkened predictably, like at her mother's house in New York, Girl would have been able to hold back her fervor. She had no rest from it, her circadian rhythm was off-kilter. The Anchorage night only faded to pale gray so her love grew unabated. Infatuation made her unable to eat, think, tie her shoes. The sun did not set and so Girl did not sleep at night. Jack did not fall in love with her, but he had been born in Alaska and was used to the cycles of the Arctic sun.

Girl knew Jack wanted to have sex, and she knew he didn't love her. Mother and Stepmother were always warning her about how a lot of girls tried to have sex to make a guy love them and that it never worked. She knew they were right, but she thought maybe if they had sex he'd keep coming around, and maybe that would be enough. "Save your virginity for someone who loves you," Jack said. "But if you really want to do something, we can have anal sex." Girl knew she didn't want to have anal sex. Nothing about it sounded good to her, but maybe if she was the only one who did it with him, he'd stop looking for a "real" girlfriend. Not that it would be enough to make him love her, and it wasn't his fault that she was such a geek. She wouldn't want to be seen with herself, either. She knew he loved her body, though. He was always talking about how she looked like a centerfold. Girl decided she'd try this thing for him. Maybe if she was willing, it might be enough. She was thirteen. At least she didn't have to worry about him telling anyone about it, because he'd never admit to having any involvement with her whatsoever.

The day before she had to return to New York to go back to school they snuck into his house when no one was home and went down into the lower level living room, where his older sister lived and which was completely off limits. He wore a white T-shirt with a cool neon Forenza logo on it. He didn't take it off.

It hurt. It hurt far worse than she had imagined, and when she looked back over her shoulder at him she could see that he had a spot of her shit on his shirt. She had been so nervous she had had diarrhea for a week. She didn't know shit would come out during sex, and she hoped he hadn't noticed. She didn't know if it stained and if she had ruined his T-shirt, which was so much cooler than any shirts she owned. After a few minutes she told him it hurt too much, and he was very sweet about stopping. He didn't push her to try a little longer at all.

Girl decided to move four thousand miles to live right down the road from this boy, even if it meant she had to live in her father's house. When she was with him she wasn't hungry. Her stomach churned and she didn't eat for days. Her heart flooded with love for this pimpled, slightly chubby boy whose hair smelled of hairspray and whose clothes left trails of fragrant Downy in her bedroom.

Girl wrote a letter to her parents, telling them that she wanted to move to Alaska. They called her immediately.

"We got your letter," Mother said. She and Stepmother were both on the phone. "You remember the rule, though, right?"

"Yeah," Girl said. The family rule was that the children couldn't just call and say they were not coming home from Alaska. They had to come back and discuss it in person, and have a waiting period of at least a month to make sure they didn't change their minds.

"I don't know if your mother will be well enough for you to go. We need you here," Stepmother said.

"We'll talk about that later," Mother interrupted. "I'm getting better."

Girl was flooded with fear. Could they make her stay in New York to be Mother's caretaker? For how long? Would she ever escape?

"I think you should stay here and start school in Alaska," Father said. "And maybe we should go to court. I called my lawyer. We could switch it so I have full custody."

Girl was uneasy. Father knew the rule about returning home, and it scared her that he wanted to break it. And custody? She didn't want to do anything that couldn't be undone. She trusted her mother implicitly, but Father was someone less trustworthy, a parent that she might need to escape from in the future.

"You know the rule," she said. "And we don't need a lawyer. Mother won't fight me moving here." Something about her father scared her. She didn't trust him—something was off. She went back to New York in time for school. Mother and Stepmother agreed that she could move in mid-October.

Girl started high school in New York. Every morning all the grades gathered in the cafeteria, and she tried her hardest to be late as often as she could.

"Come on, Girl, it's time to go!" Mother called. "And you need to eat something."

"I'm not hungry."

"At least some peanut butter on toast."

"Okay, okay." She slathered some peanut butter on wheat toast and carried it out the door wrapped in a napkin. She ate it as she slowly walked the four blocks to school. Brother was going to School of the Arts this year, so she didn't have anyone to walk with. Girl had spent most of her life walking to school with Brother, and she missed having an ally. They were the kind of kids that made easy targets for bullies. *Maybe I'll get hit by a car*, she thought. She had to cross four streets on her way to school, and she could picture stepping out in front of a moving vehicle. *Bam*—blood and a bright light. She figured if they killed you with the first hit it probably didn't hurt too much.

No such luck today, though. She entered the school and walked into the loud cafeteria where all students had to report before homeroom. Her shoes squeaked on the shiny asbestos tile floor as she walked past long Formica tables of rowdy teenagers, the waft of soured food and the antiseptic bite of floor cleaner strong in the air. Girl had to walk past the senior table to get to the freshman table. Chuck was sitting there—the blond skateboarder who was quite possibly the cutest boy she had ever seen. As Girl walked by Chuck, all the boys barked at her. She had thought the kids shouting "Lezzie" at her the year before was the worst that could happen, but she was wrong. This was even worse. "Ruff, ruff, ruff!" The room was too bright. Her stomach sickened as she kept her eyes on the shiny tile floor. She was a dog—an ugly, worthless mutt. Girl looked up and met Chuck's eyes. He was barking, too. When she moved to Alaska no one would know she was one of the biggest nerds in ninth grade. She could be anyone she wanted. Until then, she'd try harder to be late to school.

Father wrote Girl multi-page letters filled with longing for their upcoming life together, words about the culmination of love long obstructed. His cursive words made her stomach queasy and she hid the letters from her parents, but Stepmother somehow knew anyway. "He's wooing you," she said, "just like he woos his girlfriends." Girl pretended she didn't believe Stepmother, but she knew it was true. She threw away Father's letters as soon as she read them. "Your mother always nagged me, what I like about you is that you don't . . . you are so much smarter than #Five ever was . . . you understand me so much better than any woman I ever married . . ." Girl felt his tone was slightly disturbing, but she wasn't going to give up his newfound attention by questioning it. Choosing to move in with Father bumped Brother out of his role of favorite child.

Girl wore her best outfit on the eleven-hour plane ride: peach lace blouse, ruffled denim miniskirt, snakeskin shoes. She looked out the airplane window, but instead of clouds she saw only daydream-movies of her beautiful new life. Father picked her up at the airport and took her home to his apartment. Once she was settled in to the apartment, Father left to spend the night at his girl-friend Daisy's house, leaving Girl his hospital pager number in case of emergency. Daisy didn't have a phone installed yet. Girl stared at her father's red jacket and his bald spot peeking through his brown hair as he walked out the door. He didn't look back. Her bedroom mirror, stagnant and dark, reflected only an empty wall.

This became his habit—every night he would leave after dinner and not return until morning. In this void, Girl would lose her virginity, fail school, cut scars into her body. None of that was enough to make her father notice her. She could not make him stay.

Father came back to the apartment every morning to make her cinnamon toast and chit-chat as she got dressed for school. "Girl-Girl!" he'd call, walking in with a plate in one hand and a glass of milk in the other. He sat at the end of her bed and watch her strip down to nothing, never looking away, but never acting like it was a big deal. Father was a doctor; he saw naked bodies all the time. What right did she have to privacy, to not wanting her breasts and bush frankly stared at by her father every day? It wasn't like anyone wore clothes at her mother's house. Maybe if his eyes weren't such a cold, unblinking blue it would have been different. She didn't know how to ask him to turn his head away.

youth group

Girl was Unitarian, and Father had been too, when he was married to Mother and then #Four, but #Five had turned him into a Methodist. Father still went to #Five's old church, even though he had left her for the new youth minister. Girl was not supposed to tell anyone that Father and Daisy had been dating since she came up from Texas for her job interview months before. Father had shown Girl the love notes he and Daisy had sent back and forth in the months between when they met and when she moved to Anchorage, reusing the same envelope. Father had rented a secret mailbox so #Five wouldn't see the letters. Everyone liked to pretend that he just happened to fall in love with Daisy after his divorce was final.

Daisy was a mountain of a woman: close to six feet tall and shaped like a very large and fluffy bowling pin. Father had a thing for ugly women. He liked to say that he saw the beauty inside, but Girl had a feeling it had something to do with liking women who had poor self-esteem. It gave Father the upper hand. Girl and Brother called Daisy "Beluga" behind her back, after the white whales that swam in Cook Inlet, but it was more about sounding cool than meant with any real malicious intent. Daisy had shoulder-length, frizzy blond hair and a gap between her front teeth. Girl could see how batshit crazy she was about Father, but Daisy also seemed excited about being a stepmother and always called Girl "Baby Girl" with her sweet southern accent and it made Girl feel warm and small and loved. Daisy joked that if she ever married Father, she would insist on being referred to as "Mrs. C. B. Lillibridge the Sixth."

Girl was not Christian at all, and she thought the Methodist service was boring and long and the music was stupid, but Jack ran the sound board and taught her to do it, too. She liked running sound, pushing the levers up and down and making sure there was no buzzing and that everyone could hear the sermon. Plus, she had to sit through both services every week since Daisy was a minister and Father wanted to watch her "do her thing." Running the sound made time go by faster.

Her first week in Alaska she was sent to youth group on Wednesday night. Girl was excited about youth group, because although the Unitarian Church she attended back home had a solid gang of kids, they had no official youth group and no way to get together during the week. Jack picked her up in his grandfather's gold car, and they entered the parking lot fishtailing and doing donuts, like Jack always did. Girl pretended she wasn't scared and wordlessly clamped her eyes shut tight, but she felt like a movie star when she got out of the car and saw all the other kids watching them. Cool. That's all she had ever wanted to be. Jack gave her a ride because his parents made him, but as soon as they walked in he went over to the preps and left her alone.

"You know not to tell anyone we screw around sometimes," he said before they got out of the car. "You're a nice girl, but I can't be seen with you."

"I know," Girl said defensively. She knew she wasn't cool enough for anyone to be seen with. She would never embarrass him—who did he think she was? She knew her place.

Youth Group started with a prayer and a song and she could tell that none of these kids—who didn't say hi or even smile at her—were going to be anything like the Unitarians. First off, no one skateboarded or wore fedoras or dressed in tie-dyed T-shirts. They were all boring preps except for Jared, a long-haired kid wearing a jean jacket and a T-shirt that read YNGWIE WHO? YNGWIE FUCKING MALMSTEEN, THAT'S WHO! Girl sat next to him. She didn't know who Yngwie was, but she was in favor of shirts that said fuck.

After church, a tall, geeky kid named John came over to talk to her. He was kind of chubby and cross-eyed, but he invited her to party with him and his friends that Friday, and Girl said yes. She hadn't ever partied or gotten high before, but it was on her list of things to do as soon as possible.

John picked her up in a red camper van. She wore her airplane outfit again—it was still the coolest thing she owned. He introduced her to his friends: Mason, the driver; Connor, a cute brown-haired sophomore; Randy, an ugly, sullen kid. The van's back seat was sideways, facing the sliding door, and they had a mini-fridge in the back. Their first stop was a liquor store, and Girl handed John her money to add to the pot.

After some deliberation, it was decided that John should try first. He was only sixteen, but his burly frame and collared shirt made him look older. Girl watched him stand in line through the car window. What would they do if he got caught? Sure, she had snuck sips of vodka from her mother's liquor cabinet, but she never tried to buy any.

John came out of the store holding a brown bag above his head in victory, and everyone cheered. Girl took a Bartles & Jaymes wine cooler with everyone else. She liked the burgundy color of it, and it tasted pretty good. Connor was sitting next to her, and he was relatively cute—a lot cuter than John—so she kissed him. "Is this guy okay?" John asked her, and Girl nodded, not caring if John's feelings were hurt. Girl was always acutely aware of her standings on the teenaged attractiveness scale, and even if she was just a six, John was a three. He wasn't cute enough for her, and he must know it, just like she wasn't cute enough for Jack.

Mason wanted to score some weed and it was his van, so they headed downtown. The teenagers slid around on the sideways seat in the back. Mason parked downtown somewhere. Girl had no idea where she was, but there were tall buildings so it must have been close to the city center. Anchorage didn't have many buildings over five stories because they were on the Pacific Ring of Fire and got earthquakes all the time. Mostly little ones, but Father had explained how modern and smart the city planners were, and how Anchorage was built up in the seventies when they had the technology to make buildings earthquake-proof.

Mason and Randy left the van for a few minutes and came back with a baggie. The van was filled with cigarette smoke and the windows steamed up from everyone breathing. It was October, but in Anchorage October was cold like Rochester's winter. Mason used the streetlight coming in the windshield to pack his brass pipe. Suddenly there was a knock on the window. Cops. Fuck. Girl had never, ever been questioned by the police or even known someone who had. She was a geek, and geeks didn't do anything cool or dangerous or police-worthy. Father was going to kill her.

"Fuck, there's a warrant out for my arrest," Randy said. "If they ask, I'm my twin brother, Ricky."

Girl snorted. "Nice brother."

"No, it's cool, he said I could. Ricky has never been arrested."

The cops made everyone get out of the van.

"Ricky!" Randy hissed as they piled out the side door.

Girl had taken off her shoes when they were driving around, and now she couldn't find the left one. She hadn't worn a coat because she didn't own a cool one, just a big puffy blue winter jacket that she would rather freeze than wear. The pavement was cold under her bare foot, so she tried to stand on one foot, resting the unshod one on top of the other.

"Where is your other shoe?" the cop asked her.

"It's in the van somewhere," she said.

"I need to see some ID."

"I don't have any ID, I'm only fourteen," she said.

"It's the law that everyone has to carry ID, and you are out after curfew," he told her.

"Curfew? What's curfew? I just moved here," she said. Was this a Nazi state? She had never heard of curfew. It was un-American.

"All youth under the age of eighteen cannot be outside after eleven o'clock," the cop explained. "And you better get an ID."

Girl shivered and wobbled on her one shoe as they questioned the guys.

"Do any of you have any warrants?" he asked the half-dozen kids. Everyone was silent. Randy sighed.

"My name is Randy Smith, and there's a warrant out for my arrest. You can take me away," he said, holding his hands up by his face. Girl suddenly loved him so much she wanted to cry.

"Okay," one of the cops said to Mason, pocketing his bag of weed and pipe. "We can bust you, or go after the dealer. Your choice."

"Go after the dealer, go after the dealer," Mason repeated enthusiastically.

"What did he look like?"

"Um, he was black. Tall."

"Any distinguishing marks?"

"Uhhh, a red baseball cap."

"Okay, we're gonna let you go, but you kids better get out of here, and we better not see you down here again. That van will be pretty easy to remember."

They got back in the van—even Randy—and peeled out of the parking lot, the tires kicking up gravel. Connor tried to kiss Girl again, but she pushed him away. He was so dumb, she thought, and moved over next to Randy. Randy was butt-ugly but he was so brave.

Mason dropped her off at Father's apartment. After the near-miss with the cops, everyone was done for the night. She looked all over the back of the van, but she never found her shoe.

the descent

East Anchorage High was huge compared to Girl's old school, with over two thousand students. They had fifty-five-minute "hours" instead of forty-five-minute "periods" and eleven whole minutes between classes. At first, Girl just walked the halls in loops during lunch period after she bought a cinnamon roll in the cafeteria for $1.40 at the take-and-go window. No way was she standing in the hot lunch line filled with jocks shoving each other and laughing at people. She had had enough of cafeterias.

There was a cute boy in her Earth Science class named Walter. He was as muscled as a jock but wore a smooth leather jacket and had a mullet that just reached his shoulders. She knew he was out of her league but she liked him anyway. When he offered to sell her a quarter ounce of weed for twenty-eight dollars, she agreed.

"This is bud?" she asked him—not because she was questioning his product, but because she had actually never seen marijuana before. Her friend Jim had described "buds" he smoked when he went away to college at sixteen.

"Well—it's shake," Walter said, pocketing her money. It looked like oregano but she took it anyway. There was only one problem—she didn't know how to smoke weed. She'd smoked cigarettes before, but this was something different. She went to the smoking area and went up to the first guy she saw.

"Do you wanna get high?" she asked a kid with long blond hair and too big of a nose to be attractive.

"You got any?" he asked. Girl held out her bag.

"Put that away!" he said, looking quickly back and forth. "Meet me here after school."

"I don't have a pipe," Girl said.

"I'll take care of it."

After school Danny, Leonard, and two of his friends came over to her house.

"Do you have a coke can?" he asked Girl. She fished one out of the garbage and handed it to him. Danny squashed it in the middle and took a fork and carefully made a series of holes in the indention. Lastly, he poked a hole in the bottom of the can.

"That's the carb," he told Girl. Danny pinched some of the shake weed onto the holes and showed Girl how to light it and put her lips to the can opening, one finger closing off the carb hole, then releasing it. Girl tried it, but coughed out a cloud of smoke.

"You aren't inhaling," he told her.

"I'm trying!"

"No, you're breathing through your nose and taking it into your mouth. Here." He walked behind her and held the can to her lips with one hand and held her nose shut with the other. "Breathe," he told her. "Now hold it."

Girl's eyes were running when he released her, but the smoke soothed all the sad and scared feelings that lived inside her chest. She felt giggles rising like bubbles, but pushed them down. She wasn't going to look stupid. The giggling feeling went down between her legs, and she kissed Danny, even though his nose was too big and he was too skinny. She had finally found something to make all the sadness go away.

thanksgiving with father

Girl unlocked her apartment door at noon. Jenna, her favorite of her new friends, was moving to Seattle, so she had a sleepover party on her last night in town and invited Girl. It was her first sleepover since she left New York.

"I want you to meet my best friend, Suzy," Jenna had said. "Now that I am moving, you two will be best friends." The sleepover was Jenna's way of introducing the two, and both girls accepted that they would become best friends like Jenna said. They had stayed up all night talking. The girls slept till eleven, which was pretty early to wake up at a sleepover, in Girl's opinion, but it was Thanksgiving. At Mother and Stepmother's house, they watched the parade in the morning, then ate dinner in the midafternoon. She would be home with plenty of time to spare.

"Father?" Girl called as she walked into the apartment. He wasn't there—but had left a note.

"I called all twenty names on your phone list, and no one knows where you are. I went to the potluck dinner at church without you. You are grounded off the phone for two weeks, and you have to write a two-page essay on acceptable behavior," he had written on a yellow pad of paper. Girl went to pick up the phone to call her brother in outrage, but it was gone. Father had taken it with him. She couldn't talk to her mom, even. Her first holiday, and she was alone, but she was not going to be silenced. Girl picked up the yellow legal pad and ripped off her father's note. She wrote two pages on acceptable behavior, "blah blah blah, coming home on time, blah blah blah, leaving the phone number of where I'll be . . ." and then wrote two more pages on exactly what she thought of him as a father. "You never called on my birthday, you didn't tell me what time to come home, you always loved Brother more than me . . ." a long emotional vomit of old hurts and new injustices. She left her pages on top of her father's note, went into her room, and waited.

That evening she heard her father come into the apartment. *Click*—that was his key in the door, *thud*—the door shut. She stayed in her room, one ear pressed against her door. She heard the rustle of him taking off his shoes, and knew he was lining them up neatly on the mat, like always. The closet door opened and shut as he hung up his coat. Mother and Stepmother never took off their shoes neatly or hung up their coats the minute they came home, but Father was regimented about everything in his life. When she heard the crinkle of paper, she sat on her bed and picked up a book, so it would look like she wasn't nervous. She was not very good at insolence.

Father tapped lightly on her door. When she opened it, he stood there holding out the cordless phone. "I can see you learned your lesson," he said, then pulled Girl into a tight hug. "I love you so much, Girl." She didn't reply. Father reached in his pocket and pulled out his shiny eel-skin wallet and peeled off three twenty-dollar bills. "Here," he said. "I'm sorry." Girl took the money and put it in her jeans pocket.

"Love you, too, Father," she said, and listened to him talk about Thanksgiving at church. All she wanted was to call her mother.

cool

Suzy gave Girl two pairs of skintight jeans. Suzy was tiny, and the jeans were so tight on Girl that she could barely sit down, but Girl didn't care. She was finally cool. She had to lie down on her bed to zip them, and then her stomach hurt so much that she couldn't eat, which was awesome, because even though she was too tall, she figured if she kept her weight under one hundred pounds she could still be a jockey someday. Girl had never had a flat stomach even though she was thin, and not eating made her happy. Suzy showed her how to melt the tip of her eyeliner to make the line thicker and blacker. Father let her buy a pair of black satin stiletto heels, and she wore them to school every day.

Girl woke up at 5:30 every morning to catch the bus at 6:45. She curled her bangs under; even though it was no longer cool in New York to wear it that way, it still was in Alaska. She wore pale pink lipstick to accentuate the tan she acquired at the tanning beds at the mall. Every few weeks she dyed her hair a different color: first mahogany, then red, then black, then auburn. She hoped that if she found the right color, she would suddenly become beautiful.

cutting

By November, just six weeks after Girl moved to Alaska, Jack fell in love with her best friend.

She was half in love with Suzy herself, in the way that high school girls get in jealous fights when their best friend hangs out with other girls. Not in a way that involved kissing. Suzy was tiny and fragile, and had eczema and asthma and delicate bones that made everything she wore look like high fashion. It was as if she were made of glass. Suzy didn't need much makeup to be alluring with her blond hair and green eyes, and next to her, Girl felt like a big, awkward Amazon.

Do you know the sound of the wind, way up high in the atmosphere when there's a front moving in? It's a deep roar, almost like the sound of waves. That was what it sounded like when Jack kissed Suzy for the first time, in Girl's apartment, on Father's bed. They told Girl to get lost. Girl went into her bedroom and closed the door.

Dark comes early in Alaska's November. There was a window over Girl's bed, and outside she could see the lights of the snow-covered city glowing orange like sunset or a nuclear spill. Back home in Rochester their streetlights glowed yellow-white, and in Mother's house, her walls were soft pink with gauzy white curtains. Here Girl had clinical white walls and mini-blinds.

Father had converted the apartment's dining room to a bedroom with a wall made of bookcases, and he stored his clothes in the linen closet, all rolled into perfect cylinders that never wrinkled. He used the top drawer of her dresser to hold his odds and ends—old photographs, belt buckles, and pocket-knives. Father loved pocketknives. One in particular had a bone handle, and you had to push in a little button on the side to fold it closed. Girl was always afraid it would snap shut on her finger. Father had told her that it was his sharpest blade—sharp enough to shave with, which he proved one evening, using the knife to remove a few long, soft hairs from his arm. Girl took the knife from his drawer and sat on her bed. "It can cut you before you even feel it," her father had said. *Cut you before you feel it* sounded exactly like what Girl was looking for.

The blond, four-poster bed frame was her half-sister's, left behind when she moved to Seattle a few years before. The stained mattress and box spring were found at the curb in the Anchorage ghetto, her father pulling over his Subaru suddenly to ask two boys her age if they would sell it to him. Of course they would—they were throwing it out anyway. There's a look to a cheap mattress that age can't disguise: visible springs showing through the cheap fabric—this one red and bright blue, covered with a bold print featuring pilgrims —sparse threads showing needle holes at the welt, a distinctive lack of padding. Girl's mattress in Rochester was decorated with white roses embroidered on yellow satin. Mother bought the mattress new, though she didn't have money for extravagances. Father was not only a doctor, but a double specialist in pediatric gastroenterology—the only one in Alaska. He could have afforded a new mattress, but it wasn't a purchase he was willing to make.

If Girl were back home in New York, her mother would be coming home for dinner soon, she thought as she sat on her dilapidated bed. Mother would have made Jack and Suzy leave. She would have held Girl when she cried. There was no use in thinking about that. This was her father's house, and he was rarely home, leaving his dog tied up outside and only a Siamese cat to keep Girl company.

Girl sat on the bed, the shiny knife in her hands. She cried—of course she cried. Her shudders were filled with self-loathing. What was so wrong with her that she could not be someone anyone wanted? Girl wanted to pull the pain out of her body and lay it at Jack and Suzy's feet. She did not want to cry anymore—it gave her a migraine. She did not know how to make herself whole again.

Girl opened the knife. She didn't want to die, not really, nor did she want to be one of those overly dramatic girls with bandages on their barely-scratched wrists. Besides, Girl had heard that if you cut wrong, you could sever your tendons and be forced to live out the rest of your life with hands dangling uselessly at the end of your arms. If not wrists, what? Something she could hide from parents and teachers. Her ankle.

Girl still sat on the bed, her right ankle resting on her left knee. This new project dried her tears and focused her attention. "My ex-boyfriend and my best friend, my ex-boyfriend and my best friend," Girl chanted over and over in her head. Jack technically had never considered himself her boyfriend, but

Girl had no other word for this boy who broke her heart. She placed the tip of the knife against her skin, drawing it down on a diagonal. Barely a scratch. She pressed harder and produced a thin red line. She added another one.

Girl left her room to see if they were done cooing and kissing yet—they weren't. "Get out of here, Girl," Suzy said. It was dark in her father's room, and Girl couldn't see them, but Girl could hear their giggles and wet-mouth noises. Girl went back to her room and cut another line, then went back into the hall. "Girl! Go!" Suzy admonished. Girl returned to her bedroom and added another slice, each one deeper. She decided to tally up all the times they hurt her, every kiss, every giggle, every time they admonished her to leave them alone. She ended up with seven lines on each ankle. She wished she had focused more on evenly spacing her gashes, but too late. Bloody lines can't be erased.

The next time Girl walked into the hallway, she pushed up the cuffs of her jeans and turned on the light. She wanted to make sure they saw what she had done. Suzy did not break down in tears, run to hug her, or even apologize.

"What a freak show," Jack said.

"I know. Crazy. I better get home before my mom does," Suzy answered. They left the apartment fast, slamming the door behind them. Girl cried herself to sleep. Her father did not come home that night to see the lines on her ankles. Girl had given in to crazy and won nothing.

The next day Girl went to the school nurse's office and showed the nurse her legs.

"What happened?" the nurse asked.

"Um, I was carving a piece of wood, and I dropped my knife," she replied lamely.

"Fourteen times?" The nurse looked into her face hard, but Girl didn't answer.

"Look, there's a support group I run at lunch once a week. It's for kids to talk to each other about their problems. If you want to go, I won't report this to anyone."

"Okay, I'll go," she said. Relief flooded her, but she was careful not to let it show. She needed someone to keep her from falling deeper into this pit. She wasn't a bad kid. She smoked some pot and skipped some classes, but it wasn't because she didn't care about anything. Girl did it because she cared too much and life overwhelmed her and she couldn't see how to get out from inside her skin. She was willing to try the self-help group. She didn't stop getting high or skipping class, but now she felt guilty about it. She never cut herself again.

cardboard letter

Stepmother had not wanted Girl to move to Alaska, but there was nothing she could do about it. She could not argue. What if Girl's father took them to court for full custody? They were lesbians. No judge would give them custody when there was a heterosexual man there asking to keep the children. She rummaged through her desk until she found her savings account booklet and checked the balance. She always kept enough money tucked away so that if anything happened to the children when they were in Alaska, she and Mother could get on a plane and rescue them. She saw that she still had enough in the bank and tried to breathe easier.

The boy was trouble, but Girl? She was so smart—she could do anything she wanted. She was always so good, she liked getting good grades and mostly did her chores. Stepmother loved her so much. She wanted Girl to be a teacher, or a psychologist—she was smart enough and her heart was so kind. Sometimes Stepmother worried that Girl would marry some pathetic creature in a wheelchair because she just wanted to take care of all the little hurt creatures in the world. Of course she loved Brother, too, but she just wished he would apply himself for once. He didn't seem to care about anything except video games.

Girl had left for Alaska in October. She didn't call very often, not on Thanksgiving, not once a week like she had promised. But sometimes Girl would call and yell at Mother for no reason at all. She would say all kinds of hateful things until her mother cried. Then Girl would hang up. Stepmother didn't know what was wrong with the child. She thought about drugs for a moment, but that couldn't be it. Girl was an A student. She was never in trouble. The only thing to do would be to get her little girl to come home so she could talk some sense into her, explain to her how much she was hurting her mother. She wrote a letter—she would fix this.

"You must come home. I don't know what is going on up there but you must come home. You are hurting your mother. I don't know what is going on with you. Your mother and I love you so much." She signed her name as she always did, drawing little animal faces at the bottom of the page like Girl used to like before she became a teenager.

She needed to make sure that Girl got the letter. She knew Girl would come home once she remembered how much they loved her and how happy they had been. Girl used to have friends spend the night every weekend, and she'd had a boyfriend or two. The little girl was beautiful, even if she did like to wear way too much eye shadow. Stepmother had always begged her not to hide her beautiful face under all that goop, but Girl had just rolled her eyes. She must get her home. What if Girl's father was molesting her? Father was a pervert, everyone knew that. He better not touch her daughter. She would kill him.

Stepmother taped her letter to a piece of cardboard so it wouldn't get lost and sent it registered mail, even though it cost eight dollars. She knew if her daughter got the letter she'd come home right away.

Girl got the piece of cardboard, turning it over in her hands—so strange. A letter taped to a piece of cardboard, torn from a box, by the look of it. She noticed the postage and couldn't believe that Stepmother would spend extra money to send a letter. She opened it and read her stepmother's familiar round cursive. Like always, Stepmother had drawn little animals under her signature. Girl was never going home. She didn't want to live in that house and go to that school where all the boys barked at her and some kids still called her Lezzie. In Alaska, she was finally cool. She didn't have rules and she skipped school whenever she wanted. She had friends and weed and a black leather jacket. Girl didn't write Stepmother back, but she got high and called her mother, telling her how much she hated New York and everything that was wrong with the family. The next morning, she couldn't remember what she had said, only the sound of her mother crying as Girl hung up without saying goodbye.

winter

Winter is intrinsic to Alaska, cold is part of its very soul, although there had been no snow for the last three winters, only ice. The year Girl moved to Anchorage winter came back with a vengeance—snow four feet deep, and temperatures down to forty below zero. Father had a round thermometer in the yard outside Girl's bedroom window. She looked at it before she got dressed every morning. As light as it was in the summer, it was that dark in winter: the sun rose at 9:00 a.m. and set at 3:00 p.m., so when Girl had detention, she didn't see the sun at all. She walked to the bus stop in the dark, the streetlights and houselights reflected and spread on the snow, like a layer of fog. Girl wore an unlined black leather jacket over a half-shirt that always showed her belly button. She had only two pairs of shoes: blue denim high-top Converse sneakers that she wore without socks, and black satin stiletto heels. She didn't have cool socks, so she wore none at all, *Miami Vice* style. It was 1987, and while the hit TV show was losing popularity, Girl was from New York, so she was able to excuse any fashion faux pas she made at East Anchorage High as being a New York thing. She knew the other kids had no idea that although she had lived in New York state, she had never actually been to New York City. They thought the whole state was New York City, which was indisputably the coolest and toughest place in the United States. Everyone was afraid of her.

Girl always lost her gloves so she kept her hands in her pockets. She got up at 5:30 a.m. so her hair and makeup were just right. Before school she changed clothes . . . three times? Five times? Trying so hard to be perfect. Anchorage was in a valley, so the dry air was untouched by wind. Surprisingly, she was rarely too cold, even though she wasn't dressed appropriately.

Girl was fighting to be cool. She had her braces removed, because the new orthodontist had a different plan from the one in New York. Suzy gave her skintight jeans and Father bought her stretch pants, as they called leggings, and half shirts. Wayne, the boy next door, gave her a leather jacket with Michael

Jackson zippers, then Bob gave her a better, zipper-free one. Girl would do anything to be cool. She didn't mind being cold if it meant no one called her a nerd. No one barked at her in Alaska. The only kind of beautiful she wanted to be was sexy. Her breasts grew from 34C to 34D that autumn. She got her weight down from 115 pounds to 97 pounds, because skinnier was sexier, but she couldn't sustain it. Her legs were long and had a gap between her thighs. Was it good to have a gap? Was it bad? Did her legs look knock-kneed? She only knew thigh gaps were a thing to worry over because an older teenaged girl commented on Girl's. She had to remember to not lock her knees when she stood, because it made a weird concave silhouette, but it was comfortable. She walked with her weight in her heels, her feet rolled out so she wore down her shoes on the outside edge. When she walked, her boobs bounced under her shirt, but she didn't know how else to walk. She tried hard to be less bouncy, but she could not make her body behave. Always the throbbing of her crotch. The need to rub when she was home alone, the need to kiss and rip clothes off boys and feel their hands. The boys always hurt her breasts when they touched them, squeezing and sucking the nipples too hard. Only, if they weren't so rough, it felt like nothing. She thought maybe the nerves were buried too deep because her breasts were so big. But between her legs she wanted them to touch and touch and touch. She could not get the same feeling on her own, even though she had been rubbing herself to fall asleep for as long as she could remember. She needed a boy to make the light explode with their sweaty hips thrusting harder and deeper.

christmas

Girl and Father sat on the living room floor to exchange Christmas presents before she went back home to New York for winter break. No matter where she lived, home was Cooper Road, the house Mother and Stepmother bought when she was in kindergarten. Father's apartment had no tree or stockings, and he had only three packages for her to open, unlike the mountain of presents she knew awaited her at Mother's house. Girl opened the biggest box first, a navy blue sweatshirt that said LIFE IS SHORT, EAT DESSERT FIRST! It wasn't the kind of thing she would ever wear, and she pretended that she didn't know that it was the bonus gift from the catalog his girlfriend, Daisy, bought a lot of gifts from. The second gift was more her style, although it still played to Father's love of funny T-shirts. Girl smiled when she opened the mint-green sweatshirt with a puffin on it. It said, "When Puffins Go Bad," and the bird was wearing a black leather jacket like Girl's and was adorned with a real dangly earing. Girl gave him her only gift—a white bone belt buckle engraved with a mountain goat that she had stolen from the mall specifically for him. It cost $14.99, and it was the most expensive thing she ever stole, but she wanted to get him a present he would like and she didn't have much money of her own. Mother always gave her money to buy gifts for family members, but Father didn't, so she supplemented her allowance with the "five-finger discount" and the guilt kept her up all night. She knew it was wrong, and after a few shoplifting trips she never did it again. She'd rather have nothing and hate herself a little less. She had so much to hate herself for already.

Her final present from her father was a twelve-pack of condoms and box of spermicide suppositories. "Knowing you, this will be gone in a week," he said. She had just lost her virginity a few months before, and she looked down so he wouldn't see the shame his words brought. She said nothing, and he handed her an envelope containing a funny card with sixty dollars inside. Girl spent every penny of it on presents to give to Mother, Stepmother, and Brother when she went home to spend Christmas with a real tree and stockings hung by the chimney with care. She was happy to have enough money left to buy something for Suzy, too. Girl bought her a blue-and-black satin teddy that she really wanted for herself, but she would never spend that much unless it was for someone she loved. Suzy thought it was too slutty to ever wear and stuffed it in the back of her nightgown drawer so her mom wouldn't find it. At the mall, Girl found a music box in the shape of a carousel and bought it for Mother, but when she opened the box in her room at Mother's house, it looked cheap and stupid. She hid it in her closet and tried not to cry.

boys

Father didn't mind if she had boys spend the night, even if it was on the rare occasion that he was sleeping at home. Once she had gone to a party with her friend Cindy and a guy named Richard that she and Cindy both had a crush on. He had blue eyes, long chestnut hair, and broad shoulders, and he always wore a denim vest with a Harley-Davidson patch on the back over his black leather jacket. He was only fifteen, but his girlfriend had already graduated high school and had a baby, so she didn't go to parties. The three of them stood at the end of the hall at the party, peering into the living room.

"I feel so out of place," Cindy said.

"I do, too," Girl replied. She didn't even know whose apartment it was—some friend of Richard's that she had never met. But she had always wanted to go to a real party like they showed in the movies: cigarette smoke clouding the air, a keg in the kitchen sink, loud heavy metal music blaring from the silver boombox on top of the fridge.

"But you don't look out of place—look at you!" Cindy said. The apartment was filled with Native Alaskans—you didn't dare call them Eskimos if you didn't want to fight. In fact, now that Girl looked around, they were the only non-Natives there. With Girl's dyed black hair, dark eyes, and black leather jacket, she did look like everyone else there, unlike Cindy with her blond hair and preppy clothes. Girl left Cindy and Richard in the hallway and walked into the living room, feeling for the first time that she didn't stand out. Girl knew one or two of the kids from school, and obviously they knew she wasn't Native, but they didn't seem to care. Alex, a girl she hung out with in the smoking section at lunch, held a glass bong to Girl's lips and after two hits she wasn't insecure about anything. "Whoa," Girl said. She had never used a bong before, and the room was suddenly throbbing around her, like her pulse was vibrating the light. Alex held up the pipe again, but Girl shook her head, instead going over to the kitchen table where everyone was drinking beer and playing quarters.

"What's quarters?" she asked, embarrassed that she had never heard of the game.

"You bounce a quarter on the table into a cup, and if you miss, you have to drink. If you get it in the cup, you pick someone else to drink," Aidan explained. She had seen him around school, but never talked to him before. "Come sit down," he said.

"There's no room," she said.

"You can sit on my lap."

Aidan was Native Alaskan, with long frizzy black hair and slightly almond-shaped eyes. At East Anchorage High, there wasn't any tension between Native and non-Native students that she could see. The tension was between the preppy kids and the "stoners" like Girl. Aidan was definitely a stoner, and Girl had a thing for dudes with long hair.

How did people even bounce a coin on a table anyway? Girl wondered. When Girl dropped her quarter, it just lay on the tabletop and mocked her. Aidan was the only one she knew at the table, but whenever one of his friends bounced their coin into the red Solo cup, they always picked Girl to take a drink. She hated beer, but drank it anyway. She wasn't going to look like a wimp in front of a bunch of seniors. She liked sitting on Aidan's lap. She liked that he wasn't afraid to kiss her in front of his friends.

The party was apparently for some guy Stan's eighteenth birthday. He had short black hair and big wire-rim glasses.

"It's your birthday, you have to chug!" one of the women yelled, and Stan put the keg spout into his mouth. "You have to do eighteen seconds! Everyone else did twenty!" the same girl encouraged. "Chug, chug, chug, chug," everyone chanted, while the loud girl counted off the seconds. When she got to eighteen, Stan let go of the spout and slid down the cabinet to sit on the floor. "Everyone else only did four seconds, but don't tell Stan," the instigator told Girl with admiration. Stan stayed on the floor for the rest of his party.

When it was time to leave, Girl invited Aidan to come home with her. Girl, Cindy, and Aidan took a cab back to Father's condo, but she had forgotten her key and they had to knock until Father let them in. Normally Father wasn't there, so Girl had gotten lucky. She didn't have any money left for cab fare to go to someone else's house.

"Is Aidan spending the night?" Father asked in front of both of her friends. Girl had sobered up some and didn't want Aidan to sleep over now, but she was on the spot. "Yeah," she said, and that was that. Too late to back out. Girl had twin beds in her room—Cindy fell asleep in one, and she and Aidan shared the other. They had sex because that was what she was supposed to do, after inviting him over. All night, Girl had to keep getting up to pee. She was exhausted, but Father woke them all up at nine and told her she had to go to church, whether she wanted to or not. He dropped Aidan at the bus stop on their way, but drove Cindy home. Girl had assumed that he would drive Aidan home, too, but Father had refused. Girl wasn't sure why, but it embarrassed her. She didn't think Father was racist, but he always drove her white friends home. Maybe they were just running late. After that, Girl and Aidan said "hi" to each other in the halls, but neither of them wanted more.

A few months later Father had to go to an out-of-town conference. Girl's new boyfriend, Bradley, was over at her house when Father got home from work. Bradley was nineteen, and what they called a "second-year senior," a nice way to say that he had failed a grade. He had platinum blond hair down to the middle of his back, and he styled it with a curling iron and sprayed it with Aqua Net aerosol hair spray, the same brand Girl used. He didn't have a car and rode the school bus with Girl. He didn't have a job, but he played the guitar. Mother wouldn't let her date anyone over the age of eighteen, and Stepmother would never have approved of an unemployed boy with no college plans. Father liked him a lot, as he did all of her boyfriends. Not only did he like the reassurance that she wasn't gay, but he just seemed to like males more than females in general. The only weird thing was that he insisted that Girl's friends call him Dr. L, unlike her mother, who was on a first-name basis with everyone.

"So, Bradley, I have to go out of town for a week. Would you like to stay here with Girl while I'm gone? That way she won't be lonely," Father said.

"Sure, Dr. L." Bradley never said much, but he smiled a lot. Girl didn't let on that she wasn't ready to have sex with him or have him spend the night. She just went with the flow, and tried not to feel like Father was giving her as a gift to this teenaged boy in an effort to get Bradley to like him. She didn't understand Father's guilt over leaving her alone, either. Wasn't she alone every night anyway? How was this different besides not having to dress as fast as she could so that her father wouldn't walk in on her changing in the morning?

george

More than anything, Girl wanted a dog. Her father had a husky, Chuckchi, but the dog wasn't allowed in the house. Chuckchi slept outside on a long chain attached to a dog house Father had built himself. When he went to work every morning, he unlocked the padlock that connected the chain to the dog collar and brought the dog to work, where he hooked her up again outside his office window. Every day after work he took Chuckchi for a run in the park. Most of the time, Girl wasn't invited to come along. She hated that dog.

Father didn't own a television set, so when he was at Daisy's house (they had moved into the same condominium complex and lived across the street from each other) Girl read books and talked on the phone. She slept holding the cordless phone like a teddy bear, in case anyone called in the middle of the night. That year she was into horror stories—Stephen King and Dean Koontz and stories of alien abductions and true-life crime. She didn't miss the television—she had never watched much after she outgrew cartoons—but after she closed her paperback, the condo filled with creaking noises and big, scary shadows.

Girl heard a noise, and worked up her courage to get out of bed. It was probably the heat kicking on, she told herself . . . but what if someone or something was there? She was all alone, so she made herself get up and walk downstairs past the curtainless windows—was someone watching from the bushes? She locked the sliding back door and flipped the deadlock on the steel front door, then ran back to bed as quickly as she could.

But what if someone was already inside and she just locked them in with her? Her bedroom window was large plate glass, with only narrow crank-out windows on the sides. Could she get a window cranked open and jump out, landing on the dog house without breaking a leg? Better to unlock the front door, so she could get out quicker and not mess with the deadbolt. Girl crept out of bed and ran as fast as she could for the front door and unlocked it, then ran back to bed. A dog. She wanted a dog to bark at invaders and sleep in her bed at night. She could trust a dog to keep her safe.

"Can I have a dog?" she asked her father.

"Sure, but no puppies. It has to be housebroken. It has to already have its shots, be fixed, and it has to match the carpeting," he answered.

The next week she brought it up again. "So this dog . . ."

"I told you that if you want a dog, you have to vacuum the entire house every day for a week, to prove that you can be responsible."

He hadn't said anything like that, but Girl vacuumed three times a week for the next couple of weeks, and guessed that was close enough. She figured that he wasn't home enough to be able to tell the difference.

"So when can I get a dog?" she asked him.

"I never said you could get a dog," he answered.

Girl brought up the dog in her support group in the nurse's office.

"He seems to go back and forth on getting a dog," the nurse said. "Why don't you just get a dog and see what happens?"

That weekend Suzy's mother took her to the dog pound. Girl walked past the wriggling little black lab puppies—no puppies, her father had said— because she didn't know how to housebreak a dog, even if they were adorable. She stopped in front of a full-grown Newfoundland—her favorite dog of all time. She loved big dogs, but the kennel tag said he had been removed from a home for biting someone, so he wasn't up for adoption. All the dogs were barking and barking and it was making her nuts. She looked down the rows of dog cages. There was a black-and-brown dog halfway down on the right that wasn't barking at all. It was a medium-sized mutt that looked like Wimpy, Stepmother's old dog, that had died the year before. He sat and looked at Girl, his tail thumping the ground. The tag said he was six months old and already fixed. Father's carpet was dark brown, so Girl figured he'd match well enough.

"Can I see this one?" she asked the kennel attendant. The dog came out and jumped up, putting his paws on Girl's stomach.

"Sit!" She told him, and he sat, then he sat up with his paws dangling. She had always wanted a dog that could do that. Girl paid the forty-five dollars from her allowance and Suzy's mother dropped her and the dog at home.

"What are you going to name him?" Suzy asked. As soon as she got home, she had called Girl, and they were talking while the dog sniffed around her house.

"Do you remember baby Huey, from Looney Tunes?" Girl asked. "He always said, 'I will hug him, and I will love him, and I will name him George, and I will sit on him like a mother hen!'"

"And I will spank his bottom when he's bad!" Suzy answered.

"And you know George Carlin? He does that routine about how he has the name that never ends. G.E.O.R. (pause) G.E.O.R. (pause) G.E.O.R.G.E.O.R.G.E!"

"He's so funny," Suzy said. "George was my grandfather's name. I like it."

"Oh, my dad's home," Girl said. "I gotta go."

When Father walked in, he didn't say anything.

"Look, Dad! I got a dog! He's fixed and housebroken and he matches the carpeting! And look, he can sit up! Sit, Georgie!" The dog sat and pulled his back straight, his white paws dangling pathetically.

"That's nice, but he's going back," Father said, without any emotion in his voice at all.

"But you said—"

"I said you had to vacuum every day for a month."

"You said I had to vacuum for a week!"

"The dog isn't staying."

Girl took the dog's leash and ran outside. He didn't try to stop her. She walked up the hill to her old neighbor Wayne's house. Whenever she got into a fight with her dad she went to Wayne's. He was a tall, dark-skinned sixteen-year-old, and his father was never home. She thought of him as her adopted brother. She called Suzy and told her what happened.

"Hang on, I'll call you back," Suzy said. When she called back a few minutes later, she had a plan. "My mom says you and George can move in with us."

Girl moved in with Suzy, and then she had rules and chores and all the normal things that kept her from spinning out of control. She and Suzy shared a room, and one wall was covered in magazine cutouts of fashion models. Suzy had a wooden screen that hid her laundry basket and a long closet big enough for both their clothing.

Suzy was sick. She had asthma and no longer went to school—instead, a tutor came over a few times a week. Girl helped her with her homework instead of doing her own.

"All I ask is that you make sure Suzy takes her medicine," Suzy's mother had told Girl, but Suzy said the pills made her sick and she hated her breathing machine. Girl didn't have the heart to force her or make her feel bad for it.

Girl got the flu. Girl went walking in the woods with some of the boys at lunch, and she told them she wasn't getting high anymore. She didn't like feeling dirty, bad. In the shower, the soap ran down her body, but she still felt unclean. She knew she shouldn't get high. If her mother knew, she would be so disappointed. Girl would do anything not to disappoint her mother, even though she lived a quarter of the earth away. Girl swore she was done with drugs, so she told her friends she'd just keep them company as they walked into the rough tundra at the edge of school property.

"Sure you ain't gittin' high," Frank said. "Leonard, you believe that?" Girl didn't like Frank much. He was thin with long, scraggly black hair, and he wore a denim jacket instead of a leather one. His face was pointy, like a weasel's.

Leonard laughed. His straight, shoulder-length blond hair was nearly white. They were best friends, yin and yang. He packed the pipe and passed it to Girl.

"No, I told you, I'm not getting high today."

They laughed and pushed her back, so she fell against a tree behind her.

"Oh yes you are," Frank said. He held her nose shut, and Leonard held the pipe to her lips. She had no choice but breathe through the pipe. The boys were harmless, really. No one tried to kiss her or anything like that, and it's not like Girl had kicked them or fought back or anything.

When she woke up with a cough and fever the next day, she knew it was from getting high. "I should have fought harder," she thought to herself. She felt so sick—she couldn't remember ever feeling so awful. A few days later, Suzy got sick as well, but with her asthma she got it worse. She lay in her mother's bed, struggling to breathe. When she had an asthma attack, her inhaler didn't help, so her mother bundled her up and drove her to the hospital. They couldn't stop her asthma attack, so the doctors induced a coma and put her on a ventilator. Girl stood in the doorway, watching the blue machine beep and chuff as her best friend's chest rose and lowered. Her eyelids were taped shut. Girl knew it was all her fault.

Mother flew up from New York to be with Girl, because the doctors said Suzy had only a one in a thousand chance of recovering. Suzy survived, but it was decided that Girl would move back to New York, so Suzy could go to a residential hospital program in Colorado. That May, when school ended, Girl boarded a plane for New York. George traveled in baggage in a plastic crate. She wouldn't leave him behind.

notes from the fourth wall
cicadas

to survive my father, i created an exoskeleton, like a cicada

I had not seen my father in several years, and I had no aching desire to change that. When I thought about my father, I felt nothing. He wanted to visit last summer, and I didn't know how to say no, for my children's sake, if nothing else. Dementia was overtaking him, and the minute hand of the clock was stealing the person I used to know—every day he was a little less the man I remembered. But I still did not want him to come. Whatever he had or had not been to me, it no longer mattered—I was a parent now, no longer in need of parenting.

When I was a child in my mother's house, my brother and I spent our summers in the backyard. The grass was thick and dense beneath my bare feet, and the dark brown dirt always stained the pads of my toes. We carved fingernail x's in our mosquito bites, in an effort to remove the itch. The cicada buzz reverberated in my ears, the tinny radio-static soundtrack of summer. I would find their discarded robot-alien shells as clinging detritus on the tire-tread bark of the maple tree. The exoskeletons were the color of toast, slightly translucent. It took me a long time to realize the shells were empty and could not bite, and when I mustered the courage to touch them, they crackled into broken shards beneath my fingers.

I had spent a year plotting my father's death when I was fourteen—I was going to push him down the brown carpeted stairs of his condo, and then inject alcohol into his veins and make it look like an accident. He was a doctor—syringes weren't hard to come by, and I was overly confident in my ability to push a needle through someone else's skin. But in the end, I didn't have hands that would push my father down the stairs, no matter how much my rage instructed them to. My hands were useless wounded birds controlled by my heart, which still yearned for a Daddy who loved me.

The years of unrequited love drained me of all emotion toward my father. I haven't even been able to muster up anger in longer than I can remember. I have been full-grown for quite some time now. It was too late for him to return my golden-retriever-like love, to fulfill all those hastily made promises, or to take me to the father-daughter dinner dance. Whatever I hadn't gotten from him I no longer wanted. But his impending visit made me think I should try one more time, at least to appease everyone else. The night before he came into town, I thought about his recent attachment disorder diagnosis. Was it fair to shut him off if he was inherently incapable of feeling emotion? Hadn't he tried the best he was able, small though those attempts had been? He sent me stuffed animals each Christmas—weird ones, granted, like a three-foot-long snake made out of neckties or a weasel instead of the husky I had asked for—but he made time to go to a toy store and bought me something each year. He wrapped them up and wrote out a name tag with his favorite black pen. His handwriting was more familiar than his face. My father was always excited to see me, scooping me up in a tight bear hug and crushing my child-soft cheek against his black-and-red plaid Woolrich jacket.

He didn't think it mattered that I only saw him twice a year as a child, and I have learned how quickly time passes when you are an adult compared to the never-ending feel of a child's summer and the eternity of fifteen minutes when I rubbed the toes of my shoes in the brown-gray dirt and tried to guess how much time had passed.

I decided to attempt to loosen my shell. Perhaps I could learn to see him through adult eyes. Maybe his attachment disorder explained all of his past failings, if only I would stop judging him so harshly. I knew we could not make up for the lost years, but perhaps it was not too late to develop some affection for the person he had become. Maybe a relationship could be had on new terms, before his spreading dementia took the ability away entirely.

My father and I sat across the table from each other and said nothing, like strangers at a train station. I looked at his eighty-year-old hands, ropy with thick blue veins and corroded with deep lines. His fingernails were thick and clean and longer than mine. I felt nothing—not sympathy for an old, tired man, not remorse for all he had never been. I was no longer a daughter-abyss needing to be filled. We sat in silence and he looked into the distance blankly. I knew I was supposed to say something, but I had nothing left to say. My father just stared out toward my garden with unfocused eyes. When I tried to make small talk, he responded with words like "oh," words like air, words like emptiness. The cicada had flown, and the empty hard shell I had tried so hard to penetrate as a child was all that remained of my father.

My father peed on the toilet seat and I sat in it. My children asked why Grandpa got mashed potatoes all over the table when he ate. He tried to assemble a simple wooden toy with my seven-year-old and glued everything together backward. My father, formerly an airplane pilot, boat captain, and pediatrician, could no longer distinguish between his left and right hands, could not translate a map, could not follow a conversation to completion.

He asked to have a "heart-to-heart" with me before he left. I tried my best to avoid it. There was nothing he could say that would mean anything to me, and I hoped he didn't expect validation of his parenting or proclamations of my love and appreciation. I just didn't have it in me to pretend any longer. He stood up from the table where we all sat and asked to speak with me, and I could not come up with any more reasons not to. My father and I sat upstairs on my balcony, away from his wife and my family.

I could still see a tinge of brown in my father's gray hair. His face was foreign to me. He had shaved off his beard when I was twenty, and had looked like a stranger ever since. Even though I had known him clean-shaven for more years than bearded, I always saw him through the eyes of a child, and his face was no longer the face of my childhood. I wondered if his front tooth had always been longer than its mate. I noted how the extra weight he put on over the years filled in his wrinkles. He stared directly into my face, as he always had. I did not see him blink once. I could not sustain that level of eye contact, and looked at his hands instead.

My father told me about his dementia, his Parkinson's disease, and his relationship with his wife. He was sorry that he was moving closer to his stepchildren than to me or my brother. He was afraid I felt spurned. He told me that he knew he couldn't function like he used to, couldn't carry on conversations or walk with his old, easy gait. His cicada words bounced off my daughter shell. I just wanted him to go home. I stared at his folded hands and made reassuring, meaningless noises, as was expected of a good daughter. But I was no longer a good daughter.

My father's hands curled loosely on his lap, so I could not see his talon-like nails. The metacarpals rose in sharp ridges above the wrinkled red skin. His veins were bluer than his eyes. The skin on the backs of his hands was made of some material different from mine, something thinner and less opaque, like the skin of lips, that would chap and tear easily. The eighty years of his life didn't show in his face, but were betrayed by those red, fragile hands. My body remembered his hands teaching me to tie off the boat at the dock, to sew a patch on my jacket. My hands balled up so I would not reach out to stroke his fragile skin. I made an excuse to check on the children, and he followed me mutely down the stairs.

another fourth of july

On July third, they closed the street in front of Irondequoit Town Hall, set up a stage for a live band, and had the annual street dance. Girl's hair was dyed black, curled in an '80s pouf on top, and reached just barely to her shoulders if she pulled it straight with her fingers. She wished it were long—she wanted hair down to her knees, longer than her miniskirts, but she dyed it so often it was perpetually fried. She wore her Metallica half-shirt and a pair of denim short-shorts that were, to be honest, shorter than she intended when she bought them. You could just barely see the curve of her bottom from behind. She took a round black button from a band called Metal Church and attached it to the front side of her shorts, just below the left pocket, to draw the eye. She wore one lace fingerless glove on her left hand. Before the street dance, Girl applied black eyeliner on the inside rim of her eyes and pale pink lipstick, made paler by first applying a light concealer to hide her natural lip color. She was hot. Sexxy, with two Xs. She didn't look fourteen years old, that was for sure. She and Brother smoked as they walked the mile to the town hall. Brother was a real smoker; Girl only did it occasionally to look cool. Secretly she hated the taste, but she loved the look of it, and it gave her something to do with her nervous fingers. When they got to the town hall, it was swarming with people. Brother and his best friend wandered off to get high, but Girl hung back, watching the dunking booth, just like when she was a little girl. A group of boys came up and surrounded her.

"I know you," Girl said to a teen boy with curly hair down past his shoulders, like Paul Stanley, her favorite band member from Kiss.

"Yeah?" he replied with a sleepy-eyed smile.

"You're Brandon. You used to pick on my brother."

Brandon's face fell, and Girl was filled with exuberant joy. This was the revenge she had waited her whole life for.

"Your brother? Who's your brother?"

"Brother Lillibridge." Brandon was squirming, really actually squirming, his head down, his chest and shoulders moving awkwardly. Just then Brother walked up. As metalhead as Girl dressed, Brother was just as punk. His hair was naturally black, and one side was shaved to the skin. He wore cut-off army pants and a black Dead Kennedys T-shirt, with a skateboard in one hand and a cigarette in the other. Two earrings pierced his left ear.

Brandon looked up at Brother. Brandon had topped off at five foot seven, but Brother was not yet done growing at six foot four—he wouldn't stop growing until he reached six foot nine in his twenties. Girl suspected that he willfully grew so tall so no one would dare to pick on him ever again. Brandon had to bend his neck and take a half-step back to look into Brother's green eyes.

"I am so sorry, man," Brandon spluttered. "I can see you've changed. Look, let me shake your hand, and be friends, okay?" Brandon took Brother's hand and shook it. Brother looked tall and bored. Girl was exploding inside with sweet revenge. *Who's the geek now?* she wanted to ask them.

the trestles

When Girl moved back from Alaska, she became Brother's baby duck, following him everywhere. She didn't call any of her old friends—they were too "good-girl" for her now. They didn't have sex or get high or even smoke cigarettes. Liz was still gone at the foster home, and she didn't know how to find her. Brother's world became her world.

Brother made her get up early every weekday to catch a ride downtown with Mother. His friends all lived across town, and Mother's office was halfway there. From Mother's office they caught the number seven bus to Brighton or Pittsford, depending on the day. Sometimes they wandered Cobbs Hill with Brother's friends, looking for but never finding weed. If they could find a ride, they went to the trestles.

The trestles were a series of train bridges that spanned the brown water of the Erie Canal. Teenagers congregated on them to get high, play music, and watch the bravest of them jump into the water below. Brother jumped, Girl did not. Once, Girl walked down the embankment to swim in the water. The canal turned her white high-cut swimsuit the color of coffee with cream, and no matter how many times she washed it, it never turned white again.

For those who did not care to jump into the canal, there were two options when a train came by: gather on the concrete stanchion below the tracks, or sit on the iron trusses next to the train tracks themselves, where the wind and dust tornadoed around you. It was here that they sucked on torn pieces of cardboard that someone said was homemade acid. By the time Girl and Brother got home, they both regretted that decision.

"I'm gonna tell Mother," Brother said.

"Don't tell Mother," Girl said.

"She can take me to a hospital and they will give me drugs to make it stop," he insisted.

"Do what you want, but don't you dare tell her I dropped acid, too."

Girl went to her bedroom in the attic while Brother made his confession.

Mother came up shortly thereafter. When Girl looked at Mother the acid made Mother's bad eye glow extra red and loom twice the size of her normal one. Mother's mouth was the hard straight line that broadcast, "I am so disappointed in you."

"Did you drop acid too?" she asked Girl.

"Drop acid" sounded so funny in Mother's mad voice, but Girl managed not to laugh. "No. I just took some Vivarin," Girl answered. She figured Mother couldn't complain about caffeine pills because she lived on coffee.

Brother was in his bedroom, watching TV. A commercial came on for Purdue chicken, with raw chicken carcasses dancing across the screen. The carcasses spoke to Brother through the television. Brother never ate chicken on the bone again.

Alone in her room, Girl's heart was pounding so hard she could feel it in her fingertips, which she held out in front of her face. She stared at her hands, turning her head to one side, then the other. Next she looked at her feet. She had tan lines from her shoes, and her toes were white. Her two-toned feet scared her. Girl was convinced if she fell asleep, she would die, so she stared at her feet all night long, and didn't close her eyes until she heard the birds singing their morning song. She never got high again.

catholic school

As soon as Girl moved back home and it was too late to change her mind, Mother informed her that she was being sent to Our Lady of Mercy, because "you need the structure only an all-girls Catholic school can provide."

Fuck. Navy-blue-and-white uniforms. Transferring buses downtown. Most importantly: no boys. The girls here were different—you didn't have to be pretty to be popular, or even good at sports, and no one teased the geeky girls. Popularity was based on one thing only: money. Jessica was popular because she lived in a mansion on East Avenue, one that had an actual elevator inside. Girl had seen it herself at a party that Jessica threw. It was made of iron scrollwork, like a birdcage, and the boys from McQuaid, Our Lady of Mercy's brother school, hung off the bottom of it as it ascended to the second floor. So it didn't matter that Jessica had one blue eye and one brown eye, or that she was fat. It only mattered how much money her parents had. In other words, Girl was not going to fit in here. There weren't many other metalheads, and the other students were kind of afraid of Girl, which she liked quite a lot. She knew she wasn't tough, but she liked appearing tough. When they played soccer in gym class, Girl ran toward the ball and tried to kick it, but half the time she missed. The other girls assumed she kicked their shins on purpose, and let her take the ball.

Her only friends were still Brother's friends. Mother signed Brother up for a drug education class, so Girl went to all his family groups. Really, she was lonely. When Brother was required to attend an AA meeting, Girl followed along, because she knew some high school boys that went, and they were cute. Something happened at that meeting, though. Girl had always felt like she was drowning, but at that meeting, she felt like someone had grabbed her hand and was pulling her out. She asked Mother if she could go to treatment, but Mother said, "Oh, Girl, I need one of you to be a success. I can't handle both of my children being drug addicts." So she didn't go. Three months later, after attending AA meetings several times a week, she asked again. This time, Mother said yes.

diagnosis

They were sitting in a large circle of chairs at family group, everyone quiet and attentive. Ten other troubled teenagers, ten other sets of parents.

"Stepmother has clinical depression," Mother told the group. "She's been on medication for six years. For Stepmother, depression comes out as anger." Stepmother wasn't there that night. The sound of Mother's words set off a detonation inside Girl's chest.

There was something wrong with Stepmother. There was something Girl could point her finger at and say, "See? It wasn't my fault. See? I was right—she wasn't normal." It was like all the Kodak slides of her childhood were dropping into a new carousel. *Click-click-click-click*. What was wrong with Stepmother wasn't because Girl was a bad daughter.

Then her anger rolled in—the smoke from the detonation. Why had they not told her sooner? Girl already carried the secret of their sexuality, it wasn't like they were afraid to burden Girl with things she could not tell her classmates. This new secret might have actually helped. If she had known this growing up, she could have been someone different.

Girl wrote in a pink diary from September 1982 through January 1983. The book had been a gift for her ninth birthday. Girl wrote "Important" on the cover in red ink. She wrote down her pen pal's address inside the front cover, the back cover, and on a separate page. Girl only wrote seven entries in the diary before she gave up. In those seven entries, only three of them were about more than just the weather.

November 13, 1982
"I am either wacko or strange. Can someone please turn me off? Everyone acts like I am strange. Most everyone hates me. List of friends: Rebekah (D), Gwen (D), Betsy (S), Alisa (D). D= definite. S = sort of."

October 8, 1983

"Stepmother has been very depressed lately. Sometimes I worry about her."

January 12, 1984

Girl wrote "WILL" at the top of the page, and divided up her possessions between her friends. "Mom has bank book. Stepmother has silver coin. Avanga [cat] will go to Gretchen. Charlotte [hamster] to whomever."

She had been a depressed child, occasionally suicidal, raised by a depressed, rage-filled parent, but it hadn't been her fault. The whole time, Mother had insisted that everything was fine, that Girl and Brother were just difficult, intolerant children, but she knew there was more to it. Mother knew and never gave Girl absolution.

i'm just wild about harry

During February recess her junior year, Girl flew to Alaska to spend a week with Father. On the way back, she almost joined the Hare Krishnas. The man selling copies of the *Bhagavad Gita* in the Chicago O'Hare airport wore a navy blue beret over his shaved head. Girl didn't want to buy a book, but she was never good at turning away salespeople, so here she was, standing in the middle of the concourse talking to a stranger about religion. The man, who was not much older than Girl, took off his beret and long wavy hair from a patch at the back of his head fell down to his shoulder blades. Suddenly Girl was willing to leave the airport and attend his meeting. She always had a thing for long hair and shaved heads.

She had to check her flight first. She walked to her gate and saw that she had a two-hour delay, so she returned to the United terminal, but he was gone. Would she have really gone? She didn't know. At her core, she was responsible, but Girl was certainly looking for something to believe in, and she wanted more than anything to belong to something that felt like family.

But the long-haired, shaved-head man had vanished, so she had to make other plans. The two-hour delay was now a full-on cancellation. Girl waited in line for the gate attendant and rerouted her flight through Buffalo, the next-nearest airport to her parents' house. She was good at flying alone. The only problem was that she was unable to reach Mother.

That year, Stepmother had bought a cabin in the woods an hour outside of Rochester. For the first few months she went there alone, and not even Mother was allowed to visit. Soon, though, it became their hideaway, and Girl and Brother were not even given the phone number. Girl knew that her parents were at the cabin, and were planning on driving from there straight to the airport, and even though she called the phone number to the house in town, she only got the answering machine, and she couldn't leave a message when calling collect. She doubted they would check the weather and see the storm—she wasn't even sure that they had a television at the cabin.

Girl called her best friend's mother collect. Her best friend's brother refused to accept charges. One thing Girl knew from having one parent in Alaska and one in New York was that telephone operators have an unexpected degree of leeway. She pleaded with the operator and got her to reverse the charges to Mother's house even though there was no one there to approve the charges. Girl told her best friend's mother that she needed someone to keep calling Mother and tell her to pick Girl up in Buffalo, seventy miles away, instead of Rochester. All she could do was hope that her friend's mother could track Mother down. Girl could not wait to make contact before she boarded the next plane. She needed to go, and had to hope that someone would be there when she landed.

Mother and Stepmother greeted her at the gate in Buffalo, so proud that their daughter had figured everything out on her own. Girl didn't tell them about the Hare Krishnas, and secretly read the *Bhagavad Gita* in her room. The man had written his address in the back, and after she read it, she planned to write him. When she reached a section detailing celibacy and the rightful place of the man as head of the spiritual family, she closed the book and stopped dreaming of the man with the half-shaved head.

the day the word changed

They changed Stepmother's diagnosis from clinical depression to manic-depressive, and with the new word came new pills and new instructions. Do not leave her alone in stores, as she might go on a spending binge. (This doctor obviously did not know Stepmother, and how she practically wept every time she opened her wallet.) Stepmother was to avoid large crowds, as they might trigger an episode. There were new behaviors to be watchful for: compulsive spending, hypersexuality, lack of impulse control, all things that signaled a looming break with reality and descent into full psychosis. None of these behaviors had been a problem before; it was only the new word that made them possible. But it was Girl's sixteenth birthday the next week, and the invitations had been mailed to all eighty girls in her class. The party hall had been rented, the band had been hired.

"Girl, we may have to cancel the party," Mother said. "Stepmother has been diagnosed as bipolar—manic-depressive. She can't be around large crowds; it might trigger an episode."

"But we already invited everyone from school!" Girl said.

"This family's mental health comes first."

Girl's face stiffened like a mask, hard, uninhabited. Inside her rib cage was only cold, blowing wind. Not a hurricane or tornado, but the wind that whips away your body heat and pricks cold needles from the inside out. Girl stayed in the wind for three days, waiting to see if the "may have to" turned into a "we are going to." She didn't read books, she didn't talk to her friends. She waited inside her body-shell to see if this sweet sixteen party would be sacrificed for Stepmother.

It wasn't that Girl wanted presents. She didn't mean to be selfish. It was just that at Our Lady of Mercy, she had gone to her friends' parties. They were the kind of girls that parents fussed over. They didn't do their own laundry or take the bus downtown or try to hold their mother together. These girls didn't go to AA meetings at night or smoke cigarettes at the bus stop, and they certainly didn't spread their legs for boys who didn't love them. Girl wanted very much to be one of these girls—someone nurtured, protected, loved. So when Mother sat down with her one summer night and asked if she wanted a sweet sixteen party, Girl had exploded into fireworks inside. Mother had picked out light blue paper for the invitations. She ordered pizza and had the cake decorator spell her daughter's name the new way she preferred since she was fourteen—Girlh, with an added "h." Mother asked Girl if she wanted to hire one of her teenaged friend's bands to play, and of course she said yes.

A band and dancing and Girl was so excited that she even agreed to invite only her classmates, no boys, because that was how Mercy Girls did it. And maybe this party would make her acceptable to the girls at school and maybe she could learn to be sweet and protected and feel all the weight of her mother's love, and not just her fractional allocation. Job/spouse/daughter/son/volunteering/politics. Girl was only entitled to a mother-sliver, but this party meant she would get the whole share for just one day.

Mother decided to let the party go forward. She invited a few of her own friends as chaperones, but they were chaperoning Stepmother as much as the teenagers. Mother would keep Stepmother in the kitchen, where she would have friends and space and not too much chaos.

Girl pulled the top of her hair up into a tiny ponytail so you could see the shaved sides of her head. She put on her black-and-green-striped jumper over a black turtleneck. Her preppy clothes did not match her punk hair, but she wanted more than anything to be like the preppy-punk girls at Mercy—Sandy and Cyn and Sioux and the beautiful, tiny Joelle.

"Let's just put *regrets only* on the invitation," Mother had said. "That way we don't have to count everyone who is coming, just who is not coming, which is a smaller number."

Girl had only had gotten a handful of regret phone calls, and only a few girls at school had mentioned not coming, although several had said that they had thought the tri-fold 8 x 11 invitation had been junk mail and tossed it out. Girl figured there would still be around sixty people. She smoked cigarettes as she waited with Brother and her best friends, Rose-Marie and Becky, for the guests to arrive. The band placed two folding tables next to each other to create a stage and decorated it with stolen street signs, a stop sign, and one flashing yellow construction barrier.

One car pulled up and then another, then a few at once, and then they stopped coming. Only eight girls came. One-tenth of the invitations.

Mother was relieved, although she knew her daughter would be disappointed. Now Stepmother could come to the party. Now it wouldn't be teenagers running everywhere and screaming too loudly. She and Stepmother came out of the kitchen to serve the pizza and cake together. It was exactly what Mother needed. The whole family was all together in one room. Stepmother pulled Mother onto the dance floor and they did a little jitterbug. Girl never asked for a party again.

brother moves to alaska

Brother and Girl stood in the garage smoking cigarettes before he caught his flight to move to Alaska. The garage was their space where parents never ventured. When Mother and Stepmother accepted that smoking was a vocation the children were quite fond of, they dragged an old couch in there and found the children a radio. There was only one bare bulb for light and the one window hadn't been washed ever, so it was dim, brown-lit with the feeling that the ceiling was made of dust and cobwebs, even when the door was open. But yellow-brown light was warmer and more comforting than the clean white light of their house or school.

Girl was wearing her favorite earrings—wooden giraffes about an inch and a half long. She and Brother stood and smoked and tried not to talk about him leaving. Girl took off her right earring and held it in her closed hand so he wouldn't see it. Girl loved these little giraffes so much—could she break the set? Would it even matter to him? Brother went inside for a moment, and Girl carefully pried off the hook, so it was just a wood statue. When he came back outside, Girl pressed it into his hands.

Brother put the giraffe into the pocket of his black leather jacket. He didn't say anything, and Girl opened her mouth to stammer out an explanation of what she was trying to say with the giraffe. One look from him silenced her, though. Brother took off half of his slave bracelet—the chain had broken long ago between the yin-yang ring and the one on the silver wrist cuff, but he always wore them as if the chain still held them together. He kept the ring on his big finger but removed the wrist cuff and put it in her hands. Girl ran her thumb over the white and black stones and felt the crack in one of them with her thumbnail, then put it on her own wrist as their parents called the children to get in the car.

Sixteen was a bad year for Girl. Her brother was gone and Stepmother was on mental-health disability, so she was home every day after school while Mother was at work. Girl was going to visit Brother and Father in Alaska for a week. Her father had a new wife, #Six, and Girl liked her. She had even told #Six about the weird sex abuse stuff with her father.

There was that time in the bathtub with Dad that got a little weird, when he asked Girl, "Where's the penis?" And maybe let her poke it. Maybe not. She wasn't clear on what exactly happened, just that she felt squirmy inside and dirty and bad when she thought about that day. She did remember clearly the time Father and #Four had sex while the children giggled and peeked, and how he invited them into bed for a family snuggle afterward. There were all the dirty jokes he told Girl in grade school and the way he didn't make the joke about "a blond" but instead about Girl or her sister Juli, and how she felt soiled by his laughter. There was the way he sat on her bed when she lived with him in high school and made small talk while she got dressed for school without averting his gaze, or the fact that he walked around completely naked, and that Girl knew all of his mistresses by name. There were the limericks and songs he taught Girl and Brother, the naked mermaid on his cribbage board, and the mug shaped like a breast with a drinking hole in the nipple. The photograph he took of Brother on the toilet that made Brother cry. But Father never *touched* Girl.

"Covert sexual abuse," Girl's counselor informed her: an inappropriately sexual relationship between parent and child. Lack of appropriate boundaries. She told Girl that it didn't have to be worse than that. That alone counted as abuse, even if he never touched her. Girl wanted to believe her, but she wasn't sure she could.

In tenth grade Girl told her biology teacher in high school that her father raped her, knowing it was a lie. She hadn't meant to say it; it just came out when the teacher kept her after class for not turning in an assignment. Girl was crying. She didn't know why she said it. She knew it wasn't true, and she knew she was betraying every girl that had been raped, but she didn't know how to take the words back. She didn't know how to say that there was something fucked up and wrong about her father that scared her and made her feel dirty, but she didn't know what it was. She knew a lot of other girls had it worse than she did. Girl didn't have any right to complain, and all she knew was her father was coming to visit and she did not want to see him.

She told all of this to #Six: not the lying part, but the weird feelings and the jokes and the watching her dress in the morning. Of course, Brother and

Juli knew all about Father's over-sexual nature—they were the only ones who really knew. Girl was supposed to visit Father and Brother in Alaska, and the night before she was supposed to leave her father and Brother called her, both of them on the phone at the same time.

"I hear you're telling people I sexually abused you," Father said. Girl could hear Brother breathing on the phone extension. "You are a little liar! You know I never touched you. This is the worst possible thing you could ever say."

"Dad, all those jokes? And the watching me, and—"

He cut her off. "It's all in your head. I never abused you and you know it."

Girl lost her words. She breathed like she was crying, all fast and jerky and her throat was closed, but she was too angry for the tears to fall.

"I will not be the one who stands in judgment for this," Girl said at last.

"Maybe you will," Brother replied.

She hung up on both of them. She did not board the plane the next day, and she refused to send back her ticket for a refund, even when Mother asked her to.

"Girl, it's a thousand dollars. I understand how you feel, honey, but it's a lot of money," Mother said. Girl turned her back on Mother and faced the wall. Mother asked again a few weeks later, but Girl still would not give back the ticket.

bunny costume

Girl was sixteen and trying to grow out her mullet. Mom and Girl had redecorated Brother's old bedroom for her, and Mother let Girl pick out everything herself. Girl fell in love with a deep emerald green plush carpet at the remnant store. They painted her walls a clean, crisp white, and found a wallpaper border with pigs and cows and farm houses not because Girl loved farms (although she kind of loved the idea of them) but because it had that rich emerald green Girl loved so much that year. Mother bought her the white eyelet puffy comforter Girl had wanted ever since she was a little girl dreaming princess dreams and looking at J. C. Penney catalogs. Mother also bought her two throw pillows, a dusty rose one that matched the pigs in the wallpaper and a ruffled lace one that was scratchy to sleep on but pretty when Girl made her bed, which wasn't often.

Girl was sixteen and it was Halloween, and for once Girl had a boyfriend and a costume party to go to, just like she had always dreamed that she would. She was a reformed bad girl now. She wanted to be sexy and cool above all else, but still a good girl. She wanted to be pretty and sweet. Girl had stopped having sex with boys that didn't love her. She had found religion—Girl started reading the Bible in an effort to argue more effectively with the born-again Christian kids she had been hanging out with. One night she had a sore throat, and she defiantly prayed, "God, if you exist, make my sore throat disappear by morning." She figured that was probably asking too much, so she amended her request: "or at least by the day after tomorrow." The next day her sore throat was gone, and suddenly she became a believer. She prayed on her knees every night and every morning, and she prayed out loud with friends and they all held hands. Girl got nervous when it was her turn, because Rose-Marie started with "Jesus," and her boyfriend Jacob started with "Lord," but it sounded kind of like "Lerd" when he said it, and Girl knew he thought you should only pray to God and not to Jesus and she hadn't been raised Christian so she didn't have a history of words to fall back on. "God," Girl said in her little scared voice and hoped someone kind and forgiving was listening, because she was new to this good-girl stuff but she wanted it so damn badly.

Girl's family kept things they didn't have a place for on the floors of closets. In the living room closet, far back in the dark left corner, was Step-mother's old Easter Bunny costume. It was made out of terry cloth, like a towel with all the loops of thread. Brother had worn it when he went as roadkill last Halloween, covered in dirt and fake blood. He was so tall the costume's feet dangled around his knees and added to the carcass effect. But Brother was in Alaska with Dad now, and it was her turn to claim it. Girl was surprised that someone had washed it and that the terrycloth came out white and clean and fluffy.

Girl wrapped it around her arm in a bundle and brought it to her room. What could she do with it? Girl pulled it over her clothes, zipped it up, and buttoned the hood over her hair. The ears flopped down on the sides—for some reason the ears had never been wired, but you could tell it was a bunny, at least for sure you could tell from the back where it had a white yarn pom-pom tail. The bunny suit was big enough for one and a half of her—the shoe covers reached her feet and the elastic wrist cuffs landed at her wrists, in spite of her too-long, gangly arms.

Girl rummaged through her underwear drawer and found the black strapless bra she had bought to go under a prom dress freshman year. It was see-through lace and came down to her belly button, because the bra lady at the store said her boobs were too big for a regular strapless bra. Girl stretched the sides around the terrycloth suit, and the eye hooks actually met in the back on the largest setting. Girl remembered that she used to have a pair of silver lamé bikini underwear that had ripped up the back, but she thought she had kept them anyway. Girl opened her white wooden dresser that her mom had bought when she was pregnant with Girl and had glued wallpaper cutouts on—a giraffe on one side and other animals on the other, back when she was dreaming of Girl and carrying her in her belly. They had taken the animals off when Girl hit puberty, but she missed them a little, even though she was sixteen. Girl found the black-and-silver pair wadded up under all her everyday panties. The back was black mesh, and there was a slit as Girl had remembered. Girl always felt they weren't as sexy as she thought they should be—too garish—but the bunny tail fit through the rip with only a little stretching. Girl looked in the full-length mirror on the back of the door. She was marvelous. A Playboy Bunny. Anti-sexy but funny and playful, everything she wanted to be.

Girl wondered if they had a tray, and if her parents would let her use it. They had a bag of disposable champagne glasses in the kitchen left over from New Year's Eve. Maybe Girl could glue them to the tray? Like a cocktail waitress. Wasn't that what Playboy Bunnies did at the Playboy Mansion? Serve drinks and wear ears and bunny tails? Girl and her friends were sober—would her friends think Girl was glorifying alcohol? But if she didn't carry a tray, would they get that Girl was a Playboy Bunny? She went downstairs to look.

Stepmother was sitting at the dining room table, rubbing her eyebrows off as she always did. She had had half-brows for as long as Girl could remember—from the top of the arch to the outside corner of her eye was only stubble. Sometimes she wore Band-Aids over the bare half to keep herself from rubbing. Girl wasn't sure which looked worse.

"Look, Stepmother! I'm a Playboy Bunny!" Girl felt like such a fabulous tongue-in-cheek creation. It was the best costume she had ever had. It was equal to Brother's roadkill costume last year. And the only skin Girl showed was on her face and her hands—she wished she had black satin gloves. Girl used to have a pair of black gloves that were her grandmother's, but they were too tight to fit over the terry cloth sleeves. Maybe Girl could find something else in the closet.

"Girl, that is awful!" Stepmother looked at her as if Girl was a skin full of shamefulness. Like a prostitute. A stripper. A real Playboy Bunny. Her eyes were staring at Girl's silver panties like she had X-ray vision. Like they could burn through the lamé, the terry cloth, even her jeans underneath. She raised her little fist (her hands and feet were so small compared to the mountainous rest of her) and pointed her stubby finger at Girl's crotch. "Look at your shiny pussy! Judy, you can't let her wear this!" Stepmother could not stop looking at her shiny pussy. Girl hated the word pussy. She and Brother were not allowed to say pussy. Mother and Stepmother always said it was derogatory, disrespectful, that what Girl had between her legs was a vulva, a vagina. Girl could never ever say or even think the word pussy, so why did Girl now have a pussy full of shame that was drawing her stepmother's eyes like a tractor beam?

Girl ran upstairs and ripped off the costume and left it on the floor in a heap, launching herself onto that white eyelet comforter she had been so stupidly proud of, stupid little girl. Girl cried into her pillow, cried black mascara rings onto the white lace and she didn't care, she sobbed loudly, pushing the snot and mucus and shame out of her mouth into her pillow. She wasn't a dirty girl anymore, she wasn't a dirty girl, and Stepmother wouldn't stop looking at her pussy and Girl hated the word pussy and she wasn't trying to be bad.

Mother came upstairs. "I told her not to say 'pussy,'" she said. "You can wear the costume. I told her it was ironic and funny and that you weren't being too sexy." Mother stroked the back of her head. She didn't say anything about Stepmother's laser beam eyes stuck on her pussy, or how dirty her words made Girl feel. It was about vocabulary, then, not eyes like fingers running over her teenaged flesh. Girl couldn't even bear to look at the rabbit suit. She wanted to burn it. Girl never put it on again. Mother couldn't understand that words from a lesbian stepmother felt more like words from a man than words from a woman. Stepmother's whole demeanor had changed since she started lithium, but Girl was the only one who saw it.

you should masturbate

Now seventeen, Girl stood at her bedroom window smoking a cigarette, too lazy to go outside to smoke. From here she could see over the tops of the maple trees to the streetlight at the corner, and if she remembered not to daydream, she could see Stepmother's car before it turned down the lane. Girl dared herself not to flinch as the car crept closer. How long could she continue to smoke this time? Dread tightened her stomach the moment Stepmother's car turned toward their house, four blocks away. Two blocks. One block. She dropped her cigarette to the patio stones below and fled far into a book, so Stepmother wouldn't speak to her if she was lucky. Girl wished she could play chicken longer without flinching. She wished Stepmother worked full-time again, so she wasn't home so often.

9:10 a.m. and Girl was late for school. The damn snooze button was heroin, pulling her under again and again. Of course she had been up too late talking on the phone after her parents were asleep. She'd buy back an hour of that conversation and trade it for sleep if she could, but it was too late now.

"Girl! You're late again!" Stepmother said, walking into Girl's room without knocking. "You were on the phone after we told you to go to bed, weren't you?"

"I was talking to Jacob. We're having problems," Girl said.

"You are always having problems. I don't know why you need a boyfriend. You need to focus on school. If you dated girls you wouldn't have these problems."

For years, Girl had been terrified that she would turn into a lesbian in her sleep and wake up to a life of lies and hiding and would be ostracized forever. Stepmother had known she was a lesbian since she was twelve. Mother always said that she was a "political lesbian" and it wasn't until she got heavy into feminism that she became a lesbian. Girl thought being a lesbian was just about the worst thing that could happen to you, and she was strongly anti-feminist, just in case. Her boyfriend's father, just like every guy she ever met, had asked her gruffly, "Do you ever think you're a lesbian?" when he heard about her parents. No, she was not a lesbian, and no, if she was, it would not magically solve all her problems. She had enough girl drama with her best friend to know females were not any easier to get along with.

Stepmother walked out and Girl dressed quickly, rummaging through the discarded clothes on the floor. Girl had clothing crises almost every morning that required several outfit changes, but she never hung things back up, instead throwing them in piles of clean, dirty, and semi-clean laundry. Jeans and T-shirts went on easy that morning without ironing. Girl hated wrinkles so much she'd iron Brother's clothes for him, back when he lived at home. He was gone now, had moved to Alaska to live with their father.

Stepmother walked back in, one hand behind her back and an odd look in her eyes. She looked calculating, sinister, slightly unbalanced. She was grinning but it wasn't a happy look. It was a look that made Girl's hair stand up on her arms and her leg muscles yearn to run. It was a look she was intimately familiar with since Stepmother started taking lithium.

"If you masturbated, you wouldn't need a boyfriend," Stepmother said. "I understand that you want sex, but you can do it yourself. I don't know why your mother won't talk to you about this, but someone has to."

Stepmother brought her hands forward to show Girl a plastic torpedo the color of old teeth. Girl knew exactly what it was, and although catalogs listed it as a *six-inch facial massager, ivory color,* she knew better. Her brother had found their parents' vibrator years ago in the nightstand table on Stepmother's side of the bed and had showed it to his sister, but Girl wasn't going to tell Stepmother that she had seen it before.

"Have you ever used a vibrator? Your mother likes it quite a lot. You could borrow it sometimes," Stepmother said.

I have to get out of here, Girl's brain screamed, but Stepmother was blocking the door. There was no escape.

"Just give me your hand. I'm not going to use it on you, I just want you to see how it feels."

"No!" Girl pushed past Stepmother and ran for the stairs.

"I just want to show you how it works! You are being ridiculous!"

"You are not touching me with that thing! It was in Mom's vagina!" Girl thundered down the stairs, one hand on the bannister and the other on the wall for balance so she wouldn't fall. Stepmother caught up to Girl in the living room, the vibrator still clenched in her small, hairless fist.

"Stop acting like a child. I was just going to use it on your hand so you could see how it feels. I am a woman, there is nothing inappropriate about this. You are too sensitive. Don't you push your issues with your father onto me," Stepmother said. "I am nothing like your father. I have never, ever, done or said anything inappropriate. That's your issue with your father. I am a woman, not a man."

Girl shoved her bare feet into cotton boat shoes and grabbed her purse as she ran out the door, slamming it behind her.

Stepmother opened the door too quickly, banging it into the wall, her voice catching Girl before she reached the sidewalk. "There is nothing inappropriate about this! You are being silly!" Stepmother repeated, but Girl didn't look back. School suddenly didn't seem so bad now, even though she had left her book bag and hadn't made a lunch. She ran the first block, then slowed to a walk and lit a cigarette. *I cannot wait to leave this place,* she thought, too angry to cry. The cigarette distilled her shame into resolve. *I will tell no one about this, ever,* she promised herself, but of course she told her friends when she got to school. It was proof that Stepmother was crazy—one more story to sum up why Girl needed to leave home.

Girl suspected that her mother would never believe her, or if she did, she'd say Girl was overreacting. Everyone always said that Girl was always overreacting. Girl knew that a lot of her friends had it a lot worse than she did. She knew what had happened wasn't the same as being molested or raped. It made her sick and made her want to curl up and not let anyone touch her, hissing like a barnacle closing its shell when Stepmother walked by, but it wasn't like Girl had been touched. *I am just being too sensitive,* Girl told herself, trying to believe it. She didn't know how not to be too sensitive. But Girl felt that Stepmother's vibe was off—nothing she could prove—but Girl had enough unsubstantiated vibes to fill a warehouse. Now, though, she had a story she could hold in her hands, she could turn it around in the light in front of her friends. She could give herself permission to leave.

gitsis

Brother came back from Alaska with a GED and a fiancée. Brother used to have a black Mohawk past his shoulders, but his new girlfriend had encouraged him to cut it short and get a job. Girl thought he looked like a geeky Q-tip, his frizzy hair a cloud around the top of his head. She liked him better with it long, but Girl's opinion no longer mattered—she had been replaced by this fiancée and she was jealous as hell. Everything about the siblings now was oil and water, but they still kept trying to go back to how things used to be, before he moved away, before she found religion, before Stepmother became bipolar. Too much had changed.

Brother was sitting in a booth at Gitsis, his favorite diner. The place was a dive—brown, rectangular floor tiles laid in a herringbone pattern that were probably very cool in the 1970s, but now looked perpetually dirty. They served soda in dimpled, brown plastic cups; crinkle-cut fries on thick, ceramic plates; and coffee in beige mugs with one brown line drawn around the edge. Gitsis was two blocks from the High School of the Arts, where Brother used to go, and it was still his favorite hangout. He and his friends sat for hours drinking coffee, sketching in notepads, and talking about *Rocky Horror Picture Show*, music, girls, parents . . . all the usual teen discussions.

Girl had gone to Gitsis once with her uncle, and the waitress remembered him from his high school days, twenty years before. "What happened to your friend?" she asked. "The one who always ate french fries with gravy."

Gitsis never changed. Twenty-four-seven breakfast and white hotdogs and hangover food. Girl hated it, but since Brother had moved into an apartment with his girlfriend, if she wanted to see him, she had to come here. She walked over to the table in her tight jeans and baggy sweatshirt, standing awkwardly next to the booth. There wasn't room for her to sit. Brother reached up under her sweatshirt and grabbed her breast.

"What the hell?" Girl jumped back.

"I was trying to tickle you," he said. "Calm the fuck down. I was trying to tickle you and I missed."

Girl crossed her arms over her chest, willing her flesh to turn into armor. Her brother had grabbed her boob. Brother looked at her with unreadable eyes, his face tightened in his own anger. "Calm the fuck down. It was a mistake." Girl ran out of the diner, her face a dry, closed-off mask. She didn't believe in mistakes.

notes from the fourth wall
raised by wolves

"You say 'I was raised by lesbians' like you were raised by wolves," a friend commented.

"Well, that's kind of how I mean it," I answered. I always identified with Mowgli from *The Jungle Book*.

We were our own pack, a subset of the larger world in which we lived. I wasn't one of the wolves—I wasn't gay—but because I belonged to them, I didn't fit in with the rest of the society I lived in, either. I grew up straight in a gay world. I didn't fit anywhere. As an adolescent, this not-quite-fitting only manifested in the straight world. The pictures on my living room walls didn't look like my friends' family portraits. There were so many questions I was asked and I had so few answers to give. But the gay community was home. I didn't have any real extended family, and so our holidays were peopled with lesbian couples who always asked me normal questions, like what did I want to be when I grew up and how was school and did I like cats better than dogs. It was only in our group of same-sex couples that I was seen just as me, not as The Girl with the Lesbian Parents.

But once I was out of my parents' house, I no longer fit in with the gay world. If I went to a lesbian bar with friends, I was treated like an imposter. Of course I would quickly explain that my parents were gay, and then their defensiveness melted off their faces, and I was almost one of the club. Almost. My experience was slightly different, and I didn't fit in their circle anymore. Like Mowgli, I had to go find my place among my own kind. Even though I had mimicked the straight kids for most of my life, I still felt like an interloper. I spent a very long time trying to be just like everyone else, until everything that was beautiful or interesting about me had blended away to beige. I had to own my quirkiness and that of my family before I could ever find my place in the world.

But homosexuality wasn't the only differentiating feature of my wolf pack. For this metaphor to work, the wolves have to have fangs, otherwise I might just as easily say that I was raised by manatees or goats or any other herbivore. "Raised by wolves" implies teeth crunching bones and snarling at one another as they fight over the dying carcass of some unfortunate dinner item. Slightly different from a herd of goats. Like a wolf pack, we had no personal space, no boundaries or modesty. We might as well have slept in a pile at the back of a cave, scratching at each other's fleas.

Have you read about wolves marking their territory with urine? In our house it was with excrement. If my brother was pooping and Stepmother had to go, she made him get off the toilet and finish in the basement, where there was an old toilet with a pink seat. A yellow-stained shower curtain afforded a modicum of privacy, and a bare bulb hung down from the ceiling. Stepmother would never go down there herself to relieve her bowels. It wasn't her fault that my brother took so long in the bathroom.

I think most people take modesty for granted as a basic human right. There's something hard to describe about having parents that don't conform to the normal rules like wearing clothes, and who tell dirty jokes to children or discuss their sex life in intimate detail with them. Couple that with a stepmother who yelled at gas station attendants when she thought the prices are too high—"I don't appreciate your price gouging!"—and once stood up in the middle of a movie and yelled at the screen, "This sucks! It's not fair that he died! He was supposed to live!" I was permanently off-balance. I didn't know how I was supposed to act, so I watched other people. I mimicked proper behavior, like I was learning a foreign culture. I felt like a method actor, trying to pass as a normal kid. But having fuzzy boundaries gave me an unstable base, and that meant that I was always on the defensive. Like the lowest wolf in the pack, it seemed like everyone was a potential threat, except my mother. Did I snap and snarl unnecessarily at my brother that day in Gitsis? Was I too reactionary, defensive? It seems so in retrospect. No other boundary incursion occurred after that—accidental or otherwise. He returned to being the one person I was safe with in my family of origin.

It is hard to be thirteen, or sixteen. It's hard when there are no rules and you have to make them up on your own. It is hard when you aren't allowed to say that you don't want your parents to see you naked anymore. I was primed to take offense. What I did know was that I didn't have words to explain how a glance from my lesbian stepmother felt like a man's gaze. I wasn't allowed to suggest that even though my father was a doctor, I did not want to change clothes in front of him. Modesty was not an option either in my mother's house in New York nor my father's house in Alaska. Eyes like fingers traveled across my teenaged skin. Constant micro-aggressions kept my nerve endings on high alert. I hyperventilated often, and told people I had asthma, even though my doctor told me it was all in my head.

I did what any sensible kid would do—okay, maybe not what even most sensible kids would do—but I found community with the born-again Christians. The women at church made very clear rules. I was forgiven for my misdeeds and given a blueprint for staying on the right side of appropriate. I was adopted by a new pack, and had a new alpha, but it's hard to shake off your family of origin. Sure, I could go to the Christian Youth Organization meetings and sing songs about Jesus and try to pretend I didn't feel dorky, but when they told me that I was sinning by wearing stretch pants to school, I never went back. There was no way I was buying that I was responsible for causing impure thoughts in men. I had too much feminist ingrained in me for that. It seemed belonging to a group was overrated. All I ever wanted was to form a family of my own.

Once I was married and had my own children, I was finally just like everyone else. Then, the differentness of my family was one generation removed. Oh, I still played the pronoun game when talking to strangers. My stepmother's androgynous name, Pat, made it simple to mislead people, and I did it easily and with a light touch. But I only did it when I didn't trust someone. Most of the time, I mentioned my parents' sexuality casually as it came up in conversation, and if acquaintances expressed shock, their discomfort sparked my derision instead of shame. It told me that these new people would never be part of my tribe, and I no longer cared about fitting in with theirs.

It was only complicated when I visited any of my parents. Both of my ex-husbands have seen my stepmother and my father naked on multiple occasions, and as much as my ex-spouses begged me to make my parents wear pants, I had no control over either of them. Stepmother swam in the pond in a white T-shirt and white underpants with a hole showing her crack when my first ex-husband and I visited, and she often gardened in her underwear, even in the front yard. "It looks like a bathing suit!" she said. No one agreed with her. When my father came to visit, he was a fan of giving goodnight hugs in a T-shirt that ended at his navel, his full, blue-headed genitalia swinging in the wind. Neither of my husbands appreciated the "let it all hang out" philosophy.

In my house, children are allowed to remain innocent. I do not watch my ten-year-old change clothes and he is allowed to take as long as he needs in the bathroom. I do not let my youngest child do naked bottom dances in front of his older brother, because it embarrasses him. When my eldest went on an overnight school trip, I allowed him to bring a bathing suit to wear in the shower, as he requested. I teach my boys that no one has a right to look at them without clothing if they don't want them to. I let my boys wear dresses or camouflage pants or superhero costumes or whatever outfit matches the identity they want to try on that day. I let them visit all of their grandparents, but I don't let them spend the night with any of them. They are my wolf pups, and I protect them.

the fight

When Girl was seventeen and in her senior year of high school, she attended an award ceremony with Stepmother because Mother had a work conflict. It was a black-tie dinner, and Girl loved getting dressed up—she had gone to proms with everyone she could wrangle into inviting her, including Brother, when he broke up with his girlfriend the week before his junior prom. Stepmother got a lot of awards, like she did every year, and they piled up on the round table: Disability Insurance Sales Leader for the local office, the state, and the region; Million Dollar Round Table; and an invitation to the annual leader's conference for the top two hundred salespeople in the country.

Stepmother handed Girl one of her prizes, a Steuben glass cube engraved with American flags. "These suckers are worth a couple hundred dollars," she told Girl quietly. "Even though this one is ugly. I like the birds best. They'll be yours someday—you can sell 'em and make a few bucks." Girl was proud of Stepmother, and liked how the other insurance agents came up to Girl to comment on what a good job Stepmother did. "She's a firecracker!" one man said. "A pistol!" said another. Everyone treated Girl like a real grown-up, even though her white dress with the blue skirt and big off-center bow was a little more "prom" than "cocktail."

For once, she was able to let go of the resentment that was as much a part of her as her hair color or her glasses. Bitterness was hard for her to release, but this time, without Brother or Mother or anyone else around, Girl softened toward Stepmother. It had to do with the way Stepmother treated her with respect, the way her eyes shone with pride when she introduced Girl to her coworkers. And it had something to do with watching Stepmother graciously receive her praise, seeing her as a success, instead of an instigator of turmoil.

When they got home, Girl decided to confide in Stepmother. She didn't do this very often—Mother was her chosen confidant—but some things were too hard to tell her mother. Like when she went on the pill freshman year, it had been Stepmother she told first.

"Brother has been making me uncomfortable lately," Girl told her.

"What happened, honey? You can talk to me. It's okay," Stepmother said. They were both changing out of their fancy clothes. Girl was hanging her dress up in her closet, Stepmother was in the doorway. Their bedrooms were across the hall from each other.

"Well, the other day, when we were at the coffee shop, he reached up under my shirt and grabbed my breast."

"Why did he do that?" Stepmother was enraged, as Girl had counted on.

"He said he was trying to tickle me," Girl answered. He had been furious when Girl yelled at him. *You're being too sensitive*, he said, he *hadn't meant it at all*, he said, and *it was an accident. Girl was always too sensitive. Accidents happen.* She didn't know how to think about it yet.

"I always worried that he inherited some of your father's perversion," Stepmother said. She was always saying that Brother was just like their father, and she didn't mean that he was headed for a career in medicine. She thought Father was mentally unbalanced, sinisterly perverted, and a pathological liar.

"But, Girl, I always wondered if you two were too close. It's really your fault that he crosses the line, because you always let him see you in the shower."

Girl sank to the carpet and covered her ears with her hands. It was not her fault. Their house only had one bathroom, and every morning everyone in the family was in and out of it. If Girl was in the shower, Brother was on the pot and Mother was blow drying her hair at the sink. It was the only way everyone got out of the house on time. Their parents took the children to nude beaches. Mother and Stepmother raised the children not to be modest—hell, they weren't allowed to be modest. Everyone in the family walked around naked, it wasn't like Girl was parading nude to entice Brother like some sibling cock tease. How was Girl supposed to create boundaries where none existed?

"Girl, I'm just saying that it wasn't normal how you let him see you naked, or in a towel. What did you expect?"

Girl screamed to blot out her words. *It's not my fault. It's not my fault. It's not my fault.* She was balled up, her knees pulled close to her chest, her back against the closet door.

"Stop screaming! You're hysterical!" Girl wouldn't stop. Girl needed to drown out her stepmother's voice. Stepmother slapped her across the face, once, twice, four times. Girl kept screaming.

"Listen, you are crazy," Stepmother said in quiet, tightly controlled words. "I am going to call the ambulance and have them take you away in a straitjacket! They will lock you up!" Her face was red and her eyes cold and filled with fury.

Girl stopped screaming abruptly, terrified of the men with straitjackets. She was just a kid. No one would ever believe her that she wasn't crazy, wasn't hysterical, but was just trying to drown out the voice that said *it was all her fault*.

Stepmother left the room and Girl called her boyfriend. Mother still wasn't home. "Come and get me," Girl told Jacob. "I need to get out of here. She hit me." Girl hung up before Stepmother could hear her. Girl always swore that if Stepmother hit her again, she would leave and never come back. It was a relief that it had finally happened. Girl wrote a note to her mother on a napkin: "Stepmother hit me. I am moving out. I will be staying with friends." Girl always promised Mother that she wouldn't run away without telling mother first where she was headed so Mother wouldn't worry.

"You know, after you calm down, if you want to talk to me you can," Stepmother said through Girl's bedroom door. "You can even wake me up in the middle of the night if you need to."

"I'm on the phone," was all Girl said in reply.

When Jacob pulled up outside in his diarrhea-brown hatchback, Girl yelled, "I'm taking the dog out!" She left the napkin-note on the stove for her mother and ran out the door. She put the dog in the fenced-in backyard, confident that Mother would hear him bark and let him back in.

notes from the fourth wall
stepmother's side of the story

"**D**o you know the one thing I am most ashamed of?" my stepmother asked me years later. "The fight when you ran away from home."

"Yeah. I'm not sure it's going into the book," I said.

"You must write it," she told me. "If the story is to be accurate, you must write it. But here's how I remembered it: you and I went to the awards ceremony. You confided in me and we were having a nice conversation, and then you started screaming for no reason, so I slapped you because I thought you were hysterical. I had been told that when someone is hysterical you have to slap them across the face. All I could think was that the neighbors would hear you screaming and think I was abusing you and call the police. I was so afraid of losing you. We were lesbians, and if they thought I was abusing you the police could take you away and I'd never see you again. I'm so sorry for that. Really."

I made some sort of there-there noises. "It's okay," I said. It wasn't, but there weren't any words that would make it so. Throw a plate on the floor and look at the broken pieces. Tell the plate you are sorry. The plate is still broken.

"But you know, I always thought maybe you really left just to spite me. We had told you that once you turned eighteen you would be out of the house for good—either in college or working full-time. So I always thought you left first just to defy me."

"That really had nothing to do with it," I answered.

"Well, I just wanted you to know why I did what I did," she said.

We hugged awkwardly. I always hugged her sternum to sternum, with my butt sticking out so she couldn't pat it. I hated when she patted my bottom.

scraps of paper

After Girl left home—running away sounded more dramatic than she thought was justified—she stayed a week or two with one friend, then another week with a different one, always moving on before she wore out her welcome. A teacher let Girl stay in her guest bedroom for a month, until she needed the spare bed when her own mother came to town. Girl was at Sandy's house when the ice storm hit.

"Wake up, girls," Sandy's mom said. "There's been an ice storm. There's no school, and we lost power. We're going to your grandmother's, Sandy. Girl, you are going to have to call someone for a ride. The radio said over 750,000 people lost power, and no one knows how long it will take to get it back on."

Girl and Sandy looked out the frost-covered window, rubbing the pinky sides of their fists on the window to clear it. Outside was surreally beautiful. Icicles hung from every tree branch so heavily they bowed in curving arcs to the ground. Bushes were encased in ice, each twig wearing a thick coating. Whole trees had fallen over, their roots sticking out of the ground like large wheels. A black power line hung across the road. Everything was still, super quiet without traffic noises—there was a state of emergency, and roads were closed. Girl had never noticed how noisy houses were, with fans, furnaces—the electronic buzz of radios and televisions—until suddenly all the noises stopped.

Girl packed up her clothes into blue, plastic grocery bags, and Jacob came and got her. He had arranged for her to spend the day with his adult sister and her baby, because although she didn't have power either, she had a gas stove. Girl knew the sister—every Friday Jacob's older siblings and their children came to their father's for dinner, and most of the time Girl was invited, too. They all crossed themselves and recited a prayer in unison that Girl didn't know and wished she did, so she just bowed her head and looked at the red plush dining room carpeting. She was shy around them, but they were always nice, and when Jean's daughter took her first steps, it was to Girl's outstretched arms, not her mother's or grandfather's.

School was closed for a week, then two, and finally three whole weeks, but Girl wished it were in session—it would have made it easier for her to find a place to stay if people had power, and given her somewhere to go during the day at least. Jacob didn't have power either, but his father let her stay in one of his empty bedrooms: he had five children, and only two were still at home. They had a gas stove and a gas heater in the family room. The bedrooms got down to fifty degrees, but with extra blankets it wasn't that big of a deal.

Girl constantly looked through the "roommates wanted" section of the newspaper, calling every place that seemed likely. No one wanted to rent to a high school kid, even though she assured them that she had child support from her father and could make rent. Finally, Mother's best friend Marty found a coworker that agreed to take her in, but not until after the ice storm.

"I'd let her stay here," Jacob's father had told him, and that was what Girl had been hoping for, "but I don't want you to feel obligated to stay together. If she's living here and you want to break up, you won't be able to." Sigh. While Girl understood the Catholic man's position, it would have been so much simpler to be living with her boyfriend and his family. Then engaged, and then married. Fast-track to a new family. But he had said no, so she waited for the ice storm to end so that she could move in with this stranger named Ravina.

Every night, Girl wrote diary entries on little scraps of paper, then tucked them inside her student planner. She wrote practical things, like lists of people she could stay with—ranked by feasibility—and entries filled with self-doubt, like on the night she left:

"It's hard to believe I'm a runaway. I think that sounds so serious, but I guess that's what I am, technically. I wonder if I'm just making something out of nothing. Am I overreacting? I always thought runaways were either awful or came from awful families. I wonder if I'm all wrong. I am scared that they're right. Tomorrow things will be clearer. I need my toothbrush." And, on another day, *"I don't wanna ever go back. Maybe I'm sick, but I'm enjoying this. Well, maybe not enjoying, per se, but I'm comfortable within myself. I am still sort of scared that this is wrong and that I'm overreacting. I know that there are a lot of worse cases. I don't know anymore. Now I just almost hate Stepmother–especially for afterward saying that I could wake her up if I needed to.*

1. I am not crazy.

2. If I had stayed there Saturday I would have gone crazy.

I sort of feel lost and scared. I feel as though there is no going back. I miss my mother holding me but I can't be a part of her sickness."

Mostly, though, when she was all alone in the night, she wrote about how terribly she missed her mother. Some nights she cried. She tucked her diary scraps of paper into her calendar and didn't show them to anyone. It was the only time in her life that she kept a daily diary, and she wasn't sure why she did it.

She remembered once when she was so sad that she thought she would break apart, back in junior year. She just cried all the time and Stepmother thought it was hormones and she said with a voice full of fear, "Judy, I think Girl's depressed!" And Girl only cried harder because she did not want to be defective, she didn't want to be like Stepmother. And she remembered how Stepmother and Mother took her out of school for a few days and they all went down to the little cabin in the woods with a round, wooden bathtub that was too big for the hot water heater and Mother heated water on the stove so Girl could have a bath in that big, glorious bathtub. And she remembered the way Mother looked with her closed-lip smile, her eyes crinkling behind her glasses that looked just like Girl's, and how she used to sit on her mother's lap and push and pull on her mother's lips—it was a game Mother used to play with her own mother. The goal was to make the lips line up right, except Mother would always exaggerate her movements so it was impossible, and Girl would get scared that Mother's face would never go back to normal ever again. Mostly she remembered the feel of her mother around her, holding her when she cried, like sinking into a warm bowl of pudding, soft and safe and where the hole in Girl's chest was finally filled up.

When Girl first left home, she had called the Center for Youth Services, an outreach program for runaway teens. They had free family counseling, but after the first session, her mother showed up alone.

"Stepmother cannot—and I mean cannot—keep reopening old wounds. She was up crying all night. She is bipolar, and it is too hard on her," Mother told the counselor and Girl.

"She hit me in the face, Mother," Girl said.

"I choose to believe that you are lying," Mother replied. "And if I have to choose one of you, I choose her. You will be going off to college and starting your own life next year. If I chose you I'd be alone."

"If you left her I would stay with you forever," Girl said, wanting that more than anything. *Choose to believe*, Girl repeated in her head, wondering if

Mother meant that as intentionally as it sounded. She didn't say *I think* or even *I believe Stepmother.* Was she really actively choosing to believe?

"You think that, but you are growing up. Stepmother will never leave me. I have to think of my own life."

That was the end of counseling. What was interesting, though, was that Stepmother never accused Girl of lying. She never said the slapping hadn't happened, only that she was justified in her actions. Mother was the one who decided to relegate the story to something all in Girl's head. And Mother never asked Girl to come back home.

Next Girl had to check an equally hard item off her to-do list: get child support from Father. This wasn't as easy as it sounded. Father wouldn't object to the money, Girl knew that. He sent Mother two hundred dollars a month, and he had to send it to wherever Girl lived. When she had lived with Suzy, he sent Suzy's mom a check without even being asked. The problem was that she had not spoken to him in a year, and she'd have to sell herself out to get that check. Worse yet, because she was staying with friends, she'd have to call him collect.

"Hi, Dad," she started, her heart racing, her hands clammy on the white phone.

"Girl," he answered.

"I wanted to say that I'm sorry I lied about you sexually abusing me." Girl figured her heart might explode if she didn't get right to the point.

"That makes me happy to hear. It was the worst possible thing you ever could have said about me," he replied. Girl fought back rage—now wasn't the time to discuss the meaning of the term *covert sexual abuse* or talk about how she felt when he watched her get dressed every morning. She needed the money.

"Well, when I was in treatment, they kept pressuring me to say it," she said instead.

"You know I would never hurt you, Girl. I would never, ever touch you."

"I know, Dad. I'm sorry." She closed her eyes, telling herself to just get this over with so she could move on.

"It means a lot to hear you say it," he said.

"I'm sorry I lied, Dad," she repeated.

"So how are you?" he asked.

"Well, I got into a fight with Stepmother, and I moved out. I'm looking for a place to live." This was safe—Father and Stepmother had always hated each other, and she knew he was always looking for anything to make him feel superior to Stepmother—just like Stepmother was always looking for any reason to "win" over Father. They chatted briefly and he was happy to mail her checks in care of her boyfriend. He loved that she had a boyfriend—anything to prove that she wasn't going to "turn gay." He sent her a check, just as he promised, and Girl opened her first checking account and used a starter check with a picture of mountains in the background to write her first rent check to Ravina, the friend of her mother's best friend who agreed to rent her a room for $200 a month, food not included.

south wedge florist

Now that Girl had a place to live, she needed a job. She moved in on a Friday night and stayed up late, unpacking her clothes and arranging the few possessions she had onto the bookshelves that came with the room. Somehow, her things looked prettier here than they had at home. It was a nice room, and she didn't mind how small it was—it was about the size of her room at home, just enough to fit a twin bed, not a double—though it was not painted as nicely. Ravina, her landlady, was pleasant but the lines were clear—she was the tenant and neither of them were interested in pseudo-family dinners. Girl liked Ravina's twenty-one-year-old daughter, Rea, but she was rarely home. Girl missed her mother.

That first Saturday Girl dressed in a nice sweater and the plain black pants left over from when she worked at Little Caesars Pizza. She pulled her long hair into a ponytail in an effort to look more professional and then hit the streets. Without a car, she needed a job close enough to walk. She didn't want to take a bus after dark if she could help it.

A dry cleaner had a help-wanted sign, so she asked to fill out an application. Her best friend, Rose-Marie, worked at a dry cleaner's and it seemed easy. *Do you have permission to work in the United States?* Yes. *Have you ever been convicted of a felony?* No. *Have you ever used recreational drugs?* Shit. Girl checked the "yes" box, but wrote in the white space, *I have been clean and sober for over two years.* She knew they'd never hire her after reading her answer, but she couldn't bring herself to lie. She wished she hadn't even left the application for them to read.

Girl walked into a gift shop and asked if they were hiring. They weren't, but the lady behind the counter was sweet and said she'd keep her name and number in case anything opened up. Girl walked by Jacqueline's without stopping. It was an old-fashioned store out of sync with the current decade, where women made appointments to sit on a couch and sip tea while shop girls brought out expensive dresses from the back. Girl knew she would never fit in at someplace like that. Across the street was a flower shop, though, and she had floral experience, even though she wasn't skilled enough to call herself a florist. Easter was coming up, and they might need extra help for the holiday. Even a few days' work would keep her going for a little while longer. She'd skip a meal if she had to, but she was never going back home.

Heavy gold antique picture frames filled with green sheet moss instead of paintings hung in the large storefront windows. The fishing line suspending them was nearly invisible, so they seemed to float in midair. She paused in front of the glass door with gold lettering that read South Wedge Florist, took a deep breath, and pulled it open. A small brass bell jangled. The shop had glossy black floors and high tin ceilings, also painted black. Glass shelves were layered with southwestern pottery and crystal vases. She noticed a framed newspaper article about an Olympic swimmer's wedding, and another about Ronald Reagan's inaugural ball. While she waited for the manager, she read that the shop's owner had done the flowers for both of them. A short, slim man came from the back to the church-like podium they used instead of a counter. He had perfectly moussed hair and gold-rimmed glasses like Girl's, only thicker.

"May I help you?" he asked.

"Hi, I'm Girl. Are you hiring by any chance?" She sounded braver than she felt, but smiled anyway.

"That depends. Do you have any experience?" he asked.

"I worked for Flowers for All Occasions for a year and a half, but the owner won't give me a reference." She knew she shouldn't say that, but what was the point in glossing over it? If he called to check her references her old boss would give him an earful—might as well get it out in the open now.

"Jessie Santos?" His face lit up. "She fired me too! That crazy bitch with her half-a-flower-arrangements, always throwing things! I'm William, by the way. I'm the manager."

Phew, she thought. It might be okay after all. Girl had also ducked the occasional flower arrangement hurled across the shop by her old boss.

"I'll talk to Ryan and call you next week. I'm pretty sure we'll need someone soon."

Girl wrote down her name and phone number on one of the black-and-gold bi-fold cards and went home to wait. She had never seen a card that worked that way, folding in half like an empty book. She put one in her pocket before she left, promising herself to be brave and call them if she didn't hear back soon. When she got home she put it on the shelf in her room where she had arranged all her treasured things, as an offering of hope.

William called a few weeks later, and Girl started on a Saturday in May, the week before Mother's Day. She dressed again in the same pants from Little Caesars Pizza. She knew they weren't trendy or cool by a long shot, but on the phone they had said *no jeans,* and they were all she had that wasn't denim. When she walked back into the shop, she knew she should be assertive, smile, and hold her hand out firmly to shake, as Stepmother always told her, but she wasn't sure she'd be able to. She had used up all her professionalism job-hunting, and now she was left timid. She twisted her rings around her fingers and tried not to tug at her clothes.

"Hello, my name is Ryan," a tall, thin man said. The shop owner, she remembered, from talking with William. Something in Ryan's phrasing reassured her. *My name is,* a phrase from kindergarten or Spanish class, unexpected from this someone who was closer in age to her mother than to herself.

"My name is Girl," she said with a smile, parroting his phrase as she reached for his handshake. Ryan had dark black hair and the kind of thick mustache she didn't normally like, but somehow looked okay on him. He was tall, easily over six feet, but rail thin. He couldn't have weighed more than one hundred and fifty pounds, but she didn't take it to mean anything. Brother was tall and skinny like that, too. It made him less intimidating, even though he wore dressier clothes than any florist Girl had ever seen. Ryan wore gray dress pants, not just khakis, and a dress shirt buttoned to the wrists. He sported a silver and turquoise bolo tie close to his Adam's apple, the black leather strings dangling on his narrow chest.

"Come in the back and I'll introduce you to everyone," he said, and Girl followed him past the coolers into the empty space at the heart of the building where everyone worked. "This is Tony, and my partner Mike—they are our delivery and setup team. You met William, the manager, already." She followed him to one of the counters like a little duckling imprinted on the wrong mother, but devoted nonetheless. "We're getting another florist, Bob, but he hasn't started yet. He's moving here from Rhode Island.

"Do you know how to make a bow?" he asked. *Shit.* She had been trying and failing for over a year to make a bow. Jessie, her old boss, gave up on teaching her and said Girl would never learn because she was left-handed.

"Um, not really," she admitted. *Bet he's regretting hiring me,* she thought to herself, but tried to push it out of her head. She was supposed to be confident, cheerful, someone he'd like working in his shop, not some depressing girl-child.

"Here, I'll show you, and we can chit-chat while we make bows." Girl watched Ryan's long, thin fingers intently as he twisted and looped the ribbon, mimicking him as best she could. She did it! It was actually pretty easy. She didn't know why she had struggled so long.

"I love the windows," she said.

"It's the one thing no one else can touch here. I don't arrange flowers much anymore—too much paperwork—but the windows are mine. Here, when you cut the loop, cut out a tiny triangle to make the tail prettier." Everything he did was done with tiny, perfect details.

"How did you ever get the idea to frame sheet moss?"

"We were all getting high during the ice storm," he said, "and there was this pile of gold frames in the attic. Someone, I don't know, William, or Tony, or Mike, I don't remember, but one of them said we should put moss in the frames so we did." Girl didn't have a brain that thought of things like that, but then again, she didn't get high anymore. Something in the way that Ryan admitted to his drug use so casually made her protective of him, like he didn't know better than to admit to stuff he shouldn't. She was seventeen—she knew when to keep her mouth shut. Except she hadn't, when she filled out that application at the dry cleaner. But at least she was ashamed of it, not so unapologetically matter of fact.

The front bell rang, signaling a customer.

"Follow me," he said, and they walked back to the podium at the front of the store. Ryan showed her how to wrap fresh flowers in a bubble of cellophane leaving the stems exposed—the opposite of how they did it at her old shop—and tie the bottom with raffia.

"We tie everything with raffia, and attach one of our cards. It's our signature," he explained.

"When did you buy the shop?" she asked him.

"Oh, I didn't buy it, I opened it fourteen years ago," Ryan said.

"You didn't just buy it, like in the last year?"

"No. We moved here on East Avenue from the South Wedge neighborhood two years ago. Is that what you mean?" She shook her head, confused. At her last job, Girl worked with a man named Bruce, who had come to Flowers for All Occasions after he said that the last shop he worked at—South Wedge Florist—had closed. Bruce said the owner died of AIDS. Jessie, her boss at the time, had asked if any of the fixtures were for sale.

"I used to work with a guy who said he worked at South Wedge Florist—Bruce. He said the shop closed because the owner died of AIDS."

"I don't got AIDS," he said. "Bruce must have been mad I fired him."

She had never like Bruce anyway. They had worked opposite shifts, rarely seeing each other for more than a few minutes unless it was a holiday, and he was kind of weird. He wore eyeliner and would burst into falsetto unexpectedly. Plus, if Girl was late for her shift, which she generally was, he would lock the shop and leave, instead of waiting for her like he was supposed to.

"Where do you live?" Ryan asked her as their fingers twisted the white ribbons into a string of bows, ten to a length. It was quicker to just make a daisy-chain that could be hung on the wall than to cut them as they went.

"I rent a room on Beresford, near Mercy High," she answered.

"You don't live at home?"

"No, I moved out this past January," she said. He didn't ask why, and she didn't offer.

"And do you have siblings?"

"I have a brother who is a year older than I am." No sense in mentioning half- and stepsiblings at this point. It was better to keep things simple. She wished she didn't sound so awkward, but she couldn't help it.

"I have two boys, sixteen and eighteen, about your age, right? Ryan Junior is in twelfth grade at Rush-Henrietta." Ryan continued. "Manny is a sophomore. You'll meet them one of these days. They come in every now and then."

"I'm a senior, too, at Irondequoit."

"That's awfully far, isn't it?"

"I take a bus and transfer downtown. It's okay, I don't mind, and I'm saving up for a car."

"Well, if it's ever raining, one of us will drive you home from work," he said sternly. "And your parents? Are they still together?"

"My mom and stepmother." She paused. It had never been safe to just come out and say they were lesbians, but she was ninety percent sure Ryan was gay. "Mother and Stepmother have been together since I was three. They're lesbians. My dad lives in Alaska."

Ryan's fingers stopped twisting the ribbon. "Will my children hate me for being gay, do you think?" he asked. It was interesting—every man Girl had ever met asked her if she was a lesbian when they found out about her mom. Ryan was the first one who didn't. She'd come to learn that his question—about his children hating him—was the first question every gay parent would ask her the moment they found out about her family. She wondered what it would have been like to have parents that didn't hide their orientation. In her house, the secret hung over every new friendship. Being gay was about the worst thing she could imagine happening to someone, but here was an obviously gay man, running a business peopled by other obviously gay men, and it suddenly didn't seem so bleak. It seemed . . . well, not exactly mainstream, but okay, fun. Ryan smiled a lot, and the shop was filled with laughter.

"I don't know," she hedged. "Well, yes, they will," she amended, deciding to be honest. "But if you weren't gay they'd hate you for something else, like if you had an accent, or were too strict or were overweight. Teenagers always hate their parents every now and then. They'll get over it, though."

From then on, Ryan looked out for Girl like she was one of his kids. He'd cut off shoptalk that got too sexually explicit, and he'd give her a ride home if they stayed even a half-hour late. At the same time, he treated her like a fully-formed grown-up, quickly trusting her to do all the corsages and boutonnieres for the weddings, rarely double-checking her work.

Girl only worked three days a week: two half days on Thursdays and Fridays, and a full day on Saturdays. She mopped floors, dusted shelves, washed out ashtrays, and cleaned the bathrooms in addition to the wedding work. She didn't mind—she was used to working alone, so it was a nice change to have other people around.

Ryan took her along on her first wedding detail, showing her how to reach inside a woman's dress to secure the pin to her bra strap underneath, saying, "Now just let me know if I get too fresh!" Girl learned to mimic him, the teasing flirt of gay-speak putting the mothers and grandmothers of the brides at ease. He showed her how to pin down an aisle runner, how to tape bows to pews, and her favorite—how to fluff a bride's train. It was like when they did parachute games in gym class—Girl's arms went up and snapped back down, a puff of air raising and lowering the white satin fabric so the train would trail perfectly behind the bride. The gesture transformed Girl from a high school senior to a lady in waiting granted the servant's intimacy of seeing the back of the knees of the princess.

Girl spent Saturdays sending brides down the aisle, then raced ahead of the guests to the reception site, where Tony would be high on a ladder, stapling yards of fabric to the ceiling while Girl decorated the wedding cake with fresh flowers and tied gold ribbons on napkins. They placed arrangements on glass stanchions three feet above the round mirrors at their base, and she'd arrange votive candles around each one. Girl lost herself in daydreams of her own elegant wedding someday. She wanted to be a bride more than just about anything.

Because the shop serviced at least four weddings every Saturday, Girl often had to drive herself. Whenever possible, Ryan would let her use his car, a white 1978 Mercedes, instead of one of the big white vans. He didn't care that she'd only just gotten her license. Stepmother wouldn't even let Girl drive her five-year-old Toyota. "It's too special to risk at the hands of an inexperienced driver," Mother had explained. Ryan treated Girl like he treated his son. "Here's the car, be careful, fill it up on your way back, but be sure to go to full serve, so you don't get fuel on your hands." He even offered to let Girl use the Mercedes to drive to her senior prom, just like his son, Ryan Jr., did. Ryan insisted that when it was time for her prom Girl would have to come to the shop in her gown so he could see her in person, just like his son had the month before.

The florist from Rhode Island, Bob, started working there shortly after Girl did, and they shared sandwiches and played gin rummy when it was slow. Bob looked like the Marlboro man and even wore a black leather cowboy hat on occasion. He told her stories of '70s discos. "I could spin on a dime!" he said. Bob lamented the fortune his family left behind in Cuba when Castro rose to power.

All six of the men at the shop were openly gay. It was fun—even though Mother was a lesbian, Girl hadn't really met any gay men before, and the guys were always flirting with her and with each other, laughing and joking and calling each other *Mary*. Bob was the only one who minded it, which caused them to tease him even more. Whenever the shop phone rang, whoever answered would affect the deepest phone-sex voice they could muster, and Girl was almost as good at it as they were—in her mind, anyway. They all kissed each other on the lips in greeting, and the unexpected intimacy of it made Girl feel glowy and vulnerable at the same time. She had never had much extended family, or even a large group of friends. Going to work was like going to hang out with long-lost cool uncles—even on days when her fingers flew at top speed, her mouth moved just as fast, laughing, teasing, and talking about men.

"Just me!" she called as she entered the store one afternoon, a few months after she had been hired. Tony was approaching from the back to see if the ringing bell signaled a customer.

"Did you miss us?" Tony asked with a smirk. Tony's dark brown locks were pulled back into a ponytail only as thick as her index finger. His frizzy hair was receding too far to wear as long as he did, but somehow, it fit him. "Fuck you if you don't like it," Tony always said. "Fuck you with a meat hook." He was the least pretty of the six gay men she worked with, but Girl didn't think pretty was his goal. He wore his combat boots and ponytail with an appealing fierceness. There was something about his brown eyes—his gaze was somehow more intense, he held eye contact a little longer than most people. If you saw him coming in a dark alley, you'd run—he was tough and hip and still listened to death metal even though he was almost forty.

Tony wasn't a florist—he mostly did setup and delivery. Girl had learned that Tony didn't know how to read, but he knew the city streets like the back of his hand. He could create elaborate tenting out of bolts of fabric and transform rented party halls into wonderlands of bridal fantasy when he was sober. When he was drunk he had a history of knocking over expensive vases, but drinking at work was not a fireable offense. South Wedge was a family, and you don't fire family. Girl no longer drank, smoked, or did drugs, but it didn't bother her that most of the other guys at the shop did. Besides, if Ryan was high he'd sometimes pay her an extra few bucks an hour.

"Of *course* I missed you, Tony! I *always* miss you!" she said, playfully drawing out her words and over-emoting in the affectation that was the shop dialect. "I'll tell you who I didn't miss, though—William!" She didn't normally snipe, but the manager, William, was such a prig, and besides, Tony was so cool, she wanted him to like her. William—never the informal Will or the affectionate Billy—was prissy and arrogant. If alligator shirts were still in style, William would wear them perfectly ironed and buttoned all the way to the top. Now he made do with crisp designer dress shirts and creased trousers, but the snooty effect was the same. He was always shuffling papers and scuffing his feet as he walked back and forth, his dress shoes sounding like they were slippers.

"I wish he would pick up his fucking feet and walk like a normal person!" Bob always bitched to her when William was out of the room. William's sole job seemed to be waving papers around and admonishing everyone to work faster, though he rarely put a flower in a vase himself. He had criticized Girl's wardrobe several times. She wore solid color shirts with Dockers every day, but she didn't own scarves or pins to dress them up, and she didn't like how she looked in lipstick—her lips were too thin or something. She kept her hair out of her face to look neat and professional, but she knew she wasn't trendy or cool, and William never failed to comment on how she lacked the flair he felt befitted a South Wedge employee. Still, Girl loved her job. She'd rather be at work than home alone, even though it was summer and she could have lain in the sun all afternoon if she had wanted to. The only good thing about her few days off from work was not having to listen to William's voice nagging her to be better, prettier, and faster than she was capable of.

"Now, now, it's not nice to speak ill of the dying," Tony said as they walked into the back.

"What?" She was confused. She had only been off work her usual three days. They walked to the work area in the middle of the store, and she could hear the radio playing "Everything I Do, I Do It for You" by Bryan Adams. That song was so sappy, and Girl was so sick of hearing it. Apparently the DJ didn't feel the same way, because it was on the air at least once every hour.

"You don't know?"

"Know what?"

"William's in the hospital." Tony turned toward the far counter and laid flowers out next to the row of vases so Bob, the head designer, could assemble them faster.

"He might not make it this time," Tony said, his lips moving slightly as he counted off the Gerbera daisies, liatris, and Stargazer lilies that were the shop's signature look.

"Oh," she said, hating the childlike banality of her response, but not sure what she was supposed to say. "No one told me."

"You should really go visit him," Tony said. "It might be your last chance."

She set up her workstation with green florist wire, tape, and the bows she pre-made and kept on a pegboard. She was in charge of the bodywork—the corsages and boutonnieres. Ryan had taught her to mix bear grass and seeded eucalyptus in between her rosebuds and filler flowers, and now Girl was the only one who made them. She loved Fridays. Her mind could wander down any path while her fingers worked automatically, taping and wiring the stems together. Girl loved making pretty things, and she loved that Ryan trusted her enough to delegate one section of his business to her teenaged hands.

"Was this, um, self-inflicted?" Girl asked as she pulled buckets of flowers from the cooler, using her thumbnail to detach the rosebuds from their stems, leaving the headless spines in the bucket to deal with later. *William is such an arrogant asshole,* she thought. *I wonder if he tried to kill himself?* Mother always said people who acted full of themselves generally didn't have great self-esteem. Suicide was the only thing that made sense—William was young, just twenty-four. The only people Girl knew who got sick enough to go to the hospital were her mother's age or older.

"Well, I guess you could say that," Tony said. "I mean he didn't take care of himself properly. He was always out partying till three or four in the morning, and never got enough sleep. You can't burn the candle at both ends like that."

"Huh?" She was totally confused. Staying up late and getting up early was what most of her friends did in high school. It didn't seem like something that would make you wind up in a hospital.

"You know he's HIV, right?" Tony asked.

"Oh. I didn't know."

She remembered how last month Ryan had asked her to clean the bathrooms and Tony had insisted that Girl wear a pair of old, white medical gloves with stains on the fingers. It was weird—Mother never wore gloves when she cleaned. Girl had gone into the bathroom and the toilet rim was covered in diarrhea splatter. She was glad Tony had found the gloves after all. She wondered if gay men got diarrhea more often than straight people, because both toilets were in covered in such a variety of color that it couldn't have been just one person. *Ryan should hire someone to clean the bathrooms,* she thought. Then it hit her—he had. At just over minimum wage, she was the lowest-paid employee in the shop. She was probably cheaper than a cleaning service. After that Girl stopped bitching to herself when she cleaned. It was worth it to work there. She never wondered if the guys were HIV positive, but it wouldn't have kept her from cleaning the bathrooms if she had. She knew that you couldn't get AIDS from a toilet seat. At least, Mother said so, and right now Girl clung to that. Mother was so sure of it that when her seventh grade health teacher had said, "no one knows if you *can* get AIDS from a toilet seat," Mother had not only called the principal but had left work early to talk to him in person. If there was any doubt, she wouldn't have done that, right?

Girl had taken an AIDS test once, but was too scared to ever go back and get the results. In her senior government class they had debated quarantining people who were HIV positive, and honestly, Girl had been all for it. *Send 'em to an island and keep the rest of us safe*, she had thought back then, but now Girl was ashamed of herself. It was different when you knew someone who had it, someone regular and young and not a freak at all.

"What hospital is he at?" Girl asked Tony, not looking at him. The work area had two counters on opposing walls, and she was glad it wasn't set up for eye contact. They sat on tall, backless stools diagonally across from each other, and Girl kept her eyes on her work so he wouldn't see her face. For him, people with AIDS were common, and Girl didn't want him to think she was shocked or appalled or anything. She didn't want to betray herself as a dumb straight girl.

"St. Mary's."

She had heard of the hospital down in the bad part of the city, but had never been there before. Mother had had seven eye surgeries since Girl was a kid, including three cornea transplants, so she had been in most of the local hospitals at one time or another. Only one of Mother's surgeries had been at St. Mary's, the very first one, when Girl was too young to visit. Mother said the hospital was so bad that after the first surgery she always asked the doctors to schedule her at one of the other hospitals. Dirty, she had said, and under-staffed. Girl wasn't sure why William went there when Genesee Hospital was right down the street. She didn't really understand that AIDS patients weren't welcome everywhere.

"I didn't know what to bring," Girl told Mother, sliding into the blue front seat of her Toyota. William was a florist, so it seemed weird to bring him flowers. Instead, Girl got a small box of Russell Stover's chocolate and a get-well card.

"Candy is good," Mother said, "If he isn't allowed to eat it, he can give it to the nurses. It's always good to bribe the nurses, then they like you and come to your room more often."

Mother had agreed to drive Girl down to see William in the hospice wing after work, because she didn't have a car and the bus to that part of town might not be safe for a teenaged girl to ride alone. Since Girl had moved out her relationship with Mother was strained, but they still got together for lunch or dinner once a week and they talked on the phone every few days.

Girl looked at the round unicorn sticker on the glove compartment as Mother drove. Mother wasn't into frilly or girly things at all, but she always bought herself one stained-glass sticker from the museum gift shop to put on the glove box of her car. Mother wouldn't spring for power windows or even an automatic transmission, always voting for cheap and practical over luxurious, but she'd made a special trip for that one unicorn. Girl was somehow proud that her practical, short-haired mother would spend money on an expensive sticker. It spoke of dreams and yearnings for beauty that must flow inside Mother as much as they did inside Girl.

"I'll just wait in the car," Mother said when they pulled into the circular drive of the hospital. "I brought a book."

"Are you sure?" Girl asked.

"It's not really appropriate to see someone in bed that you have never met. It might make him uncomfortable."

"Well, I shouldn't be too long," Girl said, but didn't move to open the door, still looking at the unicorn on the glove box. Girl hated going to new places and feared getting lost in corridors. She was a month away from graduating high school and was living on her own, but inside, she was still small and scared.

"It's okay, I have a book, I told you. I'm fine," Mother said, and that was the end of it. Girl would have to go alone.

There was an old lady at the volunteer desk who looked up William's room number for Girl and gave her directions to the proper floor. It turned out that St. Mary's wasn't very big and it was easy to find the elevators. When Girl walked in, William was sitting up in bed, wearing a dull blue hospital gown with little anchors printed on it, the white sheet pulled over his lap. Although she had noticed the dark red spot behind his ear at work, Girl hadn't thought much about it. Now, she noticed maroon spots on his skinny, nearly hairless arms below the short sleeves of his gown. Girl had heard of Kaposi's sarcoma, the AIDS-related skin cancer, and she guessed that must have been what it was, but she didn't ask. Girl always figured William wore long sleeves every day because he was prissy and formal, not to hide his disease. He had never looked sick.

"I'm so glad you came!" William's eyes lit up. "You came at the perfect time! I have had nonstop visitors since I've been in—exhausting really. I can't believe you picked a time when no one else was here."

He hadn't been watching TV or anything when Girl came in, just sitting there in his bed, staring into space. She hadn't thought he'd be so excited to see her. He had never seemed to like her very much.

"I didn't know what to bring," she said, putting the candy on the rolling bed tray that covered his lap. It was a small box, the kind that was $4.95 and only had four pieces, but then Girl only made five dollars an hour and couldn't afford much.

"I love candy!" he said, opening the card and reading it quickly without comment. There weren't any cards or proof of other visitors in the room. Girl was sure his boyfriend, Walter, and all the guys from the shop had come by, but she guessed they hadn't brought anything.

"Did you see the flowers at the nurses' station? I had so many arrangements in here it set off my allergies. I just told the nurses to take them home. They were so excited. The nurses are really nice to me."

Girl hadn't seen any flowers, but she didn't say so. Girl couldn't have really been the only person to bring him something, could she? Not that William would have told her if she was. He needed to see himself as the life of the party, surrounded by friends, even if there was no evidence to prove it. It seemed unlikely that the flowers had disappeared so quickly, though.

"I didn't know if you were supposed to bring a florist flowers. My mom said if you couldn't eat the candy you could give it to the nurses or whatever."

"I always like to have something for visitors. I have these abscesses on my esophagus, so I can't eat a lot of chocolate. But Walter will love it."

William's boyfriend was one of the most beautiful men Girl had ever seen: tall, with dark hair and startling light blue eyes. Walter was always tan from working construction outside, and he seemed sweet; maybe because he was always really quiet when he came in the shop, never catty or condescending. Walter was the opposite of William—no one would ever think he was gay to look at him in his work jeans and flannel shirts. William looked as stereotypically gay as you could get.

"So tell me what's been going on at the shop!" William demanded.

"Well, we did the wedding for Schmidt and the Gerbera daisies came in light pink instead of raspberry and the bride had a complete meltdown! I didn't know what to do, but Ryan told her to focus on spending her life with the man she loves and sent her down the aisle. She didn't dare talk back to him." They gossiped for a while, but Girl could tell he was tired. After twenty minutes or so she stood up to leave.

"Can you turn off the light? I can't reach it." William asked. "I'm gonna sleep until Walter gets here." His skin was yellow next to the white sheet. He folded his glasses and Girl put them on the side table for him. His eyes closed before she left the room. He looked vulnerable without his glasses, and small and fragile beneath the sheets.

There was a song Girl used to sing back in ninth grade called, "A.I.D.S.— Anally Inflicted Death Sentence." It was the summer Girl was filled with hate for her parents and their gayness, when she was tired of being bullied and different and on the fringes of society. *That's what you get for having a penis up your ass. That's what you get when you swallow another man's load.* She sang it because Stepmother would hate it if she knew, but more than that, it would hurt her. Girl wanted so badly to be normal, she wished so hard to be just like everyone else. She was tired of interrupting gay jokes to tell her friends they were being insensitive, the way Stepmother had schooled her to do. She hated being called *Lezzie.* It wasn't fair that Mother had chosen to be a lesbian—she always said that she could have been just as happy with a man—so she had willingly chosen a life of ostracism and secrets. *Should have used a condom*, Girl sang angrily that summer. Now Girl wished that she could take it all back, revoke her mocking, bullying song, pull the lyrics out of her brain like threads of spider web and throw the memory away forever.

A week or so later, William was back at the shop, but now his attitude toward her had changed. On Fridays, he'd take her to the Italian restaurant next door for lunch, and they'd stay twice as long as her allotted thirty minutes. William always paid for her, but Girl was careful to order the cheapest thing on the menu, like her mother taught her.

"Hey, I have to go to the eye doctor on Tuesday," he asked. "Can you take me? I don't know if they will be dilating my eyes."

"Sure, but you know I don't have a car yet," Girl said.

"Just meet me at the shop," he said. "I'll drive us there, and you can drive us home."

William looked fragile in the deep black leather bucket seat of his car. He said he was five-foot-five, but Girl thought he was closer to five-foot-three. After his illness, he couldn't have been much more than one hundred pounds, and his wrists were bony and sharp when he gripped the steering wheel.

"Do you feel how the car just wants to go?" William asked. The silver 944 Porsche shook when it idled at red lights. She guessed that was what he was talking about.

"I just got this one a few months before you started. It's so much more powerful than my old 928. The 928 is the poor man's Porsche." William always pronounced it pore-shah, but Girl felt self-conscious and just said pore-sh. "Did you ever see my old car?"

At the next stoplight William pulled out his wallet and showed her a picture of himself standing in front of a bright yellow car.

"Nice!" she said. Girl liked it better than the one he had now, but didn't say so. She wasn't nearly as impressed with the silver 944 as he wanted her to be, but she tried to fake it. To her, the most important aspect of a car was its color.

"Do you feel how smoothly it changes gears?" William said.

"Yeah, but why would you get a sports car with an automatic transmission?" Girl had just learned to drive on a five-speed, and she scorned people who didn't drive stick.

"I had wanted a stick shift, but this was designed to be a luxury car. They mostly made automatics, so stick shifts are really hard to find used." Girl must have looked skeptical, because he went on, "Actually, I get tired a lot, so I really need an automatic. I know how to drive stick, but some days I just can't."

"Oh." Girl looked out the passenger's window and saw nothing but colors blurring by. "How long have you been sick?" Girl knew it wasn't polite to ask, but she did anyway.

"Almost five years. Since I was twenty." William didn't seem to mind talking about it.

They pulled into the mall parking lot. Girl was surprised he didn't go to a normal eye doctor in a separate office building like she did. Mother always said that mall places weren't as good.

"Can you tell I'm sick?" he asked quietly as they walked to Lens Crafters.

"No, I don't think so." He was skinny, but not as skinny as their boss, Ryan. William wore long sleeves that covered his KS spots and had a little makeup on the one behind his ear.

"I know I look gay, but I don't want to look sick."

"No, you look good. I had no idea, really." They sat side by side in a narrow hall outside the examination room.

"There're not many doctors that like to treat people with AIDS. That's why I come here. We get certain eye problems."

Girl had thought they were just there because he wore glasses like she did. His eyes didn't look infected or anything. Mother's left eye was always goopy and swollen. William's eyes looked fine behind his gold-framed bifocals.

"I like your frames, by the way."

"Twenty-four karat gold—what else!"

"Of course! What else?"

"Do you mind driving?" William asked when he left the exam room. "I still get really tired." He'd only been working half days since he got out of the hospital a month ago.

Girl wasn't really a confident driver, and it made her nervous to have him watch her. She peeled out of the parking lot, accidentally spinning the tires. Girl didn't realize that William didn't have anyone else to drive him. Walter had to work all day, and they couldn't afford for him to take time off; the same with his other grown-up friends. Without family, Girl was all he had, even if she was only seventeen and totally inexperienced behind the wheel.

"Sorry!"

"Relax! It has a lot of power!" William laughed.

William didn't even say anything when Girl accidentally drove over the curb pulling into his driveway.

"If you don't mind, I'll schedule my doctor's appointments for your days off. I like you taking me." His face was pale and worn. Although he said he was Spanish, Tony always called him a Mexican. Either way, he was tanned and dark before he got sick. Now he was slightly yellow.

"It's okay. I don't have anything else to do."

"And you should come to the birthday party I'm having for Tony next week! It's going to be *so* fabulous. You can bring a friend if you want to. Tony's turning forty, and can you believe his lover isn't having a party for him? And all the guys at work—no one offered to host! And they say they are his friends, but not one of them offered to throw him a party. I said I'd do it, because someone has to do something. Have you ever had caviar?" Girl could tell he was waning, despite his enthusiasm about the party. She handed him the embossed leather Porsche key fob and he trudged slowly up to his red front door. He didn't ask her in.

Girl was still dating Jacob, but she didn't really want to bring him to the party. It wasn't his kind of thing. Although he had come into the shop once or twice to meet the guys, he was coolly arrogant and didn't talk much. He said Ryan was the only one he liked; the rest were too *flitty*. Jacob was two years older than Girl and was born-again Christian. He didn't approve of going to parties where alcohol was served, and besides, Fridays were his jam session with all his guitar friends. She couldn't really expect him to miss the one night he looked forward to all week just to go to party where he didn't know anybody.

She had met a girl named Sharon recently, and Girl thought Sharon'd be fun to bring instead, but she was nervous to ask her. Sharon had graduated high school a semester early and already went to college. She was beautiful, too, with long red hair and perfect makeup. Sharon was one of those girls who could make jeans and a T-shirt look like high fashion. Still, she always smiled sincerely when she ran into Girl. They had talked about getting together sometime, but neither of them had followed up. Girl was too shy to go alone, though, so she invited Sharon the next time she spoke to her.

"Hey, do you want to go to a gay party this weekend with me? For the flower shop," she explained. "It's one of the guy's birthdays."

"I'd totally love to! I've never been to a gay party before! What are you wearing? Is it fancy?" Sharon asked Girl.

"William is always fancy. I promised him I'd wear a dress."

"A dressy dress? Or a regular dress? I have a cocktail dress from when my dad took us on a cruise. It's not like a prom gown or anything. I kind of like it."

"I don't think I'm wearing a dressy dress. I have this white dress. Kinda tailored, with a button lacey thing on the shoulder. I'm wearing that. I don't have a car, though."

"I'll pick you up. I love to drive. It's no big deal, really." Sharon was nice to reassure her, like she could read Girl's insecurity through the phone line.

They arranged the details, and Girl was glad she asked Sharon. Girl hadn't had that friend-chemistry in a long time, and she was kind of between best friends at the moment. Sharon was magnetic, smart, and funny. Girl wanted to be around her all the time.

William lived in the top half of a double house off Park Avenue. It didn't look like much from the outside, but when Sharon and Girl walked in it was like something from a designer magazine, with black leather sofas, gold lamé curtains, and shiny hardwood floors. It was the most stylish house Girl had ever been in. The dining room table was pushed against the wall and covered with a black linen tablecloth. Votive candles winked in round glass bowls among the trays of finger food William had displayed on risers of varying heights. Tiny black pearls of sturgeon caviar were mounded in a bowl nestled in ice. Gold Mylar balloons bumped against the ceiling, their curved edges touching, gold and silver streamers hanging to the floor straight and nearly motionless, until you parted the waterfall to walk through the room, causing the gold foil spheroids to quiver and bob.

"Oh my God, William! I love your place!" Girl said after they exchanged kisses.

"Do you like my curtains?"

"They are fabulous!" Girl said in an affected gay parody.

"I made them myself! I just got yards of gold lamé and wrapped it around the pole and stuffed it with newspapers."

He left them to go mingle with newly arriving guests, and Sharon and Girl sank side by side into the buttery-soft black leather loveseat. Tony arrived, wearing black combat boots over ripped fishnet stockings, topped with a gold lamé thrift store prom dress that he was too wide to zip up. The zipper hung open in a V to his waist, exposing his back like a high fashion designer had drawn the dress to be worn in just that way. His frizzy black hair hung loose around his shoulders, and he had a cigarette in one hand and a cocktail in the other. He had replaced the silver hoop that normally adorned his left nostril with a two-inch blue horn that reached upward toward his temple, his expression mimicking an exuberant and slightly crazed Jack Nicholson from *The Shining*.

"Who is this fabulous creature?" Tony asked Girl, taking Sharon's hand and kissing it over and over. "Mwah! Mwah!" Tony made theatric kissing noises. Sharon threw her head back and laughed with her eyes closed. She was so beautiful; her eyeliner swooping, her lipsticked lips plump in the perfect shade of mauve. Girl wasn't even jealous that Sharon was getting all the attention—Girl was just glad to be the one she came with.

Girl had met most of the guests at the flower shop, but without the camouflage of her glasses no one recognized her. At work, Girl always wore her hair up in a bun and never wore makeup, her round gold frames more memorable than any of her features. Tonight Girl had shed her glasses and let down her hair. Her makeup wasn't as skillfully applied as Sharon's, but it was deftly done and subtle.

"Hi, I'm Greg," a man said, introducing himself to Girl, not realizing they had seen each other at least twice a month since she started working there.

"I know you," she said, a flirty tease in her voice.

"You do? From where?"

"The shop. I work for Ryan."

"*You* are the shopgirl?" He was incredulous. "Oh my God! I didn't even recognize you!" Girl felt like the ugly duckling turned swan. She felt worthy to be seen with Sharon, even though she wasn't equal to her in looks by a long shot. Together they were striking, attractive, fun, like best friends in movies always were.

"I am dying to try caviar!" Sharon said. Girl didn't tell her how leery she was of trying new foods, lest Sharon think she was uncool. Sharon heaped a spoonful onto a round of dry toast, and Girl tentatively spooned a smaller mound onto her cracker. "One, two three—bite!" Sharon counted off, and they popped them in their mouths at the same time.

"Salty," Girl said, trying not to show how awful she thought it was.

"Kind of interesting, though, very posh," Sharon said, nibbling the rest of hers. "I think I like it." Girl was so glad she brought Sharon instead of her bump-on-a-log boyfriend, as the guys at the shop called him.

"So are you two a couple?" a man Girl didn't know asked.

"No, we're just friends," she said.

It surprised Girl that in this situation, sitting next to Sharon and surrounded by gay men, Girl didn't mind the lesbian assumption. Here, it didn't seem like a big deal, and if she was going to be someone's girlfriend, there was no one prettier and cooler than Sharon.

graduation

"I don't know if I can be happy with you, but I know I can be happy alone," Jacob said. It was the day before graduation, and Girl had spent the morning lying in the sun in her new Hawaiian Tropics bikini in the backyard grass. The day before, she had gone for orientation and testing at Monroe Community College. She had asked Jacob to come over to talk, and had let him go first. Now she wished she had gone first, because although she had also concluded that their relationship needed to end, it still hurt to hear him say it.

Jacob always had strong opinions on what Girl should and shouldn't do: she shouldn't wear black, she shouldn't wear makeup, and she should never wear a bikini in front of other people, because that was the same as cheating. Girl had done everything she could to please him, but he still sank into a depression that he could not rise out of.

"I think we should agree not to talk to each other for a month, so we can really see what it's like to be apart," he said.

"Okay," Girl said, although she thought that was a little extreme. "Let me get you your house key."

"No, keep it. I'll feel better knowing you have it," he answered. She watched him drive away, the CB radio antennas bouncing on his car.

Girl woke up graduation morning with a stabbing sadness. Why couldn't they have waited one more day, so she could have enjoyed graduation? She cried in the shower as she washed her hair, shampoo running into her mouth and making her spit. Girl put on her best dress, the white one with the lace and button corsage sewn on the left side. She carried her plastic-wrapped graduation gown cradled against her chest as she waited for the bus to take her to Rose-Marie's house. Every month Girl bought an unlimited ride bus pass, and just like on school days, she walked the half-mile to the bus stop, rode downtown, and transferred to one of the Irondequoit bus lines.

When she got to Rose-Marie's house, Rose-Marie's mother was taking pictures of Rose-Marie, her brother, who was also graduating, and her brother's friends. Girl unwrapped her gown and put it on for a picture with Rose-Marie. Rose-Marie was sweet to invite her over—Girl hadn't seen her much in the past few months, because Jacob didn't like her. Girl had thrown her away, but Rose-Marie was still here, ready to give her a hug and a ride to school.

"You are all wrinkled!" Rose-Marie's mother said. Girl looked down. Her gown was covered in a grid of wrinkles from being folded in the package. "I steamed all of Timmy's friends' gowns," her mother said, "and I would have done yours, too, if you had gotten here earlier. There isn't time now."

Girl posed in her wrinkled gown with Rose-Marie in her smooth one. She was embarrassed that she hadn't known enough to iron it ahead of time, sad that her mother was not a part of the day's preparation. Mother, Stepmother, and Brother were taking her out afterward, so it wasn't like they weren't celebrating. It was just when she looked at Rose-Marie's mother—so happy that she had made an appetizer buffet, like it was a real party—she wished that she belonged to someone who was excited, too. She wiped tears away with the back of her hand, hoping she didn't smear her makeup.

She and Rose-Marie had sat together for the rehearsal, and the stupid all-senior farewell dinner, and finally in the Eastman Theatre. Girl hoped someone would clap for her when she walked across the stage, but she wasn't sure anyone would. She had abandoned all her friends for Jacob, and now he was gone. She tried to push all thoughts of him out of her head and just focus on this moment, but she couldn't. She wished once again that he had just come tonight and broken up with her tomorrow.

Afterward, her parents took her to Oscars, a fancy restaurant on Park Avenue, for dessert. A pair of person-sized gold Academy Award statues flanked the door. Mother gave her a box of roses that Father had sent. Mother and Stepmother gave her a jewelry box, and a card with a check.

"Do you want to have a graduation party?" Mother asked. Girl was startled. She didn't think Mother wanted to be around her at all, let alone have a party. "We could have it at the house," Mother said. "And we could invite Marty, Shirley and Betty, all our friends."

"I'd love that," Girl said softly. It was as if she was still a part of the family. She was afraid if she said more, she'd cry.

"So when are you and Jacob getting married?" Brother asked her.

"Oh," Girl said, her eyelashes dripping tears, "you didn't hear? We broke up." She had called her mother right away, and assumed Mother had told Brother. That's how it usually worked in her family.

"Yeah, Mother told me, but . . ."

"Why would you say that then?" Girl wanted to stab him with her fork. "Is that supposed to be funny?" She had made sure not to wear her class ring on Christmas, on their anniversary, and on Valentine's day, hoping Jacob would ask her to marry him. It had been her only dream of the future. She was going to college as backup plan—what she really wanted was to be a wife and mother, the sooner the better.

"No, I just, ya know. I figured you'd get back together," Brother said lamely. Girl ignored him for the rest of dinner.

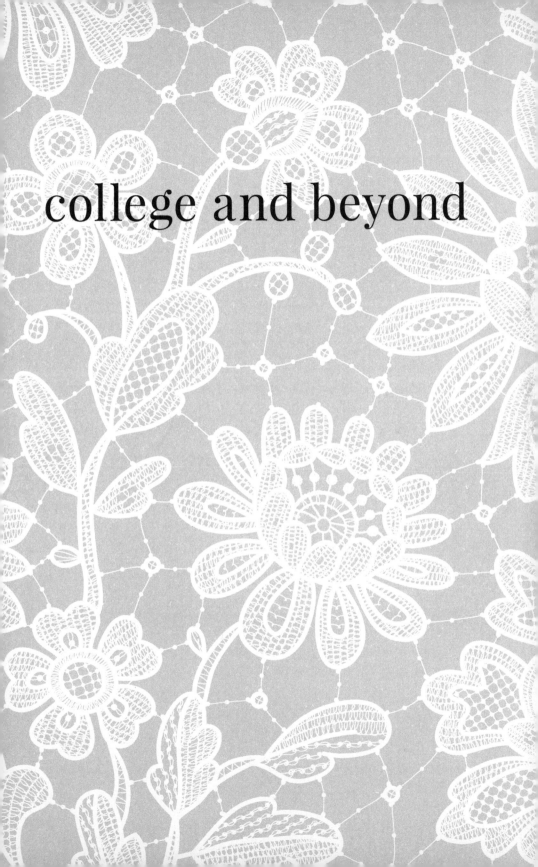

college and beyond

college

Mother had always stressed that having children was an "eighteen-year commitment," and Stepmother had made it clear that once Girl graduated high school, she had to move out and either go to school full-time and live in the dorms, or work full-time and support herself. Now that Girl had graduated high school, it was too late for them to want her to come home, so although nothing was said, the tension suddenly lifted. She was back on their agenda, no longer an embarrassing runaway.

Girl volunteered in Mother's office once a week, in exchange for using Mother's car to volunteer at a horseback riding program for children with cerebral palsy. Girl didn't actually get to ride horses, as she had hoped, but instead walked them around in circles while the children clung to the saddle. Still, it was something to do. When she and Jacob broke up Girl had filled her schedule as much as possible. At the end of the summer, Mother took Girl on a long weekend road trip to Boston. It was the only vacation with just her mother she had ever had. They stayed at a bed-and-breakfast and complained to each other about the freezing room even though it was August. It was as if the fight had never happened. Mother and Stepmother had been paying Girl child support along with father, although Girl put their checks in the bank and never spent them. At the end of the summer she gave Mother one thousand dollars as a down payment on Mother's old car.

In August Sharon and Girl got an apartment together a week before they started their freshman year of college. It was big and airy, with windows on three sides, and heated by steam radiators. There was a built-in bookcase where they arranged all of their mementos. They went to the Salvation Army and bought a wingback chair together, and melted crayons into candles. Girl loved everything about the apartment and her roommate. She had been lonely for so long.

The phone rang at three in the morning, two weeks after school started. The ringing phone woke Girl, who batted the receiver about as she struggled to awaken and find the source of noise and make it stop.

"Tigger is dead," Brother told Girl. Suddenly she was on high alert.

Tigger was Brother's best friend. He and Girl had spent half of high school dating when neither of them had anyone better around, dropping each other without malice when someone more interesting came into the picture.

"What?" Girl said, thinking, *Why does it have to be Tigger? If someone had to die, why couldn't it have been John, one of Brother's other friends, instead?*

"He was in Chicago with Karl," Brother explained. Brother was supposed to go on the trip back to Karl's hometown, but had backed out at the last minute. He was trying to get his life together, which meant working full-time at 7-Eleven and going to the same community college as Girl. She had been proud of Brother for choosing to be responsible. "They went to a party, Karl got drunk, Tigger didn't. Karl was driving. He hit a tree. Tigger was launched out the front window. When they found his body, all his clothes had been ripped off in the accident."

Girl didn't ask how he knew the details.

"I called Tigger's parents to tell them, but they hung up on me. They thought it was a joke."

Girl and Brother had drifted since she found religion in high school. She looked down on how his whole life revolved around *Rocky Horror Picture Show*; he scorned her new conservative mindset. But Brother had just decided to make a change. He had been previously living with Karl and Tigger and getting high, but he had just gotten his own one-bedroom apartment, just a few blocks from Girl's, and he had decided to get sober again. He was on the edge of the pit clawing his way out, and he had to do it without any help from their parents. Girl had a car and child support, and even though she worked, it was only part-time. Brother had a full-time job and a bus pass because Stepmother was done helping him.

"We're down at Denny's on Monroe Ave," he said. Girl got dressed and drove down to see him. She was surprised that Mother was at the restaurant, drinking coffee with all of Brother's punk friends. Mother hugged her, tears in her own eyes.

"It's been twenty years, but I wish I still smoked right now," Mother said when Brother lit a cigarette.

At the wake a few days later, Girl picked up the box of Tigger's ashes at the prompting of his sister. "Feel how light it is," the sister had urged her. It didn't feel like an entire person was contained in the metal box. It felt like nothing at all.

After Tigger died, Brother fell apart. He stopped going to work, dropped out of school, and was evicted from his apartment. He spent the next few years bouncing between friends' apartments, winding up on Girl's doorstep when he ran out of places to stay. Stepmother would not allow him to come back home, though Mother did give him a box of food every time she saw him.

Girl still worked at South Wedge Florist, and since Tony's birthday party, everyone at the shop always asked about Sharon. Her roommate hung out with William, too, taking him to doctor's appointments when Girl was busy, or going out to lunch with him.

"My two little nurses," William called them. "Sharon is so beautiful, don't you think?" he asked Girl. She was visiting William alone this time. "I want to get married before I die. Do you think Sharon would marry me? She'd be a gorgeous bride with that long red hair." Girl was uncomfortable and a little jealous.

"Why do you want to get married?"

"Oh, I have spent my life planning other people's weddings. I want to do one completely my way."

Girl understood that—she always thought about her own wedding while she put together flowers for other people's ceremonies. Girl wanted more than anything to be a princess for just one day, wearing a gown and feeling beautiful, surrounded by admiring friends and family. They always had bridal magazines around the flower shop, and at lunch she'd dream her way through the pages, trying to decide the best way to wear her hair, the best dress for her figure. Girl evaluated every church and reception hall she set up so she could pick the prettiest one when it was her big day. She no longer had a steady boyfriend, but that didn't stop her from planning everything she could, even down to the money box shaped like Cinderella's pumpkin-turned-carriage. Girl could understand William's yearning for his own wedding, but she wondered why William didn't want to marry Walter, his life partner. She didn't know why he wanted to marry a girl so badly. Girl didn't think it occurred to William to marry Walter, perhaps because of the ingrained Catholic sensibilities he was raised with, but mainly, Girl thought, because he wanted to pick out bridal gowns and attendants dresses as much as she did. He wanted to plan his big day, and straight was the only acceptable version of that in his eyes.

"Besides, I need someone to register my car for me," William said. "The insurance is too much to just have a Porsche. It's a lot cheaper if you have two cars on one policy. My friend Roselyn used to do it for me but she said she can't anymore, even though I did her drapes in her living room and everything." Oh, so there was added motivation behind it, Girl thought. There was no way she would put his car on her insurance. Mother would kill her.

Girl talked to Sharon about it the next day.

"That's funny," Sharon said. "He says the same thing to me about you. He tells me how beautiful you are. Says you are a natural beauty and I'm only pretty with makeup. And he wants to marry you but is afraid to ask."

"I only want to only get married for love," Girl said. There was more than that, though. Girl kissed William on the lips every time she saw him without thinking twice about it—all the gay guys at work gave pecks on the lips to all their friends. But if she married him would he want to have sex with her? That she couldn't do. Girl couldn't sleep with an HIV-positive man when she was only eighteen. What if she got sick, too? But he was dying. If Girl was a good friend, wouldn't she marry him? And what about money? Wouldn't she be responsible for his bills if they got married? Girl knew that William was racking them up, figuring he'd die before he had to pay them.

"Why do you think he plays us against each other like that?" Girl asked.

"I have no idea. It's weird," Sharon said. William was stirring the pot at work, too. He and Bob were constantly fighting, so he hired someone to replace Bob, but Ryan wouldn't fire him. Now they had two people who thought they were the head designer and only enough work for one of them.

"William's still kind of an asshole," Girl said. "I know you aren't supposed to say that about someone who is dying, but he is."

"Did he tell you his plan?" Sharon asked.

"What plan?"

"Well, he wanted to place an ad for a threesome in the paper and have guys come over and undress for us, and then I was supposed to say I wasn't interested. That way we'd both get to see naked penises for free."

"He didn't ask me about that. I do think he likes you better. Are you gonna do it?" It sounded predatory. Mean. Girl wanted no part of it. She understood that his time here was short and that he wanted to do everything he could in the time he had remaining, but William's requests seemed to always be at someone else's expense.

"I said I'd think about it, because I didn't know what to say. But I don't want to. I wish he'd stop asking."

"His birthday party is next week," Girl said.

"Yeah, he told me. We're going together, right?"

"Of course we are. William throws the best parties. I promised to be his bartender." It didn't matter if Girl had a boyfriend, Sharon was always her date for any of William's parties. She had made the mistake of taking a boyfriend only once, and he had just sat there, too uncomfortable to speak or even move off the sofa.

William was turning twenty-five. He seemed so grown up to Girl, so mature. She didn't realize that at eighteen she was closer in age to him than he was to any of the other guys at the shop. Girl didn't know he saw her and Sharon as his peers. It wasn't until Girl was twenty-five that she realized how it is just a breath and a week from eighteen, not all that old, not all that grown up.

A few weeks later Ryan called Girl into his office. They were so busy that she rarely spoke to Ryan one-on-one—normally he was in the back office doing paperwork and Girl was in the work area out front, and Ryan only appeared when they got too loud. Girl was a little trepidatious, but she couldn't think of what she had done wrong.

"I'm not a brave man," Ryan began. "I told William I'm closing the shop, but I'm not. I just need to get rid of him. So if you talk to him, pretend you're sad about the shop closing and that you're looking for a new job. But don't worry, I'm not firing you."

Girl nodded. She remembered Bruce, the man she worked with years ago, saying that South Wedge had closed. Apparently this was how Ryan fired people. When push came to shove, it was Ryan that Girl was loyal to, and not just because he signed her paychecks. She wished Ryan had been her father. Even his words—*I am not a brave man*—made her love him more, and want to protect him. She would play his game.

"Cleaning house!" Tony said gleefully when Girl exited the office. He was obviously in on it too. William was livid though, and not fooled for a minute. As soon as he was told the story, he called Girl.

"They all have AIDS, you know. I don't know what Ryan is thinking—I've been sharing my AZT with him, but I'm not going to do that anymore. And

Tony? I was teaching him how to read. I was the only one to throw a party for him when he turned forty. His lover couldn't be bothered."

William found another job, but he and Girl drifted apart. Not because she didn't love him, but because he was so angry and hard to be around. She didn't know how to reconcile it. Every time they got together Girl left fuming, resolving never to see him again, but then he'd get sick, or need a ride to the doctor's, and she'd always go when he called.

By May of 1992 William was bedridden, yellow and swollen from liver disease, nearly twice his original girth. William could no longer pretend to come from a close family that just happened to live too far to visit often. None of his relatives came to see him in his last few weeks, not even his mother. William couldn't hide the fact that most of the people who drank his champagne and ate his caviar at parties didn't want to see him in his final days. He couldn't hide the smell of his disease as it ate his body away, or cover up the pallor of his skin, or pretend his bloated figure was due to too much pasta.

"I'll come back tomorrow, after school," Girl said, after one visit.

"Bring me raspberries," William asked.

"Of course I will. Anything you want." Girl smiled and fought back tears. She didn't want him to go on like this, but she wasn't ready for him to die either. All of her complaints about him seemed petty now, and Girl wished she had been a better friend.

The next morning the telephone summoned her from sleep, telling her it was too late to bring William raspberries ever again.

Girl asked Mother to go to the funeral, but it was Sharon who held her as they both sobbed. Girl felt guilty for making Mother go with her—she knew Mother had lost so many people, been to too many funerals. Girl tried to turn to her instead of Sharon, but it felt forced, outgrown. She shouldn't have asked her to go, even though she was willing. It wasn't fair to Mother, so Girl let Mother hold her and cried on her shoulder as well.

the right chevy

Girl met the Right Chevy at an Alcoholics Anonymous picnic when she was almost sixteen, and almost a year sober. "Met" wasn't exactly the right word; "saw" was more precise. Samson Chevy was tan, muscular, and shirtless, at least five years older and a whole lot cooler than Girl. He had a Harley bandana tied around his head and a scruffy beard. His face crinkled in laughter around his green eyes, and he was surrounded by a group of admiring men and teenagers.

Girl was there with her best friend, Rose-Marie. They were trying to impress the other high school kids at the picnic, the boys in particular. Since Girl was going to an all-girls Catholic school, AA functions were the only place she got to flirt.

"Chevy's here!" the boy Girl was talking to said, and walked off to hang around the bikers like a groupie. Girl didn't follow him—she was too cool for that.

"No girl can ever get me down!" Brandon was bragging.

"Oh, yeah?" Girl replied. She'd show him that girls could do anything boys could do. Besides, maybe that guy on the bike was watching.

Girl waited till Brandon had the football in the middle of the field, then ran full speed at him, catching him around the waist with both her arms, and knocked him flat on his back.

"No girl can get you down, huh?" She was triumphant.

"I can't believe you did that! Everyone was watching!" Brandon was livid.

"What? You said no girl could take you down."

"Everyone saw me get tackled by a girl!" Brandon stormed off. Girl looked for the bikers, but they were gone. She couldn't stop thinking about that one guy, though. Chevy. Even his name was cool.

She saw him again at an AA dance a few months later, and this time he spoke to her. Rose-Marie and Girl were wearing their matching red sweatshirts and tight black jeans and doing their synchronized *left, right, left, turn* dance moves to "Funky Cold Medina."

"Hey, I'm Chevy," he said when the song ended. He still had that bandana tied around his head, and his face was scruffy with a few days' growth of beard. The leather jacket, jeans, and cocky smile rounded out his look as Mr. Cool. Girl couldn't believe he noticed her.

"I know who you are," she said, trying not to sound impressed. "I saw you at the picnic last summer."

"Dance with me. I'll come and find you for the first slow song," he said, walking away in his black cowboy boots that made him just an inch taller than Girl was in her white sneakers.

Girl kept looking for him as she and Rose-Marie danced to "Wild Thing," "Mony Mony," and other eighties hits, but he never came back as promised.

spring 1992

Girl met another Chevy when she was eighteen, but he wasn't the right one.

Wrong Chevy and Girl were playing cards with some mutual friends at the Sober Barn, a nonprofit organization where teenagers could hang out away from the temptation of drugs or alcohol. Girl was a freshman in college, and Sharon had just taught her to play euchre. They sat around the one-room cabin on old donated sofas playing cards night after night. Wrong Chevy was a few years older than Girl, but still in college. He was preppy and muscular with thinning blond hair and freckles. Girl was surprised when he asked her over to his apartment. Jocks didn't normally go for Girl—she didn't have enough style, or confidence, or something. They kissed and he pulled off her clothing to gasp at her matching black bra and panties (thank God it was clean laundry day). When he drove her home, though, he said, "I can't believe you let me go so far. I thought for sure you would slap me."

Girl was confused. Was he just seeing how far she would go? Didn't he like her? Hadn't he wanted to mess around, or was this some sort of test she failed? He called again a few days later, when Girl was making chocolate chip cookies. She left the batter half-mixed on the counter and drove to his house. She'd finish it later—if she delayed, he might change his mind.

Girl let him borrow her car after his was stolen from the university parking lot. He brought her a rose when he returned it. She went to his apartment on Valentine's Day with a box of homemade cookies and a handmade card, and he had a pair of earrings for her, along with a card with a picture of a girl picking her nose. "I picked this one for you!" it said. They didn't go anywhere—he didn't have any money, but had too much pride to let Girl pay—but Girl bought him groceries and he cooked for her in his studio apartment. He put his arm around her in front of their friends at the Sober Barn, and to Girl, that was all that mattered.

One night a new girl, Marian, joined the gang. Wrong Chevy leaned over to Girl and whispered in her ear, "That is the most beautiful girl I have ever seen!"

Girl looked at Marian: chestnut brown hair, no makeup. Most people would probably say that Girl was the prettier of the two. But she was clean-looking, sporty, and sincerely nice to everyone, including Girl, Wrong Chevy's girlfriend. Within a few days Girl and Wrong Chevy broke up. He and Marian would marry two years later at a 9:30 a.m. ceremony in a Catholic church when Marian was twenty years old and three months pregnant.

After Wrong Chevy and Girl broke up, he and Girl remained friends. Girl still secretly hoped he would change his mind and come back. He was selling a computer and she needed one, so she agreed to buy his, even though it was older and crappier than the one at her mother's house. Girl hoped if they hung out enough, he'd remember what he had originally seen in her. When he suggested they drive to his brother's house to look for the manual to the computer, Girl agreed, even though she knew she'd never read it.

Wrong Chevy and Girl drove to the edge of the city and parked in front of a small house with white peeling paint and cracked concrete steps, the yard completely surrounded by a chain-link fence. It wasn't a bad neighborhood—small neat houses mostly—but it was a just a few blocks from Jay Street, which Mother had told Girl to avoid at all costs.

Wrong Chevy and Girl walked into his brother's house without knocking. Two women were in the living room. He introduced them to Girl as the middle brother Sammy's girlfriend and the older brother Timmy's wife. The women were just a few years older than Girl, pretty and friendly, with trendy clothes and highlighted hair. The oldest brother was at work and the one they called Sammy was asleep, so Girl and Wrong Chevy decided to come back another day.

They went back a few days later, when the middle brother, Samson, was both home and awake. Girl recognized him immediately—it was Right Chevy. He was older, bald on top but still sporting a ponytail. He was fatter and had a thick mustache, like a janitor's broom. His smile was the same, but it seemed less infectious.

The three of them hung out in the garage, looking at Samson's new bike and making small talk. Girl teased him about disappearing at that dance years ago, and he asked her to go to a meeting with him on the bike the next weekend. He seemed dorky, overly confident, and not all that bright. The shine had worn off for Girl. She was a college kid now, and she dated college kids, not factory workers with ring-around-the-head hairstyles, but she still said yes. Girl figured that maybe she would learn something about Wrong Chevy. Surely Right Chevy wasn't interested in her since she had dated his brother. Girl decided that it couldn't possibly be a date.

"You should totally go out with Sammy!" Wrong Chevy said on the drive home.

"Oh my God, I would never!" Girl answered.

"Why not?" he asked.

"He's a blue-collar worker!"

Girl's parents wouldn't have cared if she brought home a woman, an Asian- or African-American, a Hindu, a Muslim, or a Catholic, but no way would they approve of her dating "Johnny Lunch Bucket," as Stepmother called factory workers. She was expected to go to college and marry a boy (or girl) with a college degree.

Still, Girl was looking forward to their maybe a date/maybe not a date that Friday. She and Sharon discussed what Girl should wear, and decided she shouldn't look like she was trying too hard, just in case. Girl chose jeans, a muted green polo, and sneakers, her chin-length hair smooth and curled under. She didn't want to look like she thought it was a date if he didn't think it was a date, regardless of whether Girl had decided if she wanted it to be a date. Girl told her parents, and they begged her not to go anywhere with some strange man on a Harley.

"Girl, if you seriously want to remain friends with Wrong Chevy, you can't date his brother," Mother said.

"He wants me to," Girl said.

"He may say that now, but trust me, dating your ex-boyfriend's family never works out well." Mother replied.

Girl blew off her parents' concern. After all, Stepmother had two motorcycles and used to take Girl and Brother on rides around the neighborhood all the time—it's wasn't like they really thought bikes were dangerous. Even though Girl had had her share of boyfriends, she hadn't been on many dates—they had all been more the hang-out-in-the-living-room types, not the kind where you go to dinner or a movie or something, and she had never been on the back of a real Harley. Who cared if it was raining?

Stepmother called Girl at work Friday afternoon to try once more to talk her out of it.

"Girl, you have to cancel tonight. It's raining."

"It's supposed to stop," Girl said.

"At least promise me you won't go on I-90," she begged.

"Fine, whatever," Girl said, just to get off the phone. There was no way Girl could tell her maybe date that she wasn't allowed to go on the expressway. She was almost nineteen, and Chevy was going to be twenty-eight in a month's time. He was a man. He owned his own home. He wouldn't respect a girl whose mother wouldn't let her go on the highway in the rain.

Girl drove herself over to Right Chevy's house to get suited up in a leather jacket, helmet, and oilskin raincoat, though the rain had stopped. It turned out he thought it was a date.

"I wasn't sure if you were pretty or not," he confessed. "I've never dated a girl with short hair. But Tina thought you were pretty, so I looked at you again and decided she was right. I think you grow on people. Like algae."

"Algae?" Girl repeated, offended.

"You are a diamond in the rough—just like me. That's what my mother always said about me—I was her diamond in the rough."

It wasn't exactly flattering, though algae sounded better than mold. Chevy explained that his girlfriend had moved out that month. He hadn't known until the morning of their ride that she had dated his brother, but he wasn't concerned. There had been a lot of overlap in the three Chevy brothers' lists of ex-girlfriends. It was no big deal, he said.

They met up with Sharon and some friends to play cards, and Samson was loud and dorky and irritating. Every time he started to lose, he cheated, but so obviously that everyone called him on it and the hand had to be re-dealt. He laughed too loudly and rubbed his hands together like he was trying to start a fire, or thumped the person sitting next to him on the back so hard they cringed. But when the rain started on the ride home, he covered her hands with one of his to protect her from the needlelike drops of water, and that made up for all of his shortcomings.

The next weekend they rode to the locks on the Erie Canal, and Samson put his arms around Girl and rocked back and forth as they talked—he was a man who could not stay still, and she was a girl who had longed to be held and swayed. "I'm sorry," he said, "I rock when I'm happy." The night was dark. She could just barely see the water glimmering in the moonlight. Samson smelled of oiled leather and warm skin. Later, he picked Girl up and carried her over his shoulder without a grunt or change in breath. It was the first time she had ever felt dainty.

A few days later, Samson took Girl to Red Lobster and bought her a yellow rose wrapped in fragile cellophane. So far in life, the most romance Girl had received was dining in at Pizza Hut and a half-dead rose from 7-Eleven. Samson seemed so strong and grown-up with his full-time job. Ten years before, he had been the captain of his high school's hockey team and a star in football. For the first time, Girl was finally accepted by the cool kids, even if it was a decade too late.

Samson talked loud, rode fast, and vowed to protect Girl from the world. She had been scared of so much for so long. Broad-shouldered, barrel-chested, now completely bald with a goatee—he lifted weights, loved to fix things, and laughed about how stereotypically male he was. He knew he was a caricature of a man as much as Stepmother was a caricature of a lesbian, but he just thought it was funny.

Girl and Samson Chevy spent the summer riding around on the motorcycle while he applied for loans and opened lines of credit at various banks. Girl didn't really understand why, but she figured he was a grown-up and knew what he was doing. It probably had something to do with homeownership. He bought Girl thigh-high leather boots and a leather miniskirt. No guy had ever taken her to the mall and bought her things before.

One Sunday they went to meet some friends of his in Syracuse, about an hour away. It was cold and the bike wasn't running right so they took Girl's car, because Samson didn't own one. Samson always drove when they took her car, but she didn't mind. She'd only had her license for a year, and she didn't feel entirely competent yet. As with so many things in life, she preferred to let someone else be in control.

The car ahead of them was driving too slowly, so Samson honked and crept up closer and closer, until their bumper was a mere six inches from the car in front. He was yelling out the window and flipping off the other driver the whole time. Girl had never seen someone act this way—as crazy as Stepmother was, there were limits to what she would do in public.

Both men pulled their cars over and a screaming fight ensued. Girl cowered in the car, the doors locked. *Grown-ups do not act like this! This is my car, mine!* Girl thought, her fear turning to rage and pushing tears to the edges of her eyes, where pride refused to let them fall. Samson swung his fists at the taller stranger, who jumped out of range and dashed back in his car, speeding away as fast as he could.

"The secret to street fighting is to hit first and not be afraid to be crazier than they are," Samson said when he got back in the car. "When I was a kid, my father always said, if someone hits you, hit them back. And if they are too big for you to hit, hide behind a tree with a stick. When they walk by, hit them with the stick from behind, but walk around in front of them and make sure they knew you were the one who did it." He rubbed his hands together as he laughed.

Girl was so enraged she couldn't speak. How dare he? She wanted to get away from him right that minute, but they were seventy miles from home. She couldn't just leave him at the side of the road—he'd have no way back. It would be cruel. She told herself that she'd break up with him the moment they got back home. People didn't get into fistfights with strangers for driving too slowly—not people Girl knew. It wasn't *rational*, and in Girl's world, acting rational was more important than anything else.

They had to stop for gas, and Girl discovered that the envelope containing her pay for the week (which she had foolishly left lying on the back seat) was gone. They had had the windows open and her cash had blown out the open window, all eighty dollars of it. She was going to throw up. She hadn't brought her ATM card, had no way to get money, and they were out of gas. She couldn't breathe, she didn't know what to do. Her head was filled with condemnation: she was such an idiot, she was always doing stupid things like this—she didn't know what was wrong with her, how she could have been so dumb? She was supposed to be smart, but she was such a moron. She just didn't think. Why wasn't she using the air conditioning anyway? Why had she insisted on rolling down the windows, so much less convenient than just turning on the air? What was her problem? Why hadn't she just put the envelope in her purse like a normal person?

Samson took his last twenty out of his wallet and filled up Girl's tank.

"I'll just have to be careful grocery shopping this week," he said. Suddenly Girl wasn't so mad anymore.

They moved on from the incident like it had never happened. Samson and Girl became inseparable, spending nearly every minute together outside of work and school. Although she still had her apartment with Sharon, Girl only went home to grab clothes and read the nasty notes Sharon had left and write self-righteous ones back. Sharon thought Samson was irritating and stupid; Girl thought Sharon was too needy and demanding of her time. After a year cohabitating, Sharon and Girl could no longer see what had made them best friends in the first place. Sharon would get furious with Girl for not being there for her, once hurling a chair across the living room. Girl met her passionate feelings with icy silence. Girl withdrew, refused to talk, pretended that she didn't know why Sharon was so upset—that it was totally acceptable to vanish on her best friend now that Girl had a boyfriend. She started hanging out at Samson's house while he was at work, watching TV with his brother until the shift change released him at midnight.

They fell in love in the dark. Every night at midnight Girl picked him up from the factory and they'd drive back to his house. After work Samson always had a weird metallic smell and black grease deep in the folds of his skin. Fine metal dust would cling to the top of his head. As soon as they got home he'd shower while Girl sat on the bathroom floor—she didn't want to be away from him for even ten minutes. They rode to the grocery store on the motorcycle, her arms wrapped around his waist and her cheek pressed against his back in the warm summer air. Night surrounded them like a cocoon, the bike's headlight creating a bubble of space just big enough to keep the dark from getting too close.

They had midnight cookouts: grilling steaks, corn on the cob, and potatoes on a charcoal grill in the driveway, eating cherries while they waited for the meat to brown. He taught Girl how to season a steak, how to grill corn, and how long to cook a foil-wrapped potato over open flames. They talked and laughed while he tinkered with some project in the garage. When Samson revved the bike's motor too loudly the neighbors would knock on their bedroom window and he'd be quiet for a while, until he really needed to listen to the engine run.

When she met him, Girl could make Hamburger Helper and homemade whipped cream, but that was about it. Samson was Italian, and taught her how to make spaghetti sauce from scratch, alfredo sauce, and homemade macaroni and cheese. They bought ham on the bone, and made soup with the bone the following week. He worked alongside Girl, teaching her how to cut carrots with a rocking motion, instead of chopping like the knife was an axe. She learned to sauté vegetables instead of boiling them, how to time a meal so it would all be done at the same time. She even learned how to light the pilot light in the old stove without too much anxiety. Samson was a patient teacher and always complimented her on her results, no matter how questionable. Occasionally Girl would melt a bowl or burn a pot beyond recognition, but he never yelled. Afterward they cleaned up together, and he'd try his best to rehabilitate the pans she decimated, filling them half-full with soapy water and simmering them on the stove.

When they were home, they were never more than three feet apart. Girl read books in the garage while he worked on his bike, and she was happy to make dinner for the various men who were always appearing in the garage. Girl was proud of her subservience; she kept her thoughts to herself and never interrupted the men. Samson's slogans were "I'd rather have a broken-down Harley than a woman who doesn't know the meaning of silence" and "If it has tits or wheels, it'll give you problems." Girl tried her hardest never to cause him any problems.

Girl loved the smell of his sun-warmed skin, the feel of wind on her shoulders as they rode the Harley. They made up silly songs and sang them off-key together as they rode down random country roads, not caring who heard them or where they wound up. Girl became a fixture at the bike shop as well, where the storeowner would flirt with her outrageously and she would blush and smile back, too shy to say much of anything in return. One of Samson's friends humped her leg every time she saw him, another said things like, "I'd love to bend you over right here." Girl was flattered. It made her feel like a real girl, sexy. It made her feel pretty.

The bike broke down nearly every week, it seemed, and for some reason it always cost $300 to fix it, never $189, or $310, but exactly $300, every single time. The only thing that helped Samson feel better was making the bike go faster. That way he wasn't spending money to just fix stuff, he was improving it. When the bike broke down Samson was volatile and unpredictable. One minute they would be having a normal conversation in the kitchen and the next he'd be screaming at the top of his lungs, provoked by some random comment. Girl never knew what would set him off, and she had never seen anyone go from calm to furious so quickly. She came to view the repair bills as necessary for his mental health, and gave the Harley precedence over all other expenses, paying for groceries and gas with her own money, even though they weren't living together. She wanted him to be able to pour all his earnings into the bike, if that would let him be the happy, laughing man she fell in love with.

Samson didn't just swear, he raised it to an art form. "Mother fucking son of a bitch!" echoed out of the garage, and Girl would know that his rage-o-meter had gone through the roof. She always ran toward the screaming.

Sometimes Girl yelled back, slamming doors and storming off. This was a surefire way to break his mood. The sight of Girl standing up to him, "like a little mouse yelling at a lion," as he said, made him laugh and calm down, instantly breaking the tension.

a quick lesson in motorcycle clubs

Samson was in a bike club called the Fifth Chapter. It was started by a group of people in AA who helped each other stay sober and who talked to treatment centers to help spread the message of sobriety. The name referred to the fifth chapter of the *Big Book* of Alcoholics Anonymous, which details reaching out to the newcomer. Samson and Girl both went to AA regularly. Samson had been sober a year longer than Girl, although she followed a stricter adherence to the twelve steps than he did. Members of his club went on camping trips and bike rides together, and Samson was always expanding the club by starting a new local chapter, so the two of them went to a lot of planning meetings, where women and non-members sat outside and waited. Girl learned to always bring a book in her purse. The Fifth Chapter members all had "biker names" like Doobin, Mutt, Butch, and Hound Dawg. Samson's name was Bookkeeper, though everyone called him Chevy. He picked the name from an old western movie—it had nothing to do with recordkeeping.

For those who don't know anything about bike clubs, it is the official term for what most people call gangs, and "club" can mean outlaw bikers like the Hell's Angels or the Outlaws, or it can mean a tame group like the Fifth Chapter. If you wanted to start a bike club, though, even a sober one, proper protocol entailed going to talk to the dominant outlaw club, which in our case was the Hell's Angels. The Angels had to give permission for clubs to wear "colors," as they called the patches on the backs of their jackets, and no one wanted to be in a club that didn't get to wear patches. Hell's Angels–approved patches were really cool to a lot of people. Interestingly, Hell's Angels themselves rarely wore patches in public, because it would mark them to rival gangs and the police.

Before Girl met Samson, he was very active in a local chapter that was inclusive of all people who rode motorcycles or trikes of any manufacture, and where women and men were treated equally. Apparently, Samson got into a heated fight with one of the founding members, a heavyset "butch" woman married to his sponsor. (Later Girl learned that this particular type of woman triggered the worst of his temper.) The fight was so bad that Samson left the club to start his own chapter. The two chapters he founded when Girl was with him both had the same rules: no female members, no foreign bikes. New prospective members had to "prospect" for a year, during which time any full member could ask them to do anything they wanted and they had to do it— mainly washing bikes and giving up comfortable chairs at meetings. Although the members that Girl knew were mainly married older men, they had specific rules about women. For example, if someone wanted to date someone's ex-girlfriend, they had to ask their permission and give their biker brother two dollars in exchange. Samson's ex, the one Girl had met previously, was riding around with one of his biker brothers and the man had failed to give Samson the courtesy of the two-dollar payment, and Samson was livid. Worse still, the guy was only a prospect.

The bikers Girl knew in the Fifth Chapter called their wife or girlfriend "Old Lady" and if they were really serious about them, the biker could buy their Old Lady a "Lady Patch" she could wear on the back of her jacket to show she was the property of the club and deserved a higher level of respect than hang-around girls. Girl wanted one so badly, but she didn't let on. She even picked out her biker name: Belle, from *Beauty and the Beast*. After all, Belle had brown hair and brown eyes and always had her nose in a book. Samson's temper made him a Beast, but a loveable one, in Girl's eyes.

The guys liked to talk about "passarounds" and a class of girl called a "house mouse" who were granted the privilege of living with a bunch of bikers in exchange for having sex with whomever wanted it, but Girl never actually met any of these women. She only saw a bunch of guys in their forties riding around feeling tough, sometimes accompanied by nice, normal wives.

Samson soon gave up the bike club scene entirely. He said he joined because he needed family, but after he met Girl he didn't need them anymore. Girl was more than happy to fill the void, though she secretly longed to go on the big rallies and poker runs he talked about so often and which were now consigned to his past.

ryan
fall 1992

Ryan and Girl sat in his car in a church parking lot. It was bitter cold outside, gray and un-wedding-like, though it was only the end of September. They had finished setting up for the service, but instead of leaving for the next stop Ryan lit a cigarette.

"We're running ahead of schedule," he said. "Let's talk for a minute."

"Okay," Girl said. During the summer they rarely talked much at the shop—everyone was running in different directions. She was glad to have time alone with Ryan.

"T-cells are like soldiers," he said. Girl knew all about T-cells from William, but instead of being her usual know-it-all self, she let Ryan talk.

"Infections are like bad soldiers in your blood, and T-cells are the good soldiers. A normal person has like five hundred to a thousand T-cells. My last count was seventy-five."

Girl knew what he was telling her. Although William had said Ryan was HIV positive, Girl still clung to that comment he made on her first day at work—*I don't got AIDS.* She had so hoped those words were true.

"I'll die of lung cancer. No one is to ever mention that I have AIDS. I don't want my kids to have to live through that stigma. Lung cancer isn't so bad." He flicked an ash out the window. Ryan only owned two coats—a black leather jacket and a long 1970s raccoon fur coat. He wore the leather jacket, because it was more masculine, even though it was so cold and he was so thin.

"How long have you been sick?" Girl asked.

"Two years."

William lived five years, Girl thought. There was still time.

"I've picked out my funeral home," Ryan said. "They have these emery boards with their name and phone number printed on them. I told them I want the emery boards out in bowls so everyone can have a souvenir." He coughed his deep hacking cough with which Girl was so familiar and flicked his cigarette butt out onto the ground, rolled the window up, and put the car in drive.

A few weeks later Girl came into work and everyone was quiet.

"Ryan is in the hospital," Tony said. "But he doesn't want visitors. He says he needs to rest."

No one talked much at the shop, and when Ryan returned no one mentioned it. He went back into the hospital again a few weeks later, then was sent home on oxygen. He never returned to work after that second hospital stay.

"You need to go visit him," Tony said one day. "This is it."

Girl didn't want to. More than anything, she didn't want him to die. Her first semester in college Brother's best friend had died in the drunk driving accident. Second semester, it had been William. Now it was her third semester, and she couldn't go through that again, not now. It was too many deaths. Girl didn't think she could take any more.

She knew she had to, though. After work Girl went to the grocery store and got some Pedialyte in what Tony had told her was Ryan's favorite flavor, and a dozen Sonia roses—his favorite color—tied with a pale peach ribbon. Girl stopped at the fancy soup store on Park Avenue and bought some soup and crackers, then drove over to Ryan and Mike's house. She rang the bell, but no one answered, so she set her brown paper bag on the steps and left.

Ryan called her later.

"You should have called first! I can't hear the bell over the oxygen, and besides, there needs to be someone to let you in because I can't get downstairs anymore."

"I'm sorry," she said. "I didn't think about that." She was nineteen.

"Well, thank you for the flowers and the Pedialyte. It cheered me up."

Girl had a dream a few days later that Ryan was talking to her. *You have to pull yourself together and face this*, the dream-Ryan said. *It's time.* Girl woke to the telephone ringing in the kitchen, telling her what she already knew. Ryan was gone.

Girl hadn't spoken to Sharon in months, not since their lease ended. They had fought for months leading up to it, and after they moved out neither of them wanted anything to do with each other. That night, after dark, Girl rang Sharon's doorbell.

Sharon's boyfriend answered the door. Girl had always liked Phil. He went upstairs to find Sharon in their second-story apartment. When Sharon came down the stairs, her face was both angry and indignant, but she opened the glass door anyway, arms folded across her chest, leg out in the pissed-off stance Girl had seen so many times lately.

"Ryan," Girl said, and started to cry. Sharon put her arms around Girl and they sobbed together.

Ryan had wanted a closed casket, but the funeral home had a private showing just for immediate family, and South Wedge employees were considered family. Ryan was dressed, as always, in black dress pants, a white long-sleeved shirt, and a bolo tie. Girl was glad they hadn't put him in a suit. He had always been thin, but she hadn't noticed how skeletal he had become. Girl thought about how her biker boyfriend had thumped him hard on the back in an overenthusiastic hug the last time he saw him and sent Ryan into a coughing fit. Girl should have told Samson how fragile Ryan was. She should have protected him. She thought of Ryan's long raccoon coat that he always wore to parties. She wished it was in the casket with him to keep him warm.

The South Wedge employees worked all day at the shop, servicing the weddings still on the schedule. The phone rang so many times with friends and customers wanting to send flowers to the funeral home that they had to turn them away, and eventually just left the phone off the hook. After work, they all went to the viewing together.

Every tabletop and mantel in the whole first floor of the funeral home was filled with vases of Casablanca lilies and Sonia roses. There were so many people you could hardly move. Girl took an emery board from one of the bowls and put it in her purse, like Ryan had wanted.

The day of the funeral they had to set up a wedding. When Girl got there, the bride was furious.

"I specifically requested regular eucalyptus, not seeded eucalyptus! This is the wrong green! And there was supposed to be silk eucalyptus in my sister's bouquet because she's allergic! I should never have let them hand my wedding over to Bob. Where is Ryan anyway?"

"Ryan is dead," Girl said. "After I'm done here I'm going to his funeral."

The bride's face got all crazy-looking as the anger and shock fought for control over her features. Shock won.

"Oh, I didn't know," she said. Girl just walked away. She shouldn't have done that. She shouldn't have told the bride that Ryan died just five minutes before she walked down the aisle. Girl knew she had spoiled the woman's wedding, but she couldn't help it. She knew Ryan wouldn't have approved.

Tony, Bob, Mike, and Girl drove together, racing to get to the funeral on time. They were always late. When they passed a hearse on the expressway, Tony laughed.

"Ryan always said he'd be late to his own funeral, and look—he is!" After that they slowed down and followed the hearse. The church wouldn't start the service until the casket arrived.

The obituary said that Ryan died of lung cancer. He was thirty-eight. Two months later the shop closed. According to the Internet, his partner Mike died in 1997, though Girl never saw him again after the shop closed. The online entry says he never married, the twenty years he spent with Ryan unrecorded.

Girl couldn't bear to work around flowers after Ryan died. Instead, she went to work for a veterinarian for less money—cleaning cages, assisting with surgeries, and mopping floors. When an animal was euthanized, Girl had to bag the still-warm body in a garbage bag and take it to the freezer, tears flowing down her cheeks. Perhaps Girl would have been better off finding a new gay family, but she couldn't stand to watch them die, too. At least here she had live animals to take care of most of the time, and death was sporadic, not guaranteed.

christmas
december 23, 1992

Girl picked up Samson at midnight and they drove to the grocery store. The night was crisp with a hint of expectation that always materialized with the snow in late December.

"When do you want to do gifts?" Samson asked.

"I don't know. We could bring everything to Mom's, or we could do them alone ahead of time," Girl answered. She was really excited about their first Christmas together. She had bought Samson a black sweater with black leather trim and bottles of both his favorite cologne and a new one she had liked at the store as well. She had bought the nut-driver tool set he asked for, spending all of her extra money on presents, as she did every year. Samson had warned Girl that if he found any presents hidden in the house that he would open them right away. Girl wrapped his presents and then hid them under the seats in her car and piled old McDonald's bags on top of them. Samson always called her car the "B. F. Dumpster" so she knew he would never think to look there. She was proud of her trickery but she didn't know how she was going to wait two more days. She loved Christmas.

They were having the three Chevy siblings that lived in town—Timmy, Carson, and Cindy—over for dinner Christmas Eve, then were going to church with Girl's parents for the late service.

"I think we should open them at home Christmas Eve," Girl said. She really didn't want to wait any longer.

"I think we should open them tonight, so it's just us," Samson said.

"Okay!"

They stopped at a red light, waiting for the left turn arrow, when Samson looked at Girl strangely—his mouth was somehow wrong and his eyes looked watery.

"I want you to be my wife," he said, pulling a box from his pocket.

It wasn't really a question, but she said "yes" anyway and started to cry. The ring was a small marquis-cut diamond that he had picked out with his sister that afternoon, while Girl was at school. Girl thought it looked like a glittering snowflake plucked from the Christmas air and set on a fine gold band. Married. It was all she had ever wanted in the world.

clash of the titans

Girl finished her associate's degree that summer and joined Sharon at St. John Fisher, a four-year college. She and Samson had been engaged for a year but were waiting for Girl to finish her bachelor's degree to get married. Father, Stepmother, and Mother were all contributing to her expenses: paying tuition, making her car payments, and giving Girl enough child support so that she could go to school full time and work only part time. Girl had lunch with Mother nearly every week, and on Sundays she went to their house for family dinner.

"Mother, I like having lunch with you, but I don't want to come to family dinner anymore. I just can't deal with Stepmother," Girl told Mother over the phone.

"That's fine," Mother said, her voice evenly modulated. "But Stepmother pays half of your tuition and car payment. If you refuse to see her, don't expect her to continue to support you."

Girl was sick of them holding money over her head. She did the math during class—now that Samson was collecting unemployment plus working under the table at the bike shop, they had more money than they ever had before. Girl was working part time at a new flower shop, and they liked her there. If she worked full time instead of part time, they'd only be short about $100–$200 a month, and she could still take a class or two at night. Girl wanted to be a real grown-up, not dependent on anyone. She wanted to have her own family. She wanted a wedding. She wanted to be Mrs. Somebody.

If Girl stopped taking Stepmother's money, she wouldn't have to play "happy family" anymore. So what if it took her as extra year or two to finish? She told Samson her plan, and he agreed. He had only gone to college for a few semesters and then dropped out, so he didn't see a four-year degree as essential, and she already had an associate's degree. They decided to push the wedding up to the next summer, just under a year away.

Stepmother's parents—Girl's grandparents—were in town from West Virginia. Even though they were not thrilled that their daughter was gay, they always acted like real grandparents toward the children. They were somewhat conservative and profoundly religious, so everyone agreed not to tell them that Samson and Girl were living together. It seemed easiest.

Girl and Samson went to her parents' house for dinner. They pulled extra chairs from the dining room to make places for everyone in the living room. Everyone was sitting around and talking, and Samson was needling Stepmother. She had made her living selling life insurance, though she had been receiving mental-health disability for years, selling policies under Mother's name. Samson was collecting unemployment from his factory job, but working six days a week at the bike shop. They were both scamming the system, as far as Girl was concerned. Samson was going on about how insurance was all a racket, and that people who sold insurance were even worse than used car salesmen. Girl was in a side conversation with her grandmother and not really listening. Samson liked to provoke people when he was bored, and he and Stepmother had no great love for each other. Stepmother looked down on his lack of education, and he looked down on her lack of couth. He might have chosen a blue-collar job, but he'd been raised in the country club set. When Samson and Girl went to leave at the end of the evening, Stepmother got up and followed them out.

Girl and Samson had made it as far as the sidewalk and Stepmother was at the top of the kitchen steps. Her face was red and taut, her hands on her beefy hips. She was only five foot two but outweighed Girl by at least fifty pounds. While female, she exuded masculine strength and, at that moment, anger. She called down to them, "You need to know that before you can marry my daughter, you need a full-time job with benefits!"

Girl just stood there. She was five inches taller than Stepmother, but when Stepmother yelled, Girl turned small. It made her lose her words.

Samson didn't pause for a moment—he unleashed a tirade on Stepmother that ended with "I'm going to rip off your head and shit down your throat!" After which he slid into the driver side of the car, Girl hastily hopped into the passenger's side, and they drove off. Girl was shaking like a naughty puppy, like she always did when people fought, but inside, she was overflowing with exaltation. She had waited her whole life for someone to not just stand up to Stepmother, but to win. Samson might have been too aggressive, but he protected Girl from all the people she was afraid of, and the number one person she was afraid of was Stepmother. He had slayed Girl's dragon.

"She came at me. She was above me, looking down. She was trying to intimidate me by staying up on the steps where she thought she was safe. I showed her!" Samson crowed on the car ride home.

"You didn't even do anything to deserve it!" Girl said, defensive of him.

"Sure I did. Didn't you hear me needle her about what a scam insurance is? She thinks I'm Johnny Lunch Bucket, but she's no better than me. I was provoking her and she knew it, and she wasn't gonna let us leave till she pissed on her territory. She wants to act like a man, I'm going to treat her like one."

Mother called Girl the next day.

"We were up all night terrified that Samson was going to come and kill us. Every time we heard a noise Stepmother would grab her gun. You know we really need to talk about Samson's anger."

Girl didn't see it that way and said so. She didn't think Samson had done anything worse than Stepmother had. It was just that for once, someone had out-bullied the bully.

"Girl, he threatened us," Mother said. "How can you think that's okay?"

"Come on, Mom, that wasn't a real threat. Ripping someone's head off is superlative."

"No, I meant it," Samson said when she relayed the conversation to him later. "They were right to be scared. But I was just defending myself."

Girl and Mother didn't speak for two months. They had never gone this long without making up—they had always spoken at least a few times a week on the phone, even after she ran away back in high school. For Girl, every day was marked with an undercurrent of sadness. She missed her mom. She didn't know what to do. Christmas came, and they made up just enough for Girl to go over to their house on Christmas morning, but without Samson.

Spring came, and although Girl and Mother talked every now and then, they didn't see each other in person. Girl asked Mother to look at wedding dresses with her, but she replied, "I can't picture all four of us in the same room together, let alone at the wedding."

Girl went dress shopping alone, without a single friend or relative who thought this union was a good idea. It didn't matter. Girl would marry this man no matter what anyone else thought.

Mother's anger finally broke.

"What can you and I do to get Stepmother and Samson to make up?" she asked Girl. Within a week the four of them met at a restaurant, and no one mentioned the fight, or apologized. They just went on like it hadn't happened. When Stepmother reached her spoon into Samson's bowl of ice cream, he didn't say a word, though he didn't eat any more of it.

name change

Girl walked down the aisle in her white princess dress. She had bought it from a classified ad in the newspaper—the only bridal gown she could afford—but it was beautiful, and thick satin, not that flame-retardant crap a lot of bridal stores sold. It didn't have a train, but you can't have everything. When Girl walked out of the church—ran, actually, holding hands with her new husband—she became Wife. She had always wanted to be Wife, had decided to change her name as soon as she could, but now . . . let's be honest, it was a little weird. Part of her missed being Girl, like when she wrote a check and had to stop and think for a minute, sometimes starting the first letter wrong and having to draw that "W" over the beginnings of the "G." The "G" had more grace to it. The "W" was stiffer, less round. Now her high school friends would not know how to look her up in the phone book, but that was a small price to pay. She was starting her own family. She belonged somewhere now.

moving on

"I need you and Brother to come over for dinner tonight," Mother told Girl one night. "We have something to tell you." Girl could not imagine what was too important for a phone call, but she sensed it wasn't something good.

"We were on vacation in Mexico, and I saw a little sailboat bobbing on the water. It looked so peaceful," Mother said.

"Then I realized that I wasn't depressed in Mexico," Stepmother added.

"So we bought a twenty-eight-foot catamaran," Mother said.

"I was a small watercraft instructor back at Camp Ononda," Stepmother interrupted.

"I gave my notice at work, and we are going to live on a sailboat," Mother said. "My parents died at sixty-one and sixty-six. If I only have ten years left, I'm not spending it in the office."

"I already got us a contract doing sunset sails for gay and lesbian couples in Mexico," Stepmother added.

Girl and Brother looked at each other. This was insane. They both knew that Stepmother's experience sailing dinghies on a lake twenty years before was nothing compared to the open ocean.

"And the dogs?" Girl asked. George, the dog she brought back from Alaska, still lived with Mother, and Stepmother had a snaggletoothed Shih Tzu that she had impulse-bought on one of her manic shopping binges.

"They are coming with us," Mother said.

"And the cat, too, of course," Stepmother added, picking up the twenty-pound cat and placing him on her lap.

"We are putting the house on the market this week, so you'll need to clean out any of your old things that you still want," Mother said.

You weren't depressed because you were on vacation, Girl thought, but said nothing. She understood that her parents deserved freedom. Girl was engaged and Brother was in college and they were twenty and twenty-one, respectively.

Girl understood that Mother had done her time parenting—she always told Girl that children were an eighteen-year commitment. Girl still felt abandoned. She didn't feel like she had moved past needing a mother. Girl was sad to her bones.

But oh, the irony of it! She had prayed for years, "Please, God, let Stepmother move somewhere far, far away, like Antarctica." Now she finally got her wish and Stepmother really was moving far away, but Girl forgot to specify that she didn't want her mother to go, too. Better she had not prayed at all.

That January, Mother and Stepmother paid to fly Girl and Samson down to Key West to visit them on the boat. Brother had gone for Christmas. "He's not in a relationship, Girl, so I think it's really important that Brother isn't alone for Christmas," Mother had explained. There wasn't room for all of them on the boat, and Samson and Girl couldn't afford a hotel. It had been Girl's first Christmas without her mother, but she had managed. The worst part had been singing Christmas carols without her in church.

When Mother picked them up at the airport, she was deeply tanned. When the gray in Mother's hair stopped being premature and became age-appropriate, she had started dyeing it, and the sun had bleached the dye in her hair to a weird yellow that was half-grown out. Stepmother was wearing a black captain's hat and a nose ring. Girl tried not to comment—she tried not to even look at it—but she couldn't help herself.

"You pierced your nose?" she asked.

"I got you! I have been waiting to get you and Brother back for embarrassing me my whole life! I finally got you!" Stepmother laughed. "It's a fake," she explained, taking the ring out of her nostril. "See? It's a magnet. But it was broken, so I got it on sale, and it hurts. I was waiting and waiting for you to say something so I could take it out." Stepmother had always thought Girl's and Brother's hair and clothing choices were done "just to spite me," even though, as teenagers, they were far more concerned with being cool than they were about embarrassing Stepmother.

They rode in a gray, inflatable boat out to "the hook." Mother and Stepmother had tried to rely on their anchor at night, but after drifting twice into other boats, they had given in and rented a mooring—an underwater concrete pillar with a cable running to the surface.

Their catamaran looked fat and stunted, not sleek like a motorboat, nor graceful like a sailboat. They had lost their mast. It was the oddest-looking thing Girl had seen on the water.

"So we were feeling pretty good about ourselves, and we decided to enter the Wrecker's Race," Mother explained.

"We got talked into it!" Stepmother was seething. "And your mother wanted the free T-shirt!"

"We were at a bar with a bunch of live-a-boards and they had these T-shirts from last year's race," Mother said. "I wanted a T-shirt, too! Plus, they told us that there were free appetizers and a party after the race." She didn't look regretful at all.

"Ten-thousand-dollar T-shirt, Judy," Stepmother said, with no humor in her voice.

"We talked Madeleine and Penny into being our crew. It was a lovely, sunny day and we got there early," Mother said.

"We were right out in the front row, just bobbing up and down and waiting for the race to start," Stepmother added. "Then I turned around and looked behind us and saw all the other boats lined up for the race and I knew we were in over our heads. So I started the engine and turned around—"

. "But the race had just started and there were like fifty boats coming toward us in the opposite direction," Mother interjected.

"So we were crossing in front of one of the schooners," Stepmother continued.

"And there were tourists all up and down the rail, and their sails were full," Mother said, enjoying the story, even though she knew how it ended.

"And *they* hit *us*! It was not our fault," Stepmother said.

Samson interjected, "If you were motoring and they were under sail, they had the right of way." He had grown up waterskiing on lakes and knew more than Girl did about the rules for boating in populated areas. In Alaska, where the children had sailed with Father, there were very few other boats to contend with.

"*They* hit *us*," Stepmother repeated. "And broke off our mast."

"We ripped a hole in their side," Mother said, in a *fair's fair* tone of voice, an evilly happy look in her eyes.

Oh God, Girl thought. The tourists had paid good money for that race. There were a few tall ships in Key West, called schooners, over a hundred feet long. There was no way they could stop forward motion when Stepmother cut in front of them.

"We have a call in to the boat repair place," Mother said. "Which means we'll get to stay in a slip in the marina for free while they repair it. Did you know Lloyd's of London is the only company that insures boats? And they ring a bell every time one goes down. I wonder if they rang the bell for us."

"They keep insisting it was our fault," Stepmother said. "But I told them, we were power-sailing. Yes, we had the motor going, but we had a sail up, too. We were sailing. *They* hit *us*."

The dogs barked a greeting to Girl as they pulled abreast of the *Sea Gypsy*. They wore pet-sized yellow life vests and seemed to have adjusted to living onboard. Mother took them to shore a few times a day in the dinghy, because although Muffin had never been fully housebroken and would pee anywhere, Mother had been unable to train George to pee on a plant at the back of the boat.

Their boat was as cluttered as their house had been. Father had run a tight ship—everything had to be stowed away before they left harbor. Stepmother's papers and pens and loose coins and little shells and seeds she had gathered topped every flat surface. They had an unsecured TV, and when the family motored out to the reef, it flew from one side of the cabin to the other, crashed against the wall, and came to rest on the built-in bench.

The first thing Girl noticed was the clutter, and the second thing was the smell. Mother and Stepmother were proud of this boat—it cost more than their house had—and showed Samson and Girl their berth and the tiny "head" or bathroom. Mother explained how to pump the toilet and admonished Girl not to flush toilet paper, but to put it in the grocery bag hanging on the wall. There were two built-in beds over the pontoons, and a large cabin at the bow of the boat where Mother and Stepmother slept. Samson and Girl had one berth, and on the other side was the cat's berth, the main source of the smell. Humid sea air infused with dirty litter box and a trace of urine-soaked toilet paper flooded the entire cabin.

That night, Samson and Girl rolled back and forth in their bed to the motion of the waves. The hot smell and constant movement made Girl sick to her stomach. Samson and Girl whispered about Mel Fisher, a local treasure hunter, who lost one of his children when their boat sank due to disrepair. For the first time, Girl worried that she wasn't going to make it out of this vacation. She had never doubted her parents' ability to keep her safe, but it was obvious that they had no idea what they were doing, and she knew that the ocean could be dangerous.

Mother and Stepmother lived on the boat for two years, and in spite of Girl's misgivings, nothing that terrible ever happened. Sure, they crashed a few times, and Mother got all sorts of bruises and once even a flesh-eating bacterial infection in her thumb. Thankfully, they gave up on sailing to Mexico. "I just couldn't figure out how to deal with the dogs when we were out of sight of land," Mother explained. "George would have had to hold it for two days, and that didn't seem fair." Eventually they bought a trailer on a canal with deep water access, but once Mother got on land, she was done with sailing.

They did have one last adventure, though. Some friends of theirs were sailing to Cuba, and invited Girl's parents to follow along in the *Sea Gypsy*. They had gone so far as to hire a man on as crew, but then they decided the trip was beyond their skill set.

"It's a good thing, too," Stepmother told Girl. "He had already stowed his things on the boat, and after he left we found naked Barbie dolls and a penis pump. That wouldn't have gone over very well in customs."

Their friends invited Stepmother and Mother to crew on their larger boat, and they sailed over without much trouble.

"When we got there, customs boarded the boat," Mother said. "And they were really upset that we had brought hard boiled eggs. They have no salmonella in Cuba, so they didn't want to let American eggs come to shore. They were going to make us turn around."

"I offered to throw the eggs overboard," Stepmother interrupted, "But that got them even more upset."

"Finally, we agreed to eat the eggs in front of the customs officer, and then put the shells in a Ziploc bag and promised to bring them with us when we left," Mother said.

The trouble started on their return trip. The waves were a little rough, and Stepmother got seasick, so she went below decks.

"That's the worst thing you can do when you are seasick," Girl interrupted.

"I know, but you can't tell Stepmother anything," Mother said, continuing the story. "So Stepmother went below and the waves were rolling, and she hit her head, and must have passed out. Mary went down to check on her, and Stepmother jumped on her back and started punching her."

"I had amnesia," Stepmother explained. "I thought they were kidnapping us and taking us to Cuba."

"So I heard the noise and went down, and found Stepmother on top of Mary, and had to explain to her that we weren't being kidnapped."

"I was so confused. I kept asking, 'Am I a comuniss? Are you a comuniss?'"

"I explained to her that she hit her head, and she'd get it for a while, then a few minutes later, she'd start asking if she was a communist again," Mother said.

"Once I came back to myself I felt just terrible, and I apologized to Mary," Stepmother said. "But they turned the boat around and went back to Cuba,"

"We were closer to Cuba than the United States," Mother added.

"And they just left us on the docks!" Stepmother said. "Can you believe it? There I was with a concussion and they just left us and took off!"

"Everyone was very nice in the hospital," Mother said. "I didn't have anywhere to go, and I hadn't brought any money because it is illegal for an American citizen to spend money in Cuba. But they just assume that when you go to the hospital you bring someone with you to take care of you, so they made me a bed next to Stepmother, and every time they brought her meals, they brought me one, too. I was responsible for changing her sheets and bathing her. That's just how they do it down there. But Girl, their hospital was so poorly equipped. They only had little samples of medicine. Sometimes they gave Stepmother Tylenol, sometimes Advil, depending on what they had."

"I am going to organize a shipment of medication and send it to Cuba," Stepmother said.

"So when the doctors said Stepmother was okay to leave, we had to call Stepmother's parents to send money. They had to wire money to 'an itinerant American living in Cuba,'" Mother said.

"There I was, fifty years old, and having to wire my parents for money," Stepmother said. "It was so embarrassing."

"So we had to call the US embassy, and NASA sent a really old plane down to get us. It was the scariest looking plane I have ever seen. I didn't think it would make it back to the United States."

"I called Mary and her husband again to apologize, even though it wasn't very nice of them to leave us like that when I was injured," Stepmother said. "But they won't speak to me. I think they should apologize to me!"

Girl just rolled her eyes.

a different kind of commitment

Mother and Stepmother spent the winters in Key West, and returned north to a little cabin an hour outside of Rochester in the summer. While they were gone, Mother and Girl spoke on the phone nearly every day. Girl noticed a change in Mother. She and Stepmother were fighting more, though Mother wasn't very vocal on why.

"I started throwing dishes," Mother said. "It feels really good to throw dishes—it's really quite satisfying when they crash. You should try it." Girl was astonished, but also kind of proud of her. It was about time Mother stood up for herself. The next call surprised her, though.

"Girl, I just wanted you to know that I have committed Stepmother against her will at dePoo Hospital. I talked with her psychiatrist, and Stepmother is very angry with me, but we agreed that it was necessary." Slowly, the story came out.

Stepmother had fallen back in love with an old lover, the one with the long red hair. Stepmother was calling her and writing her love letters, and even sent the woman ten thousand dollars to help her pay her bills. Mother had asked her to stop communicating with this woman, but Stepmother refused. Mother and Stepmother had broken up, and when it became apparent that Stepmother was abusing her medication, Mother committed her to the mental-health center.

"I don't think this woman did anything wrong," Mother told Girl. "I think she was as baffled by Stepmother's behavior as I was."

"Your mother cried a lot when Stepmother was in the hospital," one of Mother's closest friends told Girl. "But she never said she missed her. She only said over and over that she didn't want to rebuild her life again."

Girl was strangely sad. She had wanted for Stepmother and Mother to divorce for her whole life, but she didn't expect to feel any sort of loss over it. Still, when they reconciled a few weeks later, she was disappointed. She wanted so much better for Mother than how Stepmother treated her. But Stepmother was regulated now—Mother had explained that Stepmother had increased her meds in order to feel high all the time, but the doctors had gotten her levels back to normal—and Mother of course took her back. The next time Mother called Girl, she told her that they had sold the trailer and bought a large house on a canal on the other side of the island. "It may seem sudden, but it was something we've discussed for a long time," Mother explained. This became a pattern: every time their relationship was on the rocks, they resolved it by purchasing something big and expensive: a new cabin, an RV, a bigger house.

an un-commitment

Girl woke up at 2:00 a.m. because Samson wasn't there. Even in her sleep, she was waiting for him to come home and pull the blankets back, waking her just enough to resettle herself against him. But he never came, and so Girl woke alone in the empty bed. She called his work and his coworker said that Samson had left on his motorcycle hours ago. Terror flushed Girl's face hot; her pulse quickened. She finally registered the missed call notification on her phone, and she dialed in to her voicemail with shaking hands. She had known it would come to this sooner or later. The recording said, "Will the family of Samson Chevy please call Strong Memorial Hospital . . ."

Just say he's not dead just say he's not dead, she chanted in her head as she dialed the emergency room. Samson was Superman. Girl couldn't imagine any instance that would keep him from calling himself. This was the man who rode a wheelie into a brick wall and gave himself a concussion, all without dropping the donuts he carried on his handlebars. This was the man who ripped his hamstring in half and was still walking around, asking if his bike was okay.

"Your husband's been in an accident," the nurse said. "He's awaiting surgery. That's all we can tell you."

Girl was wearing his red-and-black, muscle-man workout pants, one of his Harley-Davidson T-shirts, and white gym socks. She didn't stop to find a bra. Girl threw on a coat and the first pair of shoes she could find—fancy suede flats that she had kicked off by the front door when she came home from work the night before.

Girl tried to drive quickly, but she couldn't concentrate, and accidentally went the wrong way and had to loop around the city, getting directions from Mother on her cell phone as she drove—of course she had called Mother the minute she left the house, even though it was the middle of the night, and Mother calmed her down, gave her directions, helped her focus. The ten-minute drive took nearly thirty in the blowing snow. Finally, Girl reached the hospital. She had to wait until Samson was stabilized to see him. Girl spent thirty minutes in the waiting room watching a runny-nosed child climb on and off the chairs, off and on, while she waited to learn her husband's fate.

Eventually, the nurse directed her to the proper gurney. Feathers floated in the air—they had cut off his down snowmobile suit. The nurses were laughing about the feathers. He could make anyone smile, even while lying in a hospital bed.

Samson wore a hospital gown with blue ship's wheels on it, his leg wrapped in gauze bandages that were starting to seep yellow and red. Girl leaned close to his face and kissed his cheek, whispering in his ear that no matter what, they would get him a new motorcycle. A motorcycle had gotten him into this hospital bed, but she needed him to know that she hadn't turned on him—that she understood that he feared the loss of his bikes more than the loss of his leg.

Samson told her the details of riding his dirt bike home on dark, snow-covered streets. He had left work after 11:00 p.m., and a car didn't brake for a stop sign before it pulled into oncoming traffic. Samson's right leg was the point of impact. A woman from a nearby gas station had cushioned his head with her flannel shirt as they waited for an ambulance.

The doctor came in.

"Near-total amputation of the right leg just below the knee," he reported, and then asked, "Where doesn't it hurt?"

Samson raised his pinky, and everyone laughed, but once the doctor started pushing and prodding his flesh, Samson cried out in pain. The room suddenly seemed hot and Girl couldn't hear anything but the blood rushing in her ears. *Don't pass out, you can't pass out, you wuss*, she told herself over and over. Girl ran to the bathroom, barely making it before her bowels emptied. She wished her body responded by throwing up—it would have been less mortifying.

Girl returned to the room just before the doctor took Samson into surgery.

"It'll take three or four surgeries over the next few weeks," the orthopedist said. "We'll know more once we open him up, but I think we can reattach it. Then we'll send him to a plastic surgeon for the final skin grafts."

Girl was directed to the main waiting room. The chairs smelled old, though the colors were new. Everyone ignored the silent TV that was hung too high on the wall to be worth watching. They stayed as far apart from each other as they could, each of them holding their private vigils in public, keeping to the corners of the mostly empty room like rubbery macaroni stuck to the sides of a pot.

Brother came to sit with Girl, and she breathed easier when he walked in. No matter what, she would be okay now. Next to arrive was Liz—the only friend Girl could trust to explain the difference between the piles of clean, dirty, and semi-dirty-but-can-be-worn-again laundry in her bedroom. Girl needed a bra badly, but she wouldn't drive the half-hour round trip home to get one, just in case. She wouldn't read a book, just in case. She had to mark every minute, feel every tick of the second hand, just in case it was his last. Five hours later they called her name, and a doctor in clean scrubs told Girl that it would be several weeks before Samson could be discharged. They wouldn't give odds on whether or not he would ever regain the use of the leg. No one warned her that Samson would spend days in the intensive care unit, receive four blood transfusions, and never walk without pain again. She didn't know that three years later he would still be out of work, addicted to morphine, and filled with even more rage.

Two weeks after the accident Girl drove Samson home from the hospital. He had rods, pins, screws, and guide wires holding his foot and leg together. Part of his *rectus abdominis* muscle had been removed from his abdomen and grafted onto his calf. Four skin grafts covered the wounds that gaped too much for the doctors to stitch shut. His leg looked like gray, uncooked sausage. He vomited from pain four times on the ten-minute drive home. Girl learned to always keep a bucket in the car.

Girl quit her job for a few months and became his full-time caregiver, sleeping on the living room floor next to the daybed, just like she had slept in a chair by his side in the hospital. She drove him to doctor and physical therapy appointments and watched the pain etch permanent lines into his face. She tried not to cry when he screamed during dressing changes. Girl bathed his leg in Dawn dish detergent and debrided the skin grafts as gently as she could. Father sent one thousand dollars to help out. Mother and Stepmother paid their mortgage for a year. When Samson was able to take care of himself, Girl returned to work.

Two years later, Girl stood at the sink in the summer heat, a fly buzzing list-lessly around her face, neither of them able to summon the energy necessary to do much of anything. Crusted, filthy dishes littered the counter that ran the full length of the kitchen: fourteen feet of filth interrupted only by two-and-one-half feet of stainless steel sink. Her gaze traveled over the curtains she had made from Walmart fabric, the stenciling on the walls that she had spent hours creating. None of her crafts were very sophisticated or skillfully done, but they were all she could do with the abilities she had and the spare change she scrimped from the grocery budget. Pretty was way down the list of priori-ties in this house—far below bike parts and dogs and other grimy things. But that day her pretty things failed to lift her spirits.

A droplet of sweat ran down her temple, and she wiped it away with her shoulder. Life hadn't exactly turned out the way she had wanted it to. Girl was poor, depressed, and her muscles always ached. The city house they owned at the edge of the ghetto was falling apart, no matter how much she painted, sewed, and glued things together. Girl waged a constant battle to maintain a semblance of cleanliness: she cleaned up the mud, fur, and animal shit from their three dogs and four cats, and once that was done she retrieved the crusted dishes from the living room, emptied the urine-filled Gatorade bottles from the bedroom, picked the fast food wrappers up off the floor where her husband had tossed them, collected the drinking glasses scattered throughout the house, and then did the dishes. Girl looked at the filth and her heart sank further, her energy leaching out of her. That day, she just couldn't do it.

Girl wandered off to see what Samson was doing, leaving the dishes to the flies for a while. She found him in the garage, trying to fix the used Weed-wacker he had just bought. He knew Girl was depressed, knew the house was getting to her, but he just wanted to be left alone with his projects. He was happiest turning a wrench, taking apart motors, and making broken things function again. Samson didn't turn to look at her as he worked, talking out the side of his mouth, his bald head covered in droplets of sweat and smudges of black grease. "Go to the mall," he said. Girl left quickly, not bothering to look in the mirror or smooth her hair.

While she was at the mall, Girl fell in love with a jewelry box. It was a small, simple, wooden box, carved with flowers and curving lines. She didn't buy it—it was eighty dollars. She thought about all the things that Samson had: four Harley-Davidsons in the garage, the ridiculously overpriced "col-lectible" plastic motorcycle models that came in the mail every month in two

different sizes, any rare coin or stamp that caught his eye at the shops he fre-
quented while Girl was at work. He denied himself nothing, and would deny
Girl nothing as well, but she knew that they were always half a step away from
having the utilities shut off, and at least one month behind on the mortgage. So
she sighed, looked longingly at the box one more time, and then left.

As Girl drove down the street, she saw a fire truck parked at the other end.
As she drew nearer the house, she could see that she would never get through
with all the commotion, so Girl parked halfway down the block.

She smelled it before she saw it, and she half-walked, half-ran, her heart
pounding. Girl had known that something would happen sooner or later, and
in some way she was relieved that it finally had. The need for crisis had been
building, tensions simmering beneath the surface like an angry pimple that
needed to be brought to a head. Girl was just beginning to see that this was
their pattern—a mix of bad judgment, high emotions, and an unsettled energy
that seemed to draw crises to them like the unwashed dishes attracted flies.

Girl pushed through the crowd of neighbors gathered in front of their
house to find her husband sitting on the front step, the firefighters packing
up their gear. Whatever had happened, it was over. She hugged Samson even
though he was covered in black soot and sweat, and confirmed the safety of
the dogs and cats, and then ventured with him into the house as he told her
his story.

The smell was overwhelming. The stench made Girl's head hurt and the
bile rise in her throat, and it worsened the deeper they went into the house.
The house was black, blacker than black, and although it was a bright summer
day, they needed a flashlight to see inside. Everything was black: the walls, the
windows, the ceiling—every inch of every item that littered the beyond-clut-
tered, filthy home. In some ways the fire made the house seem neater, as if the
fire created the mess and gave reason for its existence. They walked through
the living room and down the hall toward the kitchen in the back of the house.
They passed the office and Girl saw that her computer was covered in soot. She
was one week away from the end of her semester and she knew her final papers
were irretrievably lost.

They paused by the bathroom and Samson opened the door. Girl hated the
pink, tiled bathroom—ironically, it remained untouched by the fire and smoke.
They entered the kitchen and he shone the flashlight over the dishes covering
the counter. The ceiling fan had melted into a dangling flower blossom. They
walked through the kitchen to the attached garage, and Samson began to talk.

That July day was hot and muggy, and Samson kept the garage door closed to keep the sun out. He was paranoid about someone stealing his Harleys, so he always secured the door with four differently keyed padlocks. While working on the Weedwacker, Samson had accidentally kicked over the gas can and gasoline soaked the old piece of carpet he was standing on. He pulled the cord to start the motor and flames shot out. After that, he decided to remove the fuel filter to see if that helped. The manual said to place the Weedwacker on the ground and pull the cord, so he placed it on the gasoline-soaked carpet and pulled the string. Flames shot out again, larger now, because without the filter the gas flowed faster, and the carpet ignited instantly. Thick, black smoke quickly filled the house and Samson couldn't see, so he propped open the side door so the cats could escape, and made his way by feel to the front door to find the dogs. As he walked, he closed every door he passed so that he would stay oriented, thus saving the ugly bathroom. He found the dogs and brought them out with him, carrying the lab who was too scared to follow. As soon as the firemen cleared the house, he went into the garage, found the fuel filter he had removed, and threw it in the bushes so that no one could blame him for the fire. Girl was struck by the notion that he did it on purpose. It somehow made sense that her husband of four years could have been acting intentionally. If he had been depressed enough, if he had craved the adrenaline of a disaster so badly, needed it so badly, then he could have been purposefully careless, acting on a suicidal impulse, consequences be damned.

She ran into the backyard, unable to process what she had been told. She called Mother first and screamed at her incoherently over the long-distance line, demanding to know why she had moved away, demanding that she answer for not being here when Girl needed her most. They were homeless with four cats and three dogs, no credit card, and only a few hundred dollars to make it until the end of the month. Samson still spent much of each day bedridden. Girl didn't get paid time off of work, and she knew that there was no way Samson would be able to handle all the necessary details so that they could resume their quasi-normal life.

Girl sobbed into the phone, "Why aren't you here? Damn you for moving away!" Mother just calmly let her rant, not arguing, and after they hung up, she called a family friend to come help Girl.

Girl called the insurance company next, surprised that she reached an adjuster on a Saturday evening.

Too angry to parse her words nicely, she asked him, "Is stupidity covered?" The adjuster just laughed and assured her that they would pay, and quickly. A Red Cross truck came and gave Girl hotel and restaurant vouchers as well as phone numbers of boarding kennels for their pets. Samson vomited from the smoke he inhaled and they gave him oxygen, trying to persuade him to go to the hospital. He refused, preferring Girl to nurse him as he coughed up black chunks of phlegm and threw up for three days straight.

Samson brought the insurance policy to the hotel, smudged with soot, and he had Girl read aloud everything that was and wasn't covered. They stayed up late while he dreamed out loud of all the money they would make from this and planned how to get the insurance company to fix his uninsured motorcycles.

The hotel pillows were too soft and the room smelled of mildew. Samson stayed up watching TV in bed with the volume on high—years of riding Harleys had left him with partial hearing loss. Girl lay on her stomach and prayed for the world to go away. Although she generally thrived on crisis, this was too much. Samson's body smell irritated her, and his loud voice invaded her head. Sleep was her sanctuary, and as much as she craved it, it wouldn't come.

They moved into an old apartment building—the only place that allowed them to bring all three dogs and four cats. Six months later, the house was repaired enough for them to move back in. Then Samson was arrested for another road rage incident, and this time, he was charged with a felony. Combined with the accident and house fire, Girl knew that she could never trust her husband's judgment enough to have children with him. She had never had career goals, but only this certainty—that someday she would have children, and that she would love them into beautiful human beings who weren't broken or scarred like she was. But more than that, he was escalating. Girl started to worry about her own safety.

Girl tried to leave Samson. She drove to Liz's office—they might drift for years without speaking, but she knew that she could always count on her. When Liz had broken her ankle, she moved in with Girl until she could climb stairs again. Now that Girl left Samson, Liz took a day off of work and helped her move some furniture and boxes into a storage unit. But one phone call from Samson was all it took, and Girl went back, though she left her things in storage. He promised to change. He begged Girl to go back to marriage counseling. He swore he would get off the morphine, help out more around the house, lose twenty pounds if only she would give him another chance. Girl didn't know how to say no. She yearned to leave him but she didn't know how, and she did not think she could live with the shame of divorce. Father was on his seventh wife. Girl didn't want to fulfill her in-laws' expectations that she was bound to repeat her parents' mistakes. Girl had promised Samson *forever*. Samson always told her, "If you think you will ever find another person who loves you as much as I do, go ahead. But you won't. No one will ever love you like I do." What if it were true? Girl told herself that staying was her only option, and went with him to see a therapist.

"You have two choices," Samson said right before he walked out of the marriage counselor's office. His face was hard, foreign, like someone who didn't love Girl at all anymore. "You can do the right thing and give me two weeks' notice. I want the house clean and decorated, and then you can leave. Or you can be a snake, empty the bank account, and sneak away. It's up to you. But I'm going home. I need my morphine." Girl collapsed in her chair like a marionette with its strings cut, her body doubled over, shoulders convulsing with sobs. Samson slammed the door as he left the room.

"I don't know what to do," Girl told the counselor. She felt so small. The counselor was softly padded in the way of women around Mother's age. She dressed conservatively and kept her face always arranged in a soothing expression. From the look of her, she didn't have any more fight in her than Girl had.

"Be a snake," the therapist said. Girl looked up in surprise. Marriage counselors were never supposed to tell you to leave, but the therapist had finally witnessed one of the rages Samson normally saved for when they were alone.

"Don't even go home," she said firmly. "Just get in your car and drive to your mother's." Girl was dumbfounded—this wasn't even Samson at his worst. This was just the everyday type of screaming, not the really bad kind. The counselor's permission to leave transformed Girl from a broken marionette back into the level-headed human being she was when she was at work. Girl stopped crying. She didn't feel small and scared anymore. She gathered her coat and went out into the winter night. She went first to the bank, where she withdrew a third of their money, trying to be fair, and hid it in the trunk for the long drive to her parents' home in Florida. Girl went back to their small house and parked in the street right in front of the chain-link gate. Their Cape Cod was dark—the only light came from the upstairs bedroom window. Girl opened the front door quietly and was greeted by their three dogs. She let them out into the fenced-in yard and culled the Rottweiler from the pack. He was the only dog that was really hers. The German shepherd and the black lab had always been Samson's. The huge dog was happy to flop on the back seat of the car and wait for Girl. There was a dusting of snow in the air—ice crystals sparkling in the streetlight. It was dinnertime, but January's dark came early.

When Girl entered the house, she found her favorite of their four cats sleeping on the sofa, so she grabbed her up and dumped her into the car, ignoring her windmilling paws and plaintive yowls. Girl wanted to take both of the female cats, Persephone and Pandora. The male cats lived outside half the time and could take care of themselves. She crept upstairs without turning on the lights and grabbed her jewelry box from her dressing room, secreting that to the car as well. Although they didn't have much money, Samson liked to buy her jewelry so that she'd look like a "high-maintenance chick." Girl hoped that she could pawn it all and, combined with the cash, pay off the debts that were in her name and maybe have something left for a security deposit and some used furniture.

Girl had packed away her summer clothes into two small suitcases a few weeks before, which she had then hidden in the storage space behind her closet wall. Before she could retrieve them, she needed to find the other cat. Suddenly, Samson spoke through the closed bedroom door.

"What are you doing, Girl?" His voice was glacial and tightly controlled, which unnerved her more than if he had yelled.

Samson had told Girl what happened to the last two girls that left him: one, he hit, and the other, he raped. She didn't know if the stories were true, but she wasn't going to take any chances. Samson always said he would never hurt Girl because he loved her too much, and so far, he had never laid a hand on her. She knew, though, that whatever love held him back in the past was gone now. The counselor had stressed that women in abusive relationships are statistically most at risk of being murdered when they tried to leave. Only a hollow-core door separated Girl from an unstable man high on morphine and in possession of four guns, two of which were semi-automatic.

"I'm looking for Pandora," Girl replied, trying not to let her voice shake.

"She's in here with me," he said. "If you want her, come in and get her."

Girl ran. She left the cat, left the suitcases, and ran down the stairs, out to her mother's old car—hers had been totaled in an accident the month before, and Mother had let her drive the 1985 Camry she kept in New York and drove in the summers. Girl careened down the icy road, jumping the curb at the corner. Her hands steered the car forward, but her eyes watched only the rearview mirror. She made it to the expressway but when she passed the exit for her storage unit she didn't stop. Samson might be following, and he might expect her to go there.

Girl just kept driving, glancing over her shoulder. She had secretly written down directions to her aunt's house in Pittsburgh, her first stop on her way to Florida, and hidden them in her car, just in case. She didn't take her foot off the gas pedal until she made it to the interstate. Girl had promised *till death do we part*. This, then, was the afterlife.

cue theme music
i will survive

Girl arrived at her aunt's house after midnight. Her aunt was waiting up for her, though her cousins were asleep. Aunt Kiki gave Girl her bedroom to sleep in, and Girl fell asleep with an aching heart, trying not to think of Samson's smiling face, of the better times, before it had all come to this. Girl didn't think she'd sleep, but she did, clinging to her giant, slobbery dog. When she woke up her aunt had gone to work, but Stepmother was there. She had flown up from Key West to drive down with Girl, and taken a cab from the airport, an expense Girl had never heard of her ever indulging, certainly not when Girl was there to pick her up. "I didn't want to stress you further," Stepmother said.

Although Girl loved her stepmother and knew Stepmother loved her, she was never the person Girl turned to in a crisis. Mother had taken a part-time job at a tax preparation company, and Stepmother didn't have to work, so she had flown up on less than twelve hours' notice to help. Girl thought maybe she and Stepmother needed a road trip to help her lose her resentments.

They turned on the Weather Channel and saw that a big storm was approaching, so they decided not to wait until Aunt Kiki got off work to leave. Girl didn't have anything to pack, didn't even have clean underwear, so they loaded up the dog and cat and got on the road. Girl was too afraid to call her boss—she couldn't deal with the guilt of leaving without any notice, so she tore five pages from her diary and handwrote a note, hoping her boss would understand. Girl fed her letter into a hotel's fax machine the first night on their four-day drive south.

They listened to the radio to drown out the cat, who cried the entire trip. Every time Gloria Gaynor's "I Will Survive" came on, which was at least once a day, they turned the knob all the way to the right and sang along at the top of their lungs. They ate at Cracker Barrel whenever there was one, and picked up some Hanes Her Way underwear and simple clothing and toiletries at Walmarts and truck stops. Girl had her emergency money in the trunk, but Stepmother insisted on paying for everything. "You'll need that later," she said. The storm they saw on the Weather Channel had left a foot of snow all the way to South Carolina, where cities didn't own many snowplows and towns were shut down. With every mile they drove, the terrible sadness inside Girl lessened. She could feel her past flowing out behind the car like long ribbons undulating in the wind, stretching all the way back to Rochester, New York. Round about Georgia she felt the ends of those ribbons fly free, the ties that bound her in helplessness ripped away by the wind. Taking action had given her strength. Girl was only twenty-six, and it could only get better from here. Finally, they pulled into the driveway in Key West, 1,600 miles from where Girl began. The January night was warm and sweetly scented with night-blooming jasmine. The change in latitude made the night sky look different—the constellations loomed closer, seemed more personal. "That's Cassiopeia," Stepmother said, pointing to the constellation. "It makes a W in the sky." From then on, it was Girl's favorite, and she looked for it whenever she looked at the stars.

key west

Every night after work, Girl went rollerblading on the bike path next to the Atlantic Ocean. She began at Higgs Beach, first changing into Lycra shorts and a tank top in the round bathhouse. She filled her water bottle at the drinking fountain and then followed the path until it ended at a stoplight at the top of the island, then turned back—seven miles round trip. Rollerblading reminded her of roller-skating as a child—it tapped into long-forgotten innocence, a place where nothing mattered as much as the vibration of concrete through her feet. When Girl got too hot, she took off her tank top and skated in her exercise bra, enjoying the honks from passing cars. She jumped over cracks in the sidewalk, but tried not to sway too much to the music in her headphones—she didn't want to be too dorky. But the sun sparkling on the water filled in all her broken pieces with joy and hope.

Key West was an island of misfits, artists, and broken people who came to "the rock" to put themselves back together again. Girl dressed in donated clothing from Mother's friends and things she found at the Salvation Army. She went to the "Gay Church" with her parents, to "Gay Bingo" at the 501 Bar on Sunday afternoons with Brother, who was spending the winter there as well, and to the straight dance club with her new friend, Lorraine. Girl got a job at a car insurance agency, and soon knew enough people to recognize faces in the grocery store. Soon she had a drag queen roommate who helped her accessorize and shared her clothes, as well as a few other close friends. She was able to say "my mom's a lesbian," without anyone acting shocked or fascinated. She hadn't known how much she needed that. For the first time, she lived in a place that wasn't segregated by sexuality—people mixed freely. She kissed a girl or two, now that she could be curious without feeling like it would be fulfilling some unspoken prophesy. In the end, though, she liked kissing boys better.

Girl found a new good boyfriend, one her parents liked, even.

"Be sure your apartment is clean every time he comes over," Stepmother told her. Girl was lying in the sun in a bikini at her parents' house, as she did most Sunday afternoons between church and Bingo.

"Are you fucking serious?" Girl asked. "My lesbian stepmother is giving me man-trapping advice?"

"I'll teach you to make Swedish meatballs," Stepmother said.

"I know how to cook, Stepmother," she said. "And whatever happened to feminism?"

"He's a nice boy, Girl."

Girl flipped over onto her back.

"You really have a beautiful body," Stepmother said, a small smile on her lips. Girl wanted to throw up. She reached quickly for her shirt.

"What? There is nothing wrong with that. Don't push your issues with your father off on me. We are both women."

Girl thought about it. She couldn't put into words this feeling that her lesbian stepmother was more like a man than a woman. She thought about how she herself talked to her friends—they complimented the outfit, not the body. "That swimsuit is so cute on you," she had said to her best friend's teenaged daughter. Not "you have a beautiful body." She opened her mouth, and closed it again. There wasn't anything she could say that would make sense to Stepmother. Girl put on her shirt and walked inside.

defective

Mother went out of town for a few days. "She can never handle it if I go anywhere without her," Mother confided in Girl. "Yet, if she goes out of town without me, she's totally fine. She doesn't even always remember to call." Girl promised Mother that she would "keep an eye" on Stepmother while mother went on the writing workshop or whatever it was that she was so looking forward to, wherever it was that she couldn't bring Stepmother along.

Stepmother called first thing Saturday morning. Girl had agreed to help her replace a mini-blind in their rental condominium.

"Well, I had a bad night," Stepmother said. "I couldn't sleep, and at two a.m. I realized I had forgotten to give the cat his medicine. So I gave him his pills, but then I got confused, and the print on the bottle was small that I couldn't read it, and I thought I had given him the dog's pills, and I thought it would kill him, so there I was, crying, completely naked, holding the cat in my arms and trying to call the vet."

Girl had seen Stepmother naked often enough to be able to picture this clearly. In her head she saw Stepmother hugging that orange tabby to her massive, lumpy body. The cat was himself the fattest cat Girl had ever seen—so fat that even the stump of his tail was fat, and his stomach dragged a hairsbreadth off the ground. He had surpassed Garfield-fat and was in the realm of Jabba-the-Hutt-fat, all except his tiny yellow-eyed head. Girl imagined Stepmother hugging him against his will, so that the skin of his eyes pulled back at the corners and his arms stood stiffly out in front of him like Frankencat.

Girl started to say, "You should have called me," but shut her mouth quickly. She did not actually want Stepmother to call when she was naked and crying at two in the morning. "Did you get through to the vet?" she asked instead.

"I'm so embarrassed," she answered. "He was very nice, and explained that even if I had given the cat the dog's pills it wouldn't kill him. But he must think I'm a total lunatic."

"Of course he doesn't," Girl lied. "I'm sure he gets calls like that all the time. They'd rather you call and be safe than to not call and accidentally kill the cat."

They agreed that Stepmother would come pick up Girl, and they would measure the window of the condo, buy a new mini-blind, then go back to the condo and put it up. There was no part of Girl that wanted to do this, but she had promised Mother, and she had no valid reason not to help out. She owed them so much.

When Stepmother picked Girl up, Stepmother was sobbing, and they did the awkward front-seat-of-the-car-hug thing. It was the sort of crying that allowed no breath left over for words: shoulder-heaving, low moaning, tears and snot dripping onto her T-shirt. Girl made useless soothing noises. The day quickly fell into a pattern: they drove to a store while Stepmother cried the whole way. When they reached a store, she instantly stopped crying, wiped her face, and blew her nose. Stepmother and Girl entered the store, but for one reason or another, they never could find the exact mini-blind Stepmother wanted, so they got back in the car, Stepmother started crying again, and they drove to the next store and repeated the process. No mini-blind was purchased, although Stepmother did buy some sandwiches that they ate on a dock while looking at seagulls. Girl didn't know how Mother did it, but she could finally see why Mother could never leave Stepmother. Girl always thought that Mother's attraction to Stepmother was her abject neediness—Stepmother was her emotionally defective child that would never leave home, and Mother had been left too many times by people she loved.

Girl knew that she should be more understanding. Although she acted gentle with Stepmother, inside Girl was emotionally removed, like she was observing a case study. When the roles had been reversed and Girl was the one who could not pull herself out of the river of sadness, Stepmother always tried everything she could to help, but unlike Girl, she acted out of love, not obligation. She really wanted Girl to escape the hold of despair, not because she was a burden, but because Stepmother knew how terrible sadness could be, and she loved Girl deeply. But Girl looked at her from inside a shell, and she could not feel the love Stepmother thrust on her. She dodged it, tried to end the conversation or get out of the room.

Girl knew that feeling of the blackness lapping at the edge like waves, and that it was sometimes soothing to let go and the sadness crash over her—to give in to the cold bleakness that pierced her chest and settled into all of her bones. Girl's hips would hurt from the terrible sadness; her face felt like a mask that didn't move into proper expressions easily. And she knew that there was an intimacy in the blackness, and although she had long breaks from it, sooner or later it always returned. No matter how long it had been, her body remembered, like riding a bicycle. But Girl would rather be alone in her shell of functional sadness than admit they had this defect in common.

a second wedding

Girl never cooked Swedish meatballs for the boyfriend her parents liked so much, and she didn't clean the house before he came over, but he asked her to marry him anyway. This time, Mother and Stepmother both went along on dress-shopping missions, even driving up to Miami for a day.

Girl tried on a simple satin slip dress, and Stepmother ran a finger down her butt-cheek. "You are going to have to wear support hose with this one. You jiggle." Girl jerked away—she hated when Stepmother touched her butt, and the irony of her fat stepmother who never wore pantyhose or even a bra telling her that she was too jiggly enraged her. Yes, she was gaining weight, and she was failing at dieting, but whatever happened to the feminist messages they lived by her whole life? Wasn't Girl supposed to love her body just as it was and fuck standards that say women have to be sexy to have value?

"You can't eat that taco salad," Stepmother told her when she took Girl to Wendy's. "You're too fat for that skirt," she said when she visited Girl at work one day. Still, when Girl tried on an A-line wedding gown in the right size so it wasn't too tight, Stepmother teared up. And when Girl married that boy her parents loved, Stepmother and Mother walked her down the aisle together. Brother stood as her "man of honor," and Liz drove nine hours to wear a bridesmaid's dress along with Girl's only other remaining childhood friend, Rebekah. The rest of the wedding party was composed of her new husband's relatives—Girl never had that many people who belonged to her, but the few she had all showed up. Even her cousin made it, after driving fourteen hours from Tennessee in a car that wouldn't restart if she turned it off. Girl cried to see everyone who loved her all gathered in one place. Her new husband's khaki pants, short hair, love of golf, and family cookouts seemed to guarantee Girl's ascension from misfit to mainstream. Her white picket fence dreams were all coming true.

Three years later, Girl, her husband, and their ten-month-old baby drove across the border into Canada for Mother and Stepmother's legal same-sex wedding. Girl and Brother signed the marriage license, and Mother and Stepmother danced together while Girl's baby son played trucks on the dance floor next to their feet. Finally, they were legal, more legal than their domestic partner registry in Vermont a few years before, and even though the United States would not yet recognize their marriage, a sovereign nation had done so. New York State voted to recognize all same-sex marriages performed outside of New York long before they legalized such unions inside their own border. President Obama ensured that the country quickly followed suit. They finally got to file joint tax returns. They would get each other's Social Security someday. No one could force them to leave a hospital if their spouse was in intensive care. More than that, though, was the feeling of legitimacy. Pride. The world's value system had finally caught up with them.

safety net

Two kids and four years later, Girl lay on her parents' living room rug and begged them to tell her what to do. All Girl's husband wanted was a house that looked just like everyone else's, a well-behaved wife, and children that didn't require too much effort. Girl's lie was in saying that was all she wanted, too. It wasn't his fault that he fell in love with someone Girl never was, but longed to be—some ordinary soccer mom with a stick-figure family on the rear window of her minivan. Girl had spent a lifetime trying to be just like everyone else, and now that she had finally managed to pull that off, nothing beautiful or interesting about her remained. The stick-figure family had empty heads and no souls. Girl no longer aspired to be one of the beige people living in beige houses, eating beige food, and having beige sex. She could not sacrifice the life she wanted in order to keep the life she had. Who would her children become if they had a cardboard cutout for a mother? Girl had drained all the color out of herself in an effort to fit in. She wanted her children to know beauty and sweat and tears and the messy meatiness of life. If she didn't revive her best self, she would never be able to mother them properly.

"Try and stay until the kids are out of diapers. Have an affair if you need to," Mother said.

"Leave him," Stepmother said, "and I will make sure you and the children are okay." Girl could not bear the weight of her wedding ring on her finger, and kept it in her car's ashtray when she wasn't home, only putting it on when her husband was around.

A few weeks later, Mother called Girl with a plan.

"We used to get four percent on our CDs, but the bank called them, and now we can't get hardly any interest at all, just one and a half percent. We could take the money out of savings and buy a house and rent it to you. Then you could have a house for a reasonable rate, and we could get the same return as we used to. I just want you to know, this was Stepmother's idea. The money is her inheritance from when her mother died last year."

Girl cried in relief. They found a small three-bedroom house with hard-wood floors and colorful rooms, and even a tiny second-floor balcony. The house was old and quirky, and she could turn on the living room light from the upstairs hallway, which gave any potential burglars time to run away before she walked down the stairs. It was the first place she did not feel afraid when she was home alone. Girl went back to college and wrote stories long into the night. She got a job, made friends, and mothered her children, all in the cradle of Stepmother's safety net.

After the divorce, Girl wanted to feel desirable again. She asked Step-mother to draw her. She didn't have money to pay someone to draw or paint her, and she really wanted a picture of herself, to reclaim her body as her own, not just as a producer of children. Stepmother was a decent artist, and she always did nudes. Girl lay naked on her parents' bed as Stepmother sketched her. Maybe this was how Girl said she was sorry for objecting to Stepmother's blurred boundaries. Maybe she just wanted free art. Stepmother sketched her in charcoal, looking at her like an artist, not as a lecherous man. In the end, Girl didn't like how puffy Stepmother made her pubic hair, or how fat her stomach looked. When friends asked her how she could let Stepmother see her naked again, she didn't have an answer.

Girl, her children, and her parents went swimming in the pond, and Girl pulled leeches off the backs of Stepmother's veiny calves. Stepmother became the one Girl talked to about dating, and sex, and newfound feminine power. For once, that blur between parent and peer, male and female, was something to cherish. It was the closest to Stepmother she had ever been, and when Girl called her parents, she spent nearly as long talking to Stepmother as she did to Mother.

When Girl was asked out for her first date, it was Stepmother who volun-teered to watch the children.

"But they've never been put to bed by anyone but me for their entire lives!" Girl objected.

"I can handle it. I'll read them stories. I'll even lay down with them if they need me to. If they can't sleep, I'll just stay up with them." And so Girl went out to dinner with a man who wrote books and was the kind of person she was sure she would find, if only she went looking.

Stepmother had infinite patience with Girl's children. Girl and her boys drove to her parents' house every weekend, and Stepmother read books and played games and was never short-tempered. She was like an entirely new version of herself, and these new memories ran into the cracks of Girl's bitterness, dissolving it like rain on hard ground. And Stepmother and Mother sang songs to each other and danced in the kitchen.

"I want to do an adult adoption," Stepmother said. "When I die, I want you and Brother to inherit everything. I worry that my sister will challenge my will as my only living relative."

Girl knew the inheritance was merely a carrot at the end of a pole, meant to lead Girl where Stepmother wanted, but she understood that underneath her words of tax law and estate planning, Stepmother wanted legitimacy in Girl's life. She wanted to be recognized as the parent she had always been—flawed, certainly, but relentless in showing up. Girl researched adult adoptions, and learned that she would not have to forsake her father.

"Okay," she told Stepmother. "You can adopt me." Surprisingly, Brother agreed to be adopted as well. A lawyer was retained, and Stepmother changed her residency from Florida, which had no state income tax, to New York, which did, but also recognized adult adoptions. Then Stepmother met Deb, and everything changed.

notes from the fourth wall
i used to believe, now i know

I used to believe that my mother was complicit in everything that went wrong in my life. I knew that she wasn't particularly interested in raising children. I never listened to her protestations that she had wanted my brother and me very badly and loved us very much. She always loved Pat, her chosen spouse, more than she loved me. Pat would never grow up and move out. Pat would never leave her. She could mother Pat longer than she could mother us. It was a fight I could never win, but I could certainly resent the struggle.

Pat came first, her career came second, and my brother and I fought like cats and dogs for a distant third place. She rarely made cookies or took us to the beach and only half-listened when we talked. I would try so hard to get her attention, saying outrageous things to make sure she was listening; like that I had gone to Europe or had a frontal lobotomy. "That's nice," she'd reply, inciting me to rage while I washed the dinner dishes by hand in our old, stained sink. The fact that she took time out of her day to sit and talk to me while I was washing dishes was lost on me.

I did not understand why she would bother having kids if she didn't want to spend time with them. I desperately wanted my mother to stay at home and bake me cookies and play with me and be the room mother in my class at school. Me, me, my mother, look at me. I swore to myself that if I ever had children, I would raise them right. We had lived in a trailer so my mom could go to college. My mother said that after all that struggle and poverty and sleepless nights she wasn't going to drop her career to stay home, even though Pat wanted her to. My mother said that we couldn't afford to live in a house if she didn't work, that we'd have to live in an apartment in the city. I would look at her accusingly and tell her fiercely that I would rather live in an apartment and have her stay home. She didn't tell me of her fear of gangs in the only neighborhood that would have been cheaper than where our tiny house was, or that high-density communities like apartment complexes have more exposure to more people, some of them sinister. My mother fought all of us for her right to work a job where she would never make as much as a man, in spite of the bachelor's and master's degrees she had worked so hard for.

My mother was a bystander in my childhood. Pat was bipolar, and the childish scuffles and failings of my brother and me often got under her skin, and a fight would erupt. Mom would leave, wordlessly storming out. It was okay, Mom explained, because Pat always knew where to find her if things got really bad. It was also okay that my brother and I didn't know where she was or when she was coming home, I guess. I'd learn later she always went to the movies when the rest of us were fighting. As soon as she left we'd all shape up, though. We kids would get quiet and scared, and Pat would calm down like a switch had been flipped.

My mother had repeated surgeries during my childhood, and never wavered in refusing to show us her fear. My mother's back held up the world, but I wanted her to sit down, turn that back to the wall, and give me her arms instead. I didn't know I was standing on her back while I was stamping my feet in anger about not being the center of her world. I thought she should give up everything. She should have kept my dad's name after the divorce, so I wouldn't feel different. She should not have spent time on charity work that took her away from us even more. She should have moved to Alaska when my father did, even though he was remarried, so we could have had a more stable life. She should have dyed her hair. She had no business going on a date night with Pat once a week.

When I had my first son, I spent an entire year mad at my mother for not loving me enough. I knew how much I loved my baby—why had she not loved me as much as I loved my own son? If she had, how had she been such a non-involved parent? Why had she repeatedly chosen Pat over us? "I believe in the parenting theory of benign neglect," she used to explain. In college I learned that was something she had made up entirely. Neglect was neglect. All I knew was my mother was never there. Hanging out with us seemed to bore her, and if she had any free time, she spent it reading a book. She should have given up everything, like I did for my baby.

I didn't care that my baby nursed every two hours for nearly two years. I didn't mind putting away all my hobbies so that he wouldn't choke on a bead or get pricked by a needle. I stopped watching all my favorite TV shows and banished the news from my house. I only listened to children's music in my car. I was a Mother with a capital M, and that was all I ever wanted to be and all I ever needed to be happy. Nothing I gave up was a sacrifice; it was a gift to my child. Why did my mother not feel that way about me?

I just did not understand my mother at all until I had my second child and I was a single parent like she had been. When I had my second son, I learned that everything I gave up for my kids left them with a hollow shell for a mother. I realized that mothers no longer exist as people. That staying home with children consists of hours and hours of mind-numbing boredom interrupted only by irritation and housework. I learned that by putting their needs above everything else in my life, I was risking running out of me, leaving them with no mother at all.

I realized that you have to have passion and drive and something of your own or your children might eat the very things that are good and arty and intrinsic to your soul. I could not see that when I was the one who was trying to eat my mother's soul.

I learned that our need for great love is as powerful as the need to create life. I did not know that before. I didn't realize that children grow up so fast, that in the scheme of a woman's lifetime, the part devoted to raising children is a small piece of your whole existence. In the blink of an eye the children are grown and gone and you have only your spouse (maybe) to keep away the great tides of loneliness washing through your kitchen. Before my mom was thirty-five she had lost both parents, her only sibling, and was exiled from her extended family. Oh, and did I mention she was divorced, too? I came to understand how all of that loss made her needy and afraid to be alone, and that choosing a spouse who was chronically ill and dependent gave her much-needed security.

I didn't realize that parenting often feels like a great battle waged between adults and children, that keeping them safe and fed and delivered to school on time often takes every little bit of gumption you have, and when there is no adult to lean back on, you have to use every last bit of strength just keeping chaos at bay. When all you do is diaper and feed and dress and cook and wash and drive and worry and teach and love these children all by yourself, you are often too exhausted to enjoy it. Having another adult evens the balance. I didn't know that when you are the only responsible adult, you still need someone to soak with your tears and tell you that you are okay. You need that very badly. You also need to know you are pretty and smart and funny and all the things that used to define you before you had children. You need someone to see you as more than just a mother, and you need to fight for that relationship, you need to have dates and you need to give him or her some of your free time and you need to not drain out all the energy from the person that is your rock. You need to give to them, too.

My mother always said that she did the best she could at the time with the knowledge and skills she had at that moment. I never knew what that really meant, or how true that was. I thought that meant that she subscribed to the best parenting theory she could find at the time. I never knew that inside, my mom didn't have all the answers, and that our childhood was not a great experiment in child development theory. Rather, my mother was just trying to get by. Some days all you can manage is to keep everyone dressed and fed, that happy is a far distant second. Some days the children eat nothing but cereal and you let them trash the house because you haven't the ability to summon the strength to parent the way you had always intended. Sometimes you can't even summon the strength to get off the couch.

I could not see that by living her values, by following the life that made her as close to whole and balanced as she could be, my mother was teaching me how to be a person of worth, not just a pampered child who would grow into a selfish adult. I didn't realize that giving your child everything can turn them into a grown-up you don't like at all.

"Your job is to make me happy!" my four-year-old screamed at me one day, and at that moment I finally realized that no, it wasn't. My job was to raise him and his brother to be good people that would tread lightly on the earth and have hearts I was proud of. My job was to love him and lead him, but most of all, to keep him alive. The bottom line of motherhood is protecting our little ones. His job was to find happiness. Until that moment, I didn't fully realize that it wasn't my mother's job to make me happy, either.

I didn't realize my mother was a woman with unfulfilled dreams and ambitions, too. That being the boss was a friendless place. That there was no one she could lean on, besides Pat. That without Pat, she might have crumbled into dust. I did not understand my mother at all until one day I, too, stood with my fragile, grown-up heart breaking in my own chest and two tiny faces looking at me to make their world okay. I did not know that mothers get lonely, too. That being a mother does not obliterate all the emotional needs you have always had.

I also learned that summers pass quickly as an adult; that you mean to go to the beach more often, and you want to go to the amusement park, but between their trips with Daddy and sports and friends, it is all gone before you do half the things you mean to. The endless summers of childhood are just ten weekends and the kids are off with Daddy for four of them, leaving only six, and you want to take the kids camping for a week and that leaves just five, and you still have to clean the house and mow the lawn and sometimes it rains. I learned that getting to the beach twice in a summer took Herculean effort. I realized all that my mother did do to give us the childhood we had, in spite of tight finances and a full-time job and a chronically ill spouse.

I did not know that although you are a mother, you are still a woman, and if you don't feed all the different parts of you, if you just mother everyone, you give away bits of your soul until you have nothing left and are of no use to anyone. I did not know the hollow aching loneliness after the children are asleep or not home, and how it can consume you, and how you need a life or else you will throw yourself under a bus, and then the children will have no mother at all, and anything you need to do to keep yourself out from under the bus tires—work, romance, art, politics—whatever keeps you out of the road-side ditch is as vital to your children's well-being as wiping their bottoms and runny noses.

You know what else? While I was figuring all this out, while I was struggling to find the balance between the mother I wanted to be and the mother I had to be, while I was fighting to not lose my soul and simultaneously having my heart burst into a thousand shiny pieces by the love of a gummy toothless smile, my mother snuck in and bought me a house. She gave my children and me the security we needed, which was only possible thanks to the career I resented. While I was busy resenting and stamping feet and coming to terms with who I was as a woman and who I was as a mother and who I should have been as a daughter, she just quietly came in and held me up, as I was trying to hold my babies up.

In the end, no matter how we manage the triangulation between woman, mother, and lover, what matters is that we hold up our babies when they need us. Even if they don't appreciate it. Even if they don't notice at the time that we're doing it. If we properly manage this thing called motherhood, we all wind up okay.

the split

Stepmother made a new friend, Deb, a barber near their summer home in rural New York. Deb was fat and butch and not above whipping off her shirt at dinner parties to discuss her breasts and how much she wanted to have them surgically removed. Stepmother wanted her own breasts taken off, too.

"What if I bind them down at my sides, like this?" she asked Girl, pushing her breasts below her armpits.

"Well, it makes you look thinner," Girl said. "Right now your boobs hang by your belly button, and make you look fatter than you really are. If you bind them, they don't get in the way so much."

"I love her breasts, I don't want them removed," Mother told Girl. Girl had mixed feelings. Stepmother never wore a bra, and when she hugged Girl, her breasts swung out like oranges in a pair of socks and hit Girl around the waist. Girl didn't like being assaulted by boobs every time she got hugged, but she also wasn't convinced that Stepmother really wanted body modification surgery. It seemed like something she said to impress Deb.

Soon Stepmother and Deb were inseparable, and Mother saw the warning signs of impending mania. Girl wasn't convinced it was mania—it seemed more like purely selfish behavior in her opinion. She wasn't sure it was a break with reality.

Stepmother stopped the car in the middle of the street, ignoring honking horns, and opened the door so she could yell "hello" to Deb as she drove by the barbershop. Stepmother wrote Deb poems. Mother traced her path through the GPS unit in Stepmother's car, and learned that she was seeing Deb when she said she was with other people.

Mother and Stepmother broke up and got back together again on a nearly weekly basis. Mother called Girl crying, then called back a few days later to announce that they had bought a new house and everything was going to be okay. The next phone call announced that they had broken up again and sold the new house to the next-highest bidder a mere three days after they bought it, losing five thousand dollars in the transaction.

Mother moved back to Rochester and rented a furnished apartment on a month-to-month lease. Stepmother apologized and moved in with her for Thanksgiving.

"This is not my bipolar issue," she told Girl. "This is your mother's manic depression."

"Mother doesn't have manic depression," Girl replied.

"I don't love your mother anymore," Stepmother said. "I am only with her because she said she would drive her car into the Erie Canal if I left her."

Mother cried on Girl's shoulder until both their shirts were wet with tears. She and Stepmother bought another house, this one in Penfield, a suburb of Rochester. Before they closed on it, they broke up again.

Girl talked to Mother nearly every day, and drove to Rochester every chance she could get. Mother came to Cleveland to see Girl at least once a month, too. The weight of Mother pressed down on Girl, but she would do anything she could to help Mother start over.

"I went to leave to come see you, but Stepmother said she was going to follow me," Mother said over the phone one night when she was scheduled to drive to Cleveland. "I told her I was going to Rochester instead, but I won't come to Cleveland if I think she is following me. I don't know what she will do." Mother sounded terrified.

"Do whatever you have to do to be safe," Girl said. In the end, Mother's ruse worked, and Stepmother did not pursue her.

A few weeks later, Mother was talking to Girl on the phone and Stepmother called in on the other line. "I have to go! If I miss her she might not call back!" Mother said and hung up on Girl quickly. It went on like this for nine months.

"Stepmother has control of our joint checking account," Mother told Girl. "I have to talk to her about repairs to the new house. I can't afford them on my own." Mother was living on her Social Security and the rent Girl paid. Stepmother refused to give her any of their joint money.

"I went to a lawyer, and thank God marriage equality passed in New York. If I had switched my residency to Florida, I'd be out of luck. But New

York recognizes same-sex marriages, so I am safe. And you damn well better believe that after thirty years I'm going to get half. But Stepmother will be back once she realizes I have a lawyer. Our net worth is one million dollars. Stepmother will never agree to be half a millionaire. Money is too important to her. Once she learns that the law is on my side, she'll be back." She wasn't though. Instead, Stepmother flew Deb down to visit her.

Girl helped Mother set up an online dating account, and within a few weeks, Mother had a new girlfriend. Girl drove up to Rochester with the kids, and Mother had a dinner party to introduce her girlfriend to her existing circle of friends. Girl liked the new woman, with her red hair and snappy clothes. She was ten years younger than Stepmother, just like Deb was ten years younger than Mother. Whenever Mother ran into a friend or acquaintance or even the mail carrier, she told them, "Stepmother traded me in for a younger model." Girl wasn't entirely sure that ten years made that big of a difference when you were sixty and fifty. It wasn't like Deb was a twenty-year-old beauty queen. But for some reason, the age difference hit Mother hard.

"If your mother gets back together with Stepmother, I will not speak to her again. I mean it," one of Mother's closest friends confided in Girl. "I cannot stand the way that woman treats your mother. Mother is one of the nicest, smartest people I know. I can't stand to watch her be abused like that."

Once Mother got a new girlfriend, something shifted in Stepmother. She began wooing Mother. She sent her flowers and mailed her cards.

"If I can convince myself that this was her manic depression I'll take her back," Mother told Girl. "I am reading this book in hopes that it will convince me." She gave Girl a copy of *An Unquiet Mind* to read as well, but Girl wasn't interested in convincing herself of anything. She could understand that Mother and Stepmother could grow apart and fall out of love, but she couldn't forgive Stepmother for lying to Mother, telling her that she was crazy, or for withholding money from her. There were respectful ways to leave someone, and this wasn't it.

Of course they reconciled. Their breakup lasted a year, and Girl had done everything she could to encourage Mother to resist, but once Stepmother turned her attention back on Mother, she melted like margarine. Girl was expected to understand and welcome her back. It wasn't that easy for Girl. She never said, "you didn't just break Mother's heart, you broke mine, too."

the basement

It was Thanksgiving. Girl and her children always stayed in her parents' basement when they visited Mother and Stepmother. Girl preferred the falling-down acoustic tiles overhead and a modicum of privacy to the guest bedroom, where she had to listen to her parents snore and fart in their sleep. She had turned off the fluorescent tube lighting in favor of a shadeless table lamp set on the floor. Dim light from a low angle turned the cobwebs into large looming shadows. Damp air fought the space heater for dominance and won.

Girl woke at 1:00 a.m. She had to pee. She glanced at her phone, as she always did whenever she woke up, whatever the hour. Girl clicked on Facebook to see who, if anybody, had liked her latest picture. She had posted a selfie taken in front of a diorama of taxidermied beavers at the museum. "Me and My Beaver," she had teasingly titled it.

There was a comment from Jim, the son of Mother's best friend back from when Girl was growing up. *Better than the picture I took of your beaver,* it said, followed by something weird about "machine-drive type animations of kids posing and interacting with aquatic animals behind glass." Girl re-read it and turned off her phone's screen. She hit the button again, re-illuminating her home page, still open to Facebook, then held the button until the phone turned completely off, buzzing in her hands. Girl ran upstairs to the kitchen powder room and her bowels exploded. Terror made some people throw up, but for Girl, it was always the other end.

She went back downstairs. Girl picked up her laptop and copied the comment to a text file, then deleted the comment from her Facebook page. She deleted the picture as well. Girl looked at her sons sleeping in the dimly lit room—one boy on an old mildewed army cot, the other child on a queen-sized inflatable bed. She retreated to the twin-size foldaway that completed their sleeping island, all pushed together so she could pet their heads if they woke up. Girl put her face close to her oldest son's cheek and breathed his sleeping smell.

She had hoped for twenty-seven years that this story would never come to light. Girl pulled the thin, department-store quilt over her shoulder and tried to think. The pictures. God, why had she ever let him take pictures? Yes, she'd been thirteen, but she had known better. It wasn't like she wanted to run for president, but she didn't want them coming to light now that she was a mother.

Girl tried to type a response to Jim. She used words like *shame, missing negatives,* and *illegal.* There were a lot of other words she wanted to type but didn't. She tried to be fair. Girl had said yes, and Jim was only a few years older than she was, not a grown-up by any means. Girl decided not to send her message until the next day, not until she could read it to someone who belonged to her life now. Girl lay on her back and looked at the dark corners at the edges of the rafters where the ceiling tiles had fallen down. She waited for dawn to dilute the night to gray so she could go home. She wanted to be back in her pumpkin-colored bedroom with her fuzzy, blue blanket, handmade pillows, and people she could talk true to. This was not a story she could tell her mother.

Girl could not get her lungs to fill properly. It hurt to breathe in her pectoral muscles, and in her constricted rib cage. It hurt her skin to remember, and memory made her clammy, damp, and cold. She wrapped her arms around her chest. She watched for daylight and the clicking of digits on the clock as she waited for morning.

Another trip to her parents' basement a few months later, and once again Girl woke at 1:00 a.m., but this time there was no buzzing phone, only choking anxiety. The untold story still hung in the basement air. She could not escape the girl she had once been.

Girl went upstairs. Stepmother was awake in the living room, watching TV.

"What's wrong, Girl?" she asked.

"I have anxiety," Girl said, and haltingly told her the story of the photographs. She thought Stepmother would rage against male abusers, insist on talking to Jim. Girl was as afraid of directing Stepmother's rage at him as she was scared of her judgment of Girl's actions. Stepmother was always the voice in her head that told her that she wasn't good enough.

"That's all? Some naked pictures? That's no big deal," Stepmother said when Girl finished the story. Girl looked at her closely—Stepmother was completely unfazed. No rage, no shaming her, nothing. "Here," Stepmother said, "take a Xanax."

"I don't know what it will do to me," Girl said. "What if I sleep all day tomorrow?"

"You won't, but if you do, I'll wake up with the kids. Just take half a Xanax if you are so worried. And tell yourself, 'what I am feeling is uncomfortable, but not dangerous.' Repeat that, and try to slow your breathing. It really helps."

Girl took the partial pill and slept until morning. Stepmother's mental illness allowed her to understand Girl's anxiety, more than if she had always been stable. Girl wasn't sure the next day if it was the Xanax or the unexpected acceptance that gave her more peace.

The next day Girl was in her parents' kitchen. She filled her glass with ice and water from the fridge dispenser. Girl had to admit it still made her happy to watch the ice cubes fall into the glass. When she was small, she thought fridge ice-dispensers were the be-all and end-all of coolness. Stepmother had wanted an ice dispenser for years, but could never justify spending the money, just like she couldn't justify replacing the kitchen carpeting, even though it was old and stained and impractical. Their new house had come with both a great fridge and shitty flooring.

"Look, it makes crushed ice, too!" Stepmother said, filling her own glass to the top with ice chips. Girl took a long swig of water. Ice-cold water was one of the simplest pleasures in life.

"What does semen taste like?" Stepmother asked. Girl choked and spit a mouthful of water on the carpet.

"What?" she said, stalling.

"I just always wondered."

"Well, it's different based on what you eat, the same with women. Salty, I guess," Girl said. Her stomach tightened in revulsion. Why did she answer? Why couldn't she just walk away?

a series of surgeries

Mother needed a hip replacement. Girl drove back to Rochester for a few days.

"I'm so glad you will sit with Stepmother during my surgery," Mother said. "It's going to be so hard on her." But Girl wasn't going out of kindness for Stepmother; she needed to be there in case something went wrong, in case it was her last chance to see Mother alive. Girl chose to stay in a hotel instead of alone with Stepmother.

"You know you hurt Stepmother's feelings by not staying with her," Mother said. But there was no way Girl would stay alone with Stepmother. Since the reunification, Stepmother had not been repentant. In fact, she still insisted that it was all an innocent mistake because "I mixed up my Paxil with my Prilosec. I just wanted a friend, I didn't know what I was doing was so upsetting." No apology was given, no act of contrition performed. Girl was supposed to play happy family and pretend nothing had changed, but she remembered how Stepmother had lied, blamed, and gaslighted Mother the last year, and Girl wasn't quick to forgive. She played her daughter role, but her shell was strong and not coming down.

While they were waiting with Mother to go into surgery, Stepmother had to get a donut. Mother wasn't allowed to eat anything, but Stepmother hung over the end of her hospital bed, dropping sprinkles on the sheet as she chewed. Girl refused to eat, so Mother didn't have to starve alone.

"If Mother dies, I am going to commit suicide," Stepmother said, when she and Girl were alone in the waiting room. "I want you to help me. I will get drugs and I want to die surrounded by my family."

"I understand," Girl said. "I promise you I'll hold your hand. I will be there and I promise you won't die alone. You will die surrounded by love."

An hour later, Stepmother had a reversal of opinion.

"Don't let me die! If something happens to Mother I'll want to commit suicide and I need you to promise me that you will save me. Don't let me die!"

Girl made soothing noises. "Of course I will help you, Stepmother. I won't abandon you if Mother dies." Stepmother clung to Girl and sobbed.

Several days later, Mother was moved to a rehab facility. "It would be too much for Stepmother to try and take care of me at home," she said. Girl called her every day. She was puzzled to hear that Stepmother didn't visit all that often.

"I got a little lonely the other day," Mother told Girl. "Stepmother was so exhausted from the stress of me being in the hospital that she just slept all day, and never came by. So the next day I told her I needed her to come and visit, and she did. I was proud of myself for asking for what I needed."

Girl wanted to kick Stepmother. Really? Mother was alone in a nursing home and Stepmother just slept all day because *she* was stressed?

"How's the food?" she asked instead.

"Well, it's not great. They said they had a vegetarian menu, but it's just grilled cheese every day, so I asked Stepmother to bring me something. She brought over the leftover Chinese."

"From the night before you went in the hospital?" Girl asked. That had been more than a week prior. She pictured dried-out rice and rubbery baby corn rattling around a paper container with a sticky sludge of old sauce flaking off the sides.

"It was still good," Mother said. "It was nice of her to bring it."

Mother had spinal fusion a few years later, then a second hip replacement. Each time, Girl drove five hours to Rochester and stayed in a hotel. After Girl returned home, Stepmother visited Mother less and less frequently. Eventually, she only showed up for dinner by Mother's bedside. Girl knew that if Stepmother was in the hospital, Mother would stay beside her in the visitor's chair all day long.

a restaurant

"**M**other, you had no business showing Brother the bill! Why can't you keep your mouth shut?" Stepmother screamed in the TGI Friday's lobby, her voice loud enough to quiet the half-dozen people chatting while they waited for a table. The greeter stood with the door half open, then backed up and closed it, keeping Stepmother, Mother, and Girl outside.

"I didn't show him," Mother replied. "He just took it." Girl knew this was a lie, but didn't defend Brother. At forty years old he was still the family scapegoat. Mother threw him under the bus to save herself. Girl was back in the duck-and-cover mode that got her through childhood.

Brother, his wife and child, Girl, her two children, and her nanny all went to dinner with Mother and Stepmother. The restaurant was busy, and the server was doing the best he could, but the food was slow to arrive. Stepmother argued with him about a coupon and made him get his manager to ensure she got a free margarita that she didn't want and tried to convince Girl to drink instead. Their table was scrunched against the wall, and the server had to stretch awkwardly to serve everyone, but he didn't complain. Stepmother refused to sit next to Girl's nanny, and refused to speak to her at all, not even replying when asked a direct question. Stepmother didn't lower herself to talk to the help.

"Stepmother must be really mad to leave a tip like that," Mother said to Brother and Girl as they were leaving. She looked embarrassed. Afraid. Mother clearly didn't want to be there when the server saw his tip. Brother was in culinary school—preparing and serving food was his livelihood, but moreover, it was his passion. He had the word "SERVE" tattooed on his left bicep. Brother glanced at the check and calculated the correct tip and threw some bills on the table. Unfortunately, Stepmother saw him and went nuclear. When Stepmother yelled at Mother like she was a disobedient child, Girl went nuclear as well. If you had cut her, Girl's blood would have glowed orange with hate. But as always, she said nothing. Her fear was greater than her rage.

"How can you let her talk to you like that?" Girl asked Mother while Step-mother went to get the car.

"It's not her fault," she said. "She has no filter because she's bipolar."

"Mom, she's verbally abusive."

Mother drew back, her face angry. "It doesn't bother me. I have learned to let it roll off my back. It's not her fault. It's her disease. It doesn't bother me at all. I don't need you to defend me."

To be loved by Mother, Girl could not say a word against her one true love.

Mother rode her motorized scooter to the grocery store to do their shopping, in case Stepmother needed their only car. Stepmother didn't like grocery shopping, and besides, Mother couldn't trust her to come home with anything on the list—she had a habit of wandering store aisles, coming out with bags of things that "looked interesting" and nothing for dinner. Mother made it clear, though, that Girl had no right to complain about it. Mother liked her life the way it was.

"I have never seen someone more determined to be happy than your mother," one friend told Girl. "She makes a conscious decision and that's the end of it."

notes from the fourth wall
fierce love and loyalty wrapped in a blanket of annoyance and discontent

Here's something that is hard for me to admit: my stepmother loves me more than just about anyone else in my life. At Christmas this past year, she bought me a hand-blown glass ornament with a tree inside, a melding of tree and sky in one continuous line. It was exactly the sort of thing I loved, more perfectly suited to me than the blue, fuzzy loungewear my mother picked out. But my stepmother spelled my name wrong on the gift tag. She spelled it L-A-U-R-A, which might be a little piddly detail, but her misspelling my name has enraged me since I was old enough to read and notice such things. My mother always tells me I'm being silly, that we all know she can't spell and I should get used to it. It would be fine if only she were illiterate, but my stepmother has a master's degree, so in my opinion, there's no excuse for misspelling a name that has only four letters. Worse still, my brother married a woman named Laura, so that letter U is the only thing that keeps my name my own, as we are both Lillibridges. Do you see how it always goes astray? I was trying to tell you the story of how my stepmother went out of her way and bought me a beautiful present for Christmas, but then my bitterness took over. This is often how it is when I try to tell stories about her.

I know that she loves me, maybe as much as she loves my mom. When she and my mother broke up for a year, my stepmother still sent me emails, and that year she bought presents for my kids all by herself and not only mailed them on time but wrapped them, something my grief-wounded mother could not manage to do. I was still her child, even though she walked away from my mother.

I always thought that if they broke up, I wouldn't miss her. Yet, during their separation, I found myself unexpectedly sad. I didn't write her letters or God forbid call her on the phone, but every now and then, I'd snap a picture with my phone and send it to her. When I was in Morgantown, West Virginia, at the bar where they broadcast the Mountaineers football show, I sat at the anchor's desk, snapped a selfie, and sent it to my stepmother, since WVU was her alma mater. When the kids were particularly cute, I'd send her a picture of them. When I was in Tennessee, I took a picture of a jar of moonshine and sent her that too, because I remembered her story of going up the holler with her friend Dorothy and getting shot at by moonshiners. It was one of my favorite stories when I was young, because my stepmother trotted out her deep West Virginian accent when she told it and there were real bullets and everything.

When I try to describe her on the page, I think of her walking in her terrible jeans—she only owns terrible jeans—that are too tight in the belly and rolled up at the hem because they are always a foot too long for her five-foot-two frame. She doesn't believe in the value of nice things, so her clothing is always bought on extreme discount and looks it—some things are put on sale for a reason. I picture the stubble at the back of her neck that sticks out horizontally, because she always gets the same haircut, one where they shave her neck, but she never keeps up on it between appointments. At seventy her hair is still more brown than gray. I think of her walking in dead autumn leaves, listening to me talk—she always has time to listen to me. I know her words have saved me. She has always felt that no one I have dated was ever good enough for me. She has pulled me out of the fire time after time, and she would do so again, if I needed it. She will always tell me I am better than I think I am. She will always tell me how proud she is of me, how much she loves me, how much she loves my children. She will always make time to listen to me talk about anything and everything. She will always encourage me to be weird and different and not just like everyone else. And she will always be the one person whose hugs make me curve my shoulders forward, my sternum sinking back, tension held in my arms, gut, and thighs.

As a child, I never felt like my stepmother loved me. Oh, she said the love word often enough, and hugged and kissed me—only on the cheek, never the lips like Mom did. She went to my school concerts and stayed home from work on occasion when I was home sick and Mom couldn't take time off. She was very invested in my brother and me. But I never felt it. There was a wall she kept between us. Now, I am the one who creates distance when she reaches toward me.

What do you do when the person who has saved you is also the person who makes you the craziest? How do I explain that great love and loyalty are at her core, yet our day-to-day interactions are constantly fraught with animosity? My children love unconditionally, and she loves them back the same way. Isn't that enough—that she can give them what she could not give me? I avoid seeing her in person, so that I can try to write her with mercy. She is easier to love from a distance.

Pat texted me today:

"My love please go to utube and listen to susan boyle sing wild horses I dedicate the song to you no matter what you have written about me in your book. Love to you my dear and only daughter, your pat."

the last fight

Girl and her boyfriend moved into a new house. The house Stepmother had bought was put up for sale. Girl paid off the five-thousand-dollar loan she had owed Stepmother for a decade. For the first time in a very long time, she was no longer beholden to her parents. They came to visit one weekend and stayed in Girl's new house.

"I'm making egg sandwiches for breakfast, do you want any?" Girl asked.

"Yes, but I don't want a sandwich," Stepmother said. "I want two eggs, over easy. And I want an English muffin." Girl turned on the stove, but Stepmother wasn't done with her instructions.

"On the plate, here's how I want it to look: I want one half of a muffin, then an egg, then the second half of the muffin, then the other egg—all laid out on the plate."

Unreal. Cooking for four adults and two children was enough to manage, now Girl had to arrange it to Stepmother's satisfaction? Ever since Stepmother had left Mother, everything about her infuriated Girl. She was still waiting for an apology, an act of contrition.

"How about I'll cook and you plate it however you want. This isn't a restaurant."

"I guess I didn't raise you to be a proper host," Stepmother said.

It was stupid, but Girl was fuming. Stepmother couldn't be bothered to pick up after herself—not even throwing out her own apple core—and she was never satisfied with just eating what she was offered. Every meal had to be slightly different. If Girl planned to serve turkey, Stepmother only wanted ham. She took up all the space in the house, napping on the sofa, so no one else could watch TV or visit in the living room. There was a bed upstairs, not that she'd use it.

Mother was happy to be subservient to Stepmother, but Girl had this crazy idea that everyone should be treated politely, even grown-up daughters. Still, she said nothing. Arguing with Stepmother wasn't something she was capable of—she shook so hard with rage that she lost her words. Besides, Girl's children loved Stepmother. Stepmother always came to visit with crafts and games and taught them magic tricks. Girl swallowed bitter bile and did the dishes, glad for a reason not to have to talk to anyone. After the children went to bed, Girl and Mother drank wine, ignoring Stepmother's comments about drunks. Girl encouraged Mother to drink more.

The next time her parents came to town, Girl asked them to stay in a hotel. Perhaps, if she had downtime at the end of each evening, she could resist throttling Stepmother.

"I never thought there would come a time that I wasn't welcome in my own daughter's house," Mother replied.

"It's not you, it's Stepmother. She's a horrible guest," Girl said. She knew she wasn't the first person to say so. Heck, one of Mother's close friends was supposed to stay with them after surgery, but left after only one night. No one would explain what happened, other than "Stepmother was tired, and she said some things she shouldn't have." Girl didn't need the details; she knew how offensive Stepmother was to the people closest to her—she didn't think they deserved common courtesy. But it reassured Girl to know that she wasn't the only one who couldn't get along with Stepmother without biting back words and grinding her teeth. "I guess we didn't teach you to be a good housekeeper . . . I'll let you carry my suitcase . . . Girl, I really need you to get me ice water, but not cubed, I like the crushed ice . . ." all of her little holier-than-thou microaggressions that added up to more than Girl could tolerate. Still, Mother was not going to make it easy.

"I don't want to pit my daughter-in-law against my daughter, but when I visited Brother, his wife was so gracious. We felt so wanted."

"She is a lovely person, Mother, and you *are* trying to pit us against each other with that statement. Leave her out of it," Girl said.

They rarely talked on the phone, only calling each other a few times a year. Their exchanges were now made via text or email. "I feel like I'm intruding," Mother explained.

"I feel like you are too wrapped up in your own life to have time for me," Girl wrote back.

"If that's how you feel, then I have failed as a mother," Mother replied.

Girl tried to explain how she felt about Stepmother, why she didn't want to spend time with her. "I love her, but I don't like her much," she wrote.

"I don't like you much either," Stepmother wrote back from Mother's email account. Girl didn't know why she was surprised that Mother had let her read their correspondence.

Girl was frustrated. Her whole life, Mother and Stepmother acted like Girl was creating drama where none existed. She knew that many people found Stepmother intolerable.

"I don't know why men have such a problem with Stepmother," Mother said.

"I don't know anyone who doesn't have a problem with Stepmother. I just think women are socialized not to say anything rude," Girl answered. Apparently they should have socialized Girl better, because she couldn't bring herself to be polite anymore. But as always, she struggled to explain what it was exactly that was so outrageous. It was myriad paper cuts, and she could not make them add up to a justifiable wound to show to Mother.

"Mother," she wrote, exhausted with the constant tense, useless rage living in her body, "Stepmother called your friend her 'slave,' and she said it in front of my children. She has no regard for anyone else's feelings." Mother was not swayed. Girl decided to pull out her biggest guns.

"She's completely inappropriate. Remember when she asked me what semen tasted like?"

"You chose to remain in that conversation. You could have walked away." *Click, click,* their fingers dashed off arguments across the Internet.

"Did I ever tell you that she showed me your vibrator back in high school and wanted to show me how to use it?" This was the one thing she had always held back, the secret she thought would destroy Mother if she knew. The only time Mother made Stepmother shut up about anything was when she talked about Mother's sex life. Mother might not care that Stepmother creeped Girl out, but she'd sure as shit care that Stepmother was talking about what Mother liked in bed. And Mother didn't know the half of what Stepmother had confided in Girl over the years on that very subject.

"I really don't see why that upset you so much," Mother typed. "Really, Girl, you are forty years old. It's time to get over your childhood."

Girl had been wrong. Mother didn't care about the vibrator story. She had held it as her trump card for years, and it turned out to hold no value—the joker in the deck of cards. Nothing Stepmother had ever done to Girl was enough to make Mother defend her child.

"I don't know why you are surprised," her boyfriend said. "Your mother has always chosen her over you. Your stepmother might not know how abusive she was, but your mother knew, and she let it happen. She's guiltier in my eyes. She was your mother, it was her job to protect you, and she didn't."

The next time they spoke, Mother told Girl that she had had a series of mini-strokes that no one noticed. Girl rarely visited, and Stepmother didn't pay close attention. They only discovered the brain damage after she got an MRI for a suspected heart problem. She was okay, she reassured Girl, and it was unlikely to happen again.

"I went to the library the other day," Mother said. "I rode my scooter because Stepmother had a sculpture class."

"Mother, isn't that like three miles?"

"It took me forty-five minutes, but I did it! I love my scooter. It's so much fun."

Girl pictured Mother riding her motorized scooter to the library in the hot Key West sun. The scooter went even slower than Girl's six-year-old did when he rode his bike. Girl closed her eyes, imagining her mother wipe sweat off her face as she rode for an hour with the sun baking down on her shoulders. Maybe she wore a hat. Girl shook her head. Mother chose the life she led willingly—she had gotten out from under Stepmother once, but ran back to her embrace as fast as her legs could carry her. Mother wasn't a victim—she was a volunteer. But Girl didn't have to play happy family anymore.

Girl realized it was time to stop acting out the same role. This was the life that made her mother happy—it was no longer Girl's place to criticize or convince her mother that she deserved better. Mother seemed completely fine with letting her relationship with Girl float away, as long as Stepmother was happy. Girl had her own family now, a life filled with art and writing, and a few close friends. She no longer had a mother-shaped hole in her chest. Girl wrote her stories, played with her children, and stopped expecting anything from her mother at all.

Of course they still saw each other a few times a year. Girl's children had a right to know their grandparents. Girl dropped the children off while she attended Liz's wedding, two hours away from her parents' house in Rochester. When she returned, the children were happily playing with Stepmother, and Mother was sitting in her recliner with a bandage on her hand.

"I was walking outside and I fell," Mother said. "Stepmother put a bandage on my hand, but it's coming off, and it won't stop bleeding. Can you fix it?"

Girl unwrapped the gauze on her mother's hand and uncovered a gash several inches long. The tissue underneath was bulging out of the wound, fat and muscle and red jello-y looking flesh.

"Mom, you need to go to the hospital. You need stitches."

"Well, I thought I might, but Stepmother and the boys were having so much fun and they don't get to see each other very often. I didn't want to be a bother."

Girl took Mother to urgent care, and made sure they X-rayed her injured knee and checked out her swollen, bruised cheekbone. She held Mother's hand as the surgeon trimmed away bits of viscera and stitched her hand closed, and this mothering of Mother made Girl want to cry. It was the most alone-time she had gotten with Mother since she and Stepmother got back together.

"Mother, you are going to die if you don't start advocating for yourself," Girl told her in the examination room. "Stepmother isn't capable of taking care of you. You have to speak up for yourself when you get hurt. You need to use your cane when you walk. You need to stop worrying about bothering other people."

"That's exactly what I would tell my mother," the nurse interjected. "Your daughter is absolutely right. You need to take care of yourself. No one else is going to, and next time you could get hurt even worse."

When they got back from the hospital, the children were already asleep. Girl and her parents sat talking in the living room. Girl tried to keep the conversation around her children, as it was the safest topic she could think of.

"It's really amazing to watch them grow up," Girl said. "I know they are smarter than I am." She and Mother often discussed the wonder they felt at watching these children develop.

"I always felt that way about you and Brother," Mother said.

"Well, I'm smarter than all of you," Stepmother said. Girl didn't bother to reply—she just excused herself and went to bed.

A month later, Mother fell again.

"Have you seen your mother lately?" a friend asked. "I saw her recently, and the whole side of her face has fallen. I could tell she'd had a stroke."

"I just talked to your parents," a relative said. "Did you know your mother fell again this week?"

Girl called her mother. "How are you, Mom?" she asked.

"Oh, we're having so much fun going out with friends. We've gotten to know a whole bunch of new people—I feel like we are real A-listers down here. We're just so busy, having so much fun."

"I heard you fell."

"Yes, but I'm taking tai chi now. It's really helping my balance. Sometimes Stepmother even comes, too. And I've lost weight. I just refuse to buy treats anymore, and it's working, as long as I don't let Stepmother do the shopping. Here, she wants to say hi, too."

"I'm so proud of you, Girl. You are a wonderful mother and a wonderful writer, and I'm so proud you finally got your master's. I love you. Kiss-kiss," Stepmother said. She said all the right words, but they only bounced off Girl's shell.

As soon as Girl heard Stepmother's voice, she knew she wouldn't be going down to visit Mother anytime soon. She knew Stepmother had saved her many times. She knew Stepmother loved her. When she closed her eyes, she could picture Stepmother and Mother dancing in the kitchen, gazing lovingly into each other's eyes—there was no question that Stepmother was Mother's one true love. But the very sound of Stepmother's voice made Girl grind her teeth. Mother had chosen a life that made her happy, it was not Girl's place to protect her or convince her that she deserved more. Mother was right, it was time for Girl to let go of her issues with her family of origin and focus on her present family. Girl was an adult, and no longer at the mercy of Stepmother, and just because they raised Girl did not obligate her to a lifetime of Thanksgiving dinners or intimate conversations. She no longer yearned for what she never had.

Girl hung up the phone and went upstairs to check on her own children. Her oldest was asleep, turned toward the wall with one arm flung sideways, his head on a ladybug-shaped pillow. Her youngest was balled up on his side, only half his face showing under the covers. She kissed their sleeping heads, the eldest oblivious—he was always a deep sleeper—but the youngest stirred a moment, his eyes flickering half open. "Shhh, it's okay," she whispered, shushing him back to sleep. She was no longer Girl, but Mama.

notes from the fourth wall
being raised by lesbians

The story everyone wants to hear isn't the story I want to tell. Everyone wants to know what it was like to be raised by lesbians, how we functioned, what made it different. I want to talk about other things, the things that formed me and shaped me and scarred me. Not my mother's sexuality. I want to say that isn't what scarred me or made me different or made me who I am today. I want to say that it didn't matter. But all of that is a lie. Of course it mattered more than almost any other aspect of my childhood.

Perhaps I don't want to write about it because I feel an obligation to represent lesbian parents well, and to show that children of lesbians are normal. I don't want to be a poster child for lesbian families. I don't want to say it is or is not okay.

It is not something you can place a value judgment on, because it is not something my moms had any control over. They are who they are, and it isn't fair to say that something that is intrinsically part of them is open to a value debate. I prefer to use my writing to scold them for things they could control.

Maybe I don't like the voyeuristic component. After all, every teenage boy I ever told asked if he could come look in my windows, even though I explained that my parents weren't people any teenage boy would want to see naked. I resented every straight adult asking me if I ever thought I was a lesbian. I don't like the reduction of my entire life to a discussion on sexuality. I wish there was a way to define who makes up your family without the connection to what happens in the bedroom.

But the case may be that I don't want to talk about having two moms because I am overshadowed by it. The most interesting thing about my life is not about me at all; it is about my parents. Perhaps I deny its importance because I want to be the most interesting character in my own story.

I can tell you what you want to hear. I can tell you about the kids that weren't allowed to play with me because of my moms. I can tell you that I was called Lara the Lezzie for most of junior high. I can tell you about the fight I had with one of my best friends in the locker room after gym class where she accused me of being a lesbian just like my mom and how I never forgave her.

I can tell you that I needed a boyfriend for years to prove I was straight to anyone who wondered during my teen years. I can tell you that I had nightmares that I would wake up one day and find I had turned into a lesbian overnight, and was no longer the person I was when I went to sleep.

I can tell you about the blue-collar, Republican parents of my friends who never batted an eye about my two moms and allowed their daughters to have sleepovers at my house. I can tell you about the time my best friend's mother caught her daughter playing doctor with me and how she didn't freak out any more than was appropriate, and how she never tried to keep us from being friends.

I can tell you about the family my parents created, made up of other lesbian women, because my cousins stopped talking to us after my mom was outed. I can tell you about the Christmas parties and New Year's Eve parties and everyone laughing and talking just like a normal family, and about how their conversations were as boring to me as a child as grown-up conversations are to children everywhere. I can tell you how both of my moms went to every school concert and even a few track meets, that the school administration accepted that I had two moms even though it was the late 1970s and it wasn't very common. No teacher ever made me feel weird when I made my moms name tags for open houses or introduced them at parent-teacher conferences. The Boy Scouts allowed my mom to volunteer with the troop when they asked for father-helpers. The Girl Scouts gave my two moms a troop to lead.

Or maybe you'd rather hear about me living in fear that I would confide in the wrong friend, and that they would tell my deep, dark family secret. A popular story of neighborhood hate can be told two ways; maybe once someone threw that rock through our window, or maybe it just was kicked up by a truck and meant nothing at all. Most people prefer to think it was a hate crime, although there was no note to clarify.

I can tell you all of it or none of it, but I can't tell you what it was like to have lesbian parents. I can't speak to some universal experience. I can't tell you what it would have been like if my parents were straight, and what parts would have been different and what parts would have been the same. I have no other point of view.